Wellness
Counseling
A Holistic Approach to Prevention and Intervention

Jonathan H. Ohrt
Philip B. Clarke
Abigail H. Conley

AMERICAN COUNSELING
ASSOCIATION
6101 Stevenson Avenue, Suite 600 • Alexandria, VA 22304
www.counseling.org

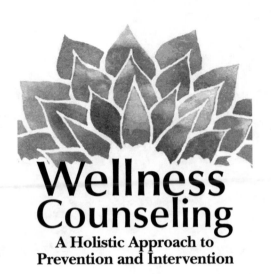

Wellness Counseling

**A Holistic Approach to
Prevention and Intervention**

American Counseling Association

6101 Stevenson Avenue, Suite 600 • Alexandria, VA 22304

Associate Publisher • Carolyn C. Baker

Digital and Print Development Editor • Nancy Driver

Senior Production Manager • Bonny E. Gaston

Copy Editor • Tyler Krupa

Cover and text design by Bonny E. Gaston

Library of Congress Cataloging-in-Publication Data

Names: Ohrt, Jonathan H., author.
Title: Wellness counseling in action : a holistic approach to prevention
    and intervention / Jonathan H. Ohrt, University of South Carolina,
    Philip B. Clarke, Wake Forest University, Abigail H. Conley, Virginia
    Commonwealth University.
Description: Fourth edition. | Alexandria, VA : American Counseling
    Association, [2019] | Includes bibliographical references and index.
Identifiers: LCCN 2018047344 | ISBN 9781556203749 (pbk. : alk. paper)
Subjects: LCSH: Health counseling. | Health promotion. | Alternative
    medicine.
Classification: LCC R727.4 .O37 2019 | DDC 613–dc23 LC record
    available at https://lccn.loc.gov/2018047344

Table of Contents

Part I
Foundations of Wellness Counseling

Part II
The Five Domains of Wellness

Preface

Most people are familiar with the term *wellness*. It is likely that most people you ask would say that wellness is important to them. Unfortunately, individuals who conduct an Internet search in hopes of finding ways of improving their personal wellness will often find a plethora of gimmicks and strategies that are not effective, unsupported by research, potentially harmful, and sometimes expensive. Most helping professionals also acknowledge that wellness is important for their clients. However, various disciplines promote different definitions of wellness. Within the counseling profession, we tend to agree that wellness consists of "a way of life oriented toward optimal health and well-being, in which body, mind, and spirit are integrated by the individual to live life more fully within the human and natural community" (Myers, Sweeney, & Witmer, 2000, p. 252). In our work with clients, we have continuously recognized the importance of viewing their concerns from a holistic perspective. Each area of an individual's life inevitably affects other areas. We also believe that now, maybe more than ever, it is important to work from a prevention approach. As mental health concerns appear to be on the rise, we can help people work toward optimal wellness in an effort to avert such concerns. At the very least, prevention and wellness promotion efforts can help build coping strategies that can help alleviate or reduce the severity of unavoidable mental health concerns.

In our experience teaching wellness courses and speaking with experienced practitioners, we have received feedback that counselors believe in promoting wellness for their clients; however, they are not quite sure what wellness "looks like," or they are not interested in learning more concrete strategies to promote client wellness. This book is designed for beginning and experienced counselors who are interested in conceptualizing clients from a holistic wellness perspective and in promoting wellness through prevention and intervention efforts. Each chapter contains up-to-date research and best practices within the wellness domains. We also provide concrete strategies for implementing wellness interventions throughout the book. In addition, we include "Practitioner Spotlights," where experienced practitioners share their personal experiences implementing wellness interventions. Some additional features of the book include reflection prompts to help the reader process the information, learning activities to help the reader participate in wellness strategies before implementing them with clients, and additional resources for the reader to explore related to the content in each chapter.

This book is divided into four parts. Part I consists of a chapter describing the theoretical foundations, empirical support, and domains of wellness. Part I also contains a chapter discussing the current trends and public policy implications related to wellness. Part II of the book includes wellness domains. We divided this part into five chapters: Mind (e.g., cognitions, intellectual stimulation), Body (e.g., physical wellness, nutrition), Spirit (e.g., religion, spirituality, meaning and purpose), Emotion (e.g., emotion regulation), and Connection (e.g., social support). Part III pertains to wellness counseling in action and contains chapters on assessment and conceptualization, treatment planning, and wellness interventions. Part IV is composed of chapters on wellness with specific populations and settings. Our goal for this section is to provide more depth and specific strategies for implementation. The section includes chapters on wellness across the life span, wellness counseling modalities, wellness counseling in educational settings, and wellness for counselors (i.e., self-care).

Reference

Myers, J. E., Sweeney, T. J., & Witmer, J. M. (2000). The Wheel of Wellness counseling for wellness: A holistic model for treatment planning. *Journal of Counseling & Development, 78,* 251–266.

About the Authors

Jonathan H. Ohrt is currently an associate professor and counselor education program coordinator at the University of South
Carolina. He earned his PhD in counselor education at the University of Central Florida in 2010 and his MA in counselor education at the University of South Florida in 2006. He is a certified
K–12 school counselor and has worked for several years providing
psychoeducation as well as individual and small group counseling
services to high school students in Florida. He has also provided
services in a university-based counseling clinic. His current research projects are related to prevention and wellness promotion
for children, adolescents, and transitional-age youths; counselor
wellness; and group work.

• • •

Philip B. Clarke earned his MS/EdS in counseling in 2004 and
his PhD in counselor education in 2012. He has been a licensed
professional counselor (North Carolina) since 2006 and a faculty member in the Department of Counseling at Wake Forest
University since 2011. He has worked and interned in multiple
counseling settings, including a group private practice, a hospital-
based intensive outpatient substance abuse program, a treatment
research clinic, and a hospital-based counseling program. He has
experience counseling clients with substance use and co-occurring
disorders. His clinical experience has also centered on providing
counseling for people diagnosed with dementia and their family
caregivers. He had the privilege of taking a course in wellness
counseling from Dr. Jane Myers, which sparked his interest in

the subject. He has presented and written about wellness counseling for people with substance use concerns, cancer survivors, and family caregivers of people with dementia. His scholarship also includes developing integrative counseling and experiential teaching approaches. In his classes, he strives to engage students through the use of actors to portray clients.

• • •

Abigail H. Conley is an assistant professor in the Department of Counseling and Special Education and is an affiliate faculty member in the Institute for Women's Health, at Virginia Commonwealth University. She earned her PhD in counselor education from North Carolina State University in 2012 and her MA in counseling psychology at Lewis and Clark College in 2006. Her clinical experience is in higher education in both community college and university settings, focusing on providing counseling and advocacy services to survivors of sexual assault. Her research interests include interpersonal violence survivorship and healing, violence prevention, and wellness and resiliency. She serves as an associate editor of quantitative research for *Counseling and Values*, the official journal of the Association for Spiritual, Ethical, and Religious Values in Counseling, a division of the American Counseling Association.

• • •

About the Spotlight Contributors

The contributors listed below are mental health professionals, educators, and human services center directors who authored the Practitioner Spotlights found throughout the book. In the Practitioner Spotlights, the contributors impart their knowledge and experience on wellness and wellness counseling with the purpose of illustrating and elaborating on key terms and concepts.

Jamie D. Aten, PhD, is founder and executive director of the Humanitarian Disaster Institute of Wheaton College in Wheaton, Illinois.

Hannah Bayne, PhD, is an assistant professor of counselor education at Florida State University in Gainsville, Florida.

Michael D. Brubaker, PhD, LICDC-CS, NCC, is an associate professor of counseling at the University of Cincinnati in Cincinnati, Ohio.

Craig Cashwell, PhD, LPC, NCC, ACS, is professor of counseling at the University of North Carolina at Greensboro.

Don Davis, PhD, is an associate professor of counseling at Georgia State University in Atlanta, Georgia.

Allison M. Forti, PhD, LPC, NCC, is an assistant teaching professor at Wake Forest University in Winston-Salem, North Carolina.

Matthew Fullen, PhD, MDiv, LPCC, is an assistant professor of counselor education at Virginia Tech in Blacksburg, Virginia.

Jessie Guest, MA, RPT, LPC, is a doctoral student and counselor in private practice in Shelby, North Carolina.

Linda Hancock, FNP, PhD, is director of Virginia Commonwealth University's Wellness Resource Center, in Richmond, Virginia.

J. Robert Nations, DMin, is an assistant teaching professor and associate director of counseling department online programs at Wake Forest University, Winston-Salem, North Carolina.

Therese L. Newton, PhD, LPCA, NCC, is an assistant professor at Augusta State University in Augusta, Georgia.

Jacy Rader, LPC, is in private practice in Dallas, Texas.

Laura Shannonhouse, PhD, LPC, NCC, is an assistant professor of counseling and psychological services at Georgia State University in Atlanta, Georgia.

Matt Shenker, MEd, is a school counselor in Hanover, Virginia.

Julia V. Taylor, PhD, is an assistant professor of counselor education at at the University of Virginia in Charlottesville, Virginia.

Cirecie A. West-Olatunji, PhD, is an associate professor of counseling at Xavier University of Louisiana, New Orleans, Louisiana.

Brooke Wymer, LISW, is a doctoral student and counselor in private practice in West Columbia, South Carolina.

• • •

Acknowledgments

First and foremost, we thank our students who have inspired this book and taught us so much about wellness. We are grateful for the practitioners who volunteered their time and were willing to share their experiences to greatly enhance this book through our Practitioner Spotlight sections. We appreciate Carolyn Baker, Nancy Driver, the American Counseling Association staff, and the reviewers for their work on this text. We are also grateful for the foundational work in our field by Jane Myers, Tom Sweeney, Melvin Witmer, and Mark Young. We are so honored to know and learn from you all.

Jonathan: I thank my advisor Dr. Mike Robinson for his mentorship and guidance. I am also grateful for Dr. Mark Young, who was the first person to introduce me to wellness from a professional perspective. I am grateful for my coauthors, Philip and Abigail. It is amazing that this book, that we first imagined at an American Counseling Association conference 6 years ago, will now be published. Thank you both for your hard work, flexibility, and persistence. Finally, I am grateful for my wife, Dodie, and my sons, Hayden and Maren, who all bring me great happiness and contribute to my own personal wellness.

Philip: I am appreciative of the opportunity to work with my co-authors Jonathan and Abigail. This was truly a thoughtful writing process and involved many long discussions because we care deeply about the topic of wellness counseling. I want to thank my parents (Ray and Lynn) and sister (Jessica) who were my first wellness role models. I thank my wife, Rebecca, for all her love and support and my son, Andrew, for teaching me so much. I am grateful to Dr. Donna Henderson for her support in my growth as a counselor educator and Dr. Sam Gladding for his advice and listening ear in regard to the writing of this book. A debt of gratitude is owed to Sara Oberle for developing the image for the five-domain wellness model. I thank Taylor Pisel and Rachel Powell for their work on developing images for the book. I thank all of my students and clients. My writing in this book has been largely inspired by you. Special thanks to the great mental health professionals and counselor educators who wrote or were interviewed for Practitioner Spotlights in the book. My biggest inspiration in writing this book was Dr. Jane Myers—thanks for the mentorship that you provided to me and many others and for pioneering counselors' understanding of wellness.

Abigail: I want to thank my amazing students and colleagues at VCU who make space for me to grow, and provide feedback on many of the ideas in this book. And, I have so much gratitude for my partner and husband, Joe; my parents, Gayle and Norm; my children, Miles and Polly; and my amazing coauthors, Jonathan and Philip, for their support and encouragement while writing this book. It was truly a labor of love. At times, late nights spent writing did not seem like the best example of wellness. However, having support to cultivate the inevitable ebb and flow of writing has given me a new appreciation for what work–life balance can look like. The word "balance" in this sense is a misnomer, really, because a fulfilling work–life ratio is anything but balanced—it's finding a way to make time for the things that need attention (sometimes that is writing, sometimes that is rocking a teething baby all night), leaning on others to help pick up the slack during the transition, being okay with asking for help, and finding ways to create space for joy and replenishment in between it all.

Part I
Foundations of
Wellness Counseling

Chapter 1

Introduction to
Wellness Counseling

When one tugs at a single thing in nature,
he finds it attached to the rest of the world.
—John Muir

• • •

Discovering theories and frameworks for counseling that fit for you and your clients is, in a weird way, like reconnecting with a long-lost love that you had never met. You are beside yourself with excitement that your paths have crossed. You share similar values and enhance each other's ways of navigating life's challenges. You enjoy spending time with this new love. As a college student trying to figure out what type of post-college helping professional education I (Phil) wanted, I searched desperately for a metaphorical connection. A friend of mine mentioned that she was applying to counseling programs. I read about many different counseling programs and their definition of counseling. I discovered the word "wellness" in many of the descriptions. "Counselors do that?" I thought to myself. "I thought they just focused on symptoms and what was going wrong with people." This idea of wellness resonated with my beliefs and values, even without a day of counselor training under my belt. Like new love, there were sparks, and I was definitely interested. The romance blossomed as I got to study with and serve as a graduate assistant for Jane Myers, one of the great scholars who has advanced our understanding and practice of wellness counseling. Wellness "completed me" as a professional. It was and is a significant part of my counselor identity—and just like a healthy romantic relationship, it made me want to be my best self as a counselor.

However, it was not until I obtained my master's degree and went into the real world of counseling that I truly appreciated how important wellness counseling was to me. Much of my work at the time was at an addictions treatment center working with clients diagnosed with co-occurring disorders. The most common struggle I saw across clients was not necessarily relapse into addiction or mental health symptomology but deficits in, and barriers to, wellness. Issues of lifestyle imbalance (e.g., poor nutrition and sleep habits, lack of meaning and purpose, spiritual bypass, conflict with family or friends or outright lack of social support, inability to identify and make sense of emotions, insufficient intellectual stimulation) not only severely detracted from my clients' lives but also seemed to perpetuate an ongoing cycle of addictive behaviors and mental health concerns.

The above is an excerpt from my story with wellness. There is a lot more to this subject matter than what I just described and that we (Jonathan, Abigail, and myself) capture in this book. The purpose of the book is to (a) provide a comprehensive overview of the theoretical background and empirical support for wellness counseling, (b) discuss current trends in wellness, (c) provide practical strategies for clinical application of wellness concepts, and (d) describe wellness counseling interventions for specific populations and settings. This book is applicable for counselors and counseling students who seek to better understand clients' holistic wellness and integrate wellness-based interventions in their practice; it also applies to educators who are teaching a course on wellness counseling or incorporating it into existing courses. In the upcoming sections, we explore the relevance of wellness and wellness counseling for all counselors. We then outline the contents and structure of this book. Along the way, we encourage you to reflect on what led you to read these pages at this time as well as your own perceived and lived benefits of wellness and wellness counseling.

The Value of Wellness

Wellness Is Who We Are

What does wellness mean to you? How do you define wellness? What are the key pieces that motivate you to work toward being well or your best self? These are a few of the essential questions that wellness counselors ask our clients. It is equally valuable for counselors to be able to define wellness and wellness counseling. First, any counselor who adopts wellness counseling as one of their counseling approaches needs to describe what it is during the informed consent process, meriting some definition of terms. Second, counselors may need to justify use of this approach to insurance providers. Additionally, clients may desire a starting point for operationalizing wellness to empower them to discover how they would define it. Myers, Sweeney, and Witmer's (2000) definition of wellness is a helpful point of departure in understanding this concept: "a way of life oriented toward optimal health and well-being, in which body, mind, and spirit are integrated by the individual to live life more fully within the human and natural community" (p. 252). We explore different definitions and offer our own definition of wellness as you proceed through the book. Moreover, we hope that you begin to formulate your own definition along the way.

As health care trends continue to move toward holistic and integrated care models, it is important for counselors to communicate their counseling philosophy and approaches to other professional helpers involved in their clients' care. The term "wellness" is in the definition of counseling: "Counseling is a professional relationship that empowers diverse individuals, families, and groups to accomplish mental health, wellness, education, and career goals" (Kaplan, Tarvydas, & Gladding, 2014, p. 368). It is an inextricable part of our professional identity. Hence, all counselors should be able to articulate what wellness is to consumers, government officials, and other helping professionals (Myers, 1992). Maintaining wellness at the forefront of counseling may aid in reducing the stigma of receiving counseling, potentially resulting in more people seeking and receiving services.

The World Needs Wellness Counselors

The world needs counselors skilled in wellness approaches now more than ever. According to an American Psychological Association (APA) survey, nearly one in four people rated their stress as an "8" or higher on a 1–10 scale in 2015 (APA, 2016). The high stress appears to be having a trickle-down effect, manifesting in symptoms including anxiety and melancholy (APA, 2016). Youths are unfortunately not free from the effects of stress, as evidenced by 31% of caregivers of K–12 students reporting high stress associated with school in their child or adolescent (National Public Radio, Robert Wood Johnson Foundation, & Harvard School of Public Health, 2013). Older students were placed in the high-stress category by their caregivers with more frequency than younger students. These findings were corroborated in a study of 11th graders (n = 128), 49% of whom endorsed feeling "a great deal of stress" every day—26% with depressive symptomology (Leonard et al., 2015). Further, more than one third of the sample had been intoxicated on alcohol or drugs in the previous month.

In 2015, the National Survey on Drug Use and Health produced findings that 43.4 million American adults have a mental disorder (Center for Behavioral Health Statistics and Quality, 2016). Several studies have demonstrated that there is a strong relationship between mental and physical health (Baughman et al., 2016; Razzano et al., 2015; Scott et al., 2016). For instance, in a sample of 457 people with mental disorders, 44% had hypertension (Razzano et al., 2015). In another study, almost two thirds of individuals with mental illness noted having chronic pain (Baughman et al., 2016). Participants also reported "not feeling very healthy" for an average of 15.7 days in the previous month (Baughman et al., 2016, p. 428).

There are several encouraging factors that accompany this concern; the primary one is that wellness issues are drawing the public's attention. According to Mattke et al. (2013), more than half of all employers with 50 or more employees offer a wellness program. Workplace wellness programs often include an initial wellness evaluation, dissemination of health information, and individual or group sessions led by a helping professional (Baicker, Cutler, & Song, 2010). Although most wellness programs center on physical health (Baicker et al., 2010), 41% of employment places have an Employee Assistance Program, enabling counselors to address mental health and other aspects of well-being (Mattke et al., 2013).

The well-being of young people is being addressed on several levels. Given Lai, Guo, Ijadi-Maghsoodi, Puffer, and Kataoka's (2016) statement that "schools are the most common entry point into mental health services in the United States" (p. 1328), efforts to enhance child and adolescent wellness are occurring through school-based mental health programs as well as through the infusion of mindfulness (Semple, Droutman, & Reed, 2017) and spirituality (Gibson, Dixon, & Myers, 2012) into the classroom. Many universities provide wellness programs for their students. Program staff can support the well-being of college students in several ways, such as distributing information as well as hosting campus events and screenings.

Medical and mental health professionals are working together in providing client services. These integrated care approaches include counselors as part of a team that conceptualizes and treats clients holistically, thereby improving care results in individuals with both mental and physical health concerns (Gerrity, 2016). Counselors are supporting clients in transcending illness and moving toward wellness. For instance, several years ago, I (Phil) was on a research team that examined the outcomes of Finding Your New Normal, a wellness-based support group for female breast cancer survivors (Shannonhouse et al., 2014). The qualitative findings revealed that for some group members, Finding Your New Normal helped "reintegrate [their] sense of self after a cancer experience" (Shannonhouse et al., 2014, p. 19). Research and life experience tell us that the stresses and struggles of life are not going away any time soon. Additionally, the advent of new technologies presents challenges and opportunities for the well-being of the public. However, there is a wave of recognition that the world needs wellness, as indicated by the use of integrated care in medical, mental health, and school settings. Wellness programs in the workplace and on college campuses also support this trend. Counselors must be informed on wellness approaches to best serve their clients, propel the identity and value of the counseling profession forward, and be active participants in the wellness wave that continues to rise.

The Wellness Platform

I (Phil) was co-lecturing in an advanced skills/crisis counseling class of 16 second-year master's students. The lecture topic was on the early stages of the goal-setting process with clients. These students had completed a practicum in which they had worked with their first clients and were now embarking on their internship in which they were seeing clients on a weekly basis. One of the students raised her hand asking, "How do we begin to set and discuss goals with clients when they don't have any goals, don't know their goals, or have vague goals?" I paused for a moment, nodding my head in agreement when the light bulb went off for me. Although the topic of my lecture was not on wellness counseling, I responded that it is one of the best solutions to this conundrum.

Wellness counseling provides a concrete platform or launching pad for discussing client-presenting concerns and goals. If I am working with a client who is unsure of what they would like to work on in counseling, I often present a paper copy of a wellness model. The client and I can then discuss strengths and stressors across the domains of the client's life (Myers & Sweeney, 2006; Sweeney & Myers, 2005. This exercise regularly results in increased clarity for the client and a focus for counseling. It also facilitates insight about (a) issues that feed into the presenting problem, (b) how this problem trickles down into other facets of the client's wellness, and (c) strengths that have been maintained in spite of the presenting concern (Clarke, Adams, Wilkerson, & Shaw, 2016; Myers, Clarke, Brown, & Champion, 2012). This incident was one of those rare moments as an educator when, instead of responding with "It depends . . . ," I had a clearer answer.

Counseling With the Whole Person

Human beings are incredibly complex. You are probably saying to yourself that this is one of the most obvious and clichéd statements that one can make. Yet, as helping professionals, we often consciously or unconsciously reduce our conceptualization and approaches with clients to isolated symptoms. We target our treatment plans at one aspect of a client's life, and we neglect to recognize the interplay/interconnectedness of the different components that compose the well-being of our clients.

The wellness counseling approach reminds the counselor to attend to the multiple aspects of each client. Hence, when I am counseling a client and reflect on the wellness model during an intake session or goal setting, I am prompted to ask not only about the presenting concern but also about factors such as the client's religion/spirituality; gender; and physical, emotional, social, and mental well-being. As noted previously, filling in pieces of the painting of the client's life informs both the counselor and client about (a) areas of the client's life affected by the presenting concern, (b) areas of the client's life exacerbating the presenting concern, and (c) areas of strength that can be channeled toward addressing the presenting problem (Clarke et al., 2016; Myers & Sweeney, 2004).

Wellness as a holistic approach positions counselors to be a part of integrated care teams. As part of integrated care models in which multiple helping professionals work in the same setting or collaborate on client care (Hooper, 2014), wellness counselors will be grounded in conceptualizing the importance and processes of these treatment teams. I landed a job launching a co-located mental health clinic in part because my interest and background in wellness counseling merged with the director's vision for his integrated care program.

Strength and Prevention Based

A lot can get lost in the counseling process. One of the first things to be neglected is client strengths. Most of you reading this book can relate to feeling overwhelmed when a client walks in your office for a first session with many different presenting concerns, and a parallel process occurs in which you feel as lost as your client. Where do we begin, and what do we work toward? It is easy for counselors to experience cognitive constriction, overlooking clients' strengths when they present with extensive stressors. Wellness keeps both client and counselor anchored, grounded in the strengths possessed by the client. Without recognizing and mobilizing these client strengths, the counselor might be lost at sea, and the client might drift away, literally, from returning for further sessions. Attending to strengths can be empowering to clients. It sends a meta-message that things can get better—and hope is a big slice of the counseling pie (Asay & Lambert, 1999).

Client strengths and resources are essential elements in the counseling process. You may already be familiar with the data on common factors that show that 15% of counseling outcomes are related to what the client expects from counseling, 15% to the counselor's techniques, 30% to the helping relationship, and 40% "to factors outside of therapy" (Lambert & Barley, 2001, p. 358). The outside-of-therapy factors can include both client struggles and strengths. As shown later in this book, a significant portion of the wellness approach pertains to a rigorous exploration of the client's strengths as both prevention and response strategies in wellness counseling.

Applicable Across the Life Span

Wellness counseling fits mental health needs across the life span. More than one in five children have experienced two or more adverse childhood experiences, such as being present during an occurrence of domestic violence, having an incarcerated parent, or residing with an individual who abuses substances (Child and Adolescent Health Measurement Initiative, 2013). The ripple effect for some children can spread to different aspects of their well-being. Building wellness into support systems for children, such as the school environment, has shown promise (Villalba & Myers, 2008). For instance, 55 elementary school students attended three classroom guidance sessions filled with wellness activities and information. Increases in well-being resulted across several wellness factors (Villalba & Myers, 2008).

The presenting concerns of the adolescent clients who enter your office may affect them across all aspects of their well-being. Adolescents ($n = 114$) attending outpatient counseling scored lower on wellness than the 1,142 adolescents who formed the norm group for the Five Factor Wellness Inventory—Teenage Version that was used in the study (Watson & Lemon, 2011). Yet again, however, wellness approaches are increasingly being incorporated to address critical problems.

For example, Saul and Rodgers (2016) recommended wellness-based, holistic approaches to weight-loss-focused approaches in addressing childhood obesity. These approaches ranged from family involvement to fostering self-esteem and social skills, to mindful eating.

The well-being of older adults is of paramount importance. The high rates of substance abuse among aging populations is concerning because substance use can exacerbate health issues and be dangerous in combination with medication (Kuerbis, Sacco, Blazer, & Moore, 2014; Mattson, Lipari, Hays, & Van Horn, 2017). However, researchers have found a positive relationship between aging into older adulthood and wellness (e.g., Blanchflower & Oswald, 2008). Furthermore, rates of mental disorder are at their lowest in older adulthood (Center for Behavioral Health Statistics and Quality, 2016). Wellness counselors build on the strengths of older adult clients, aid them in pursuit of the full spectrum of goals inherent in a wellness perspective, and prevent the magnified effect of any mental health problems (Fiske, Wetherell, & Gatz, 2009).

Applicable Across Presenting Concerns

Wellness counseling is a versatile approach for working with clients. Wellness is frequently assumed to be appropriate for prevention or clients with subclinical or lower severity mental health concerns. However, we argue and demonstrate that wellness counseling can be effective as prevention or intervention. As a form of prevention, wellness counseling allows clients to examine components of wellness that they would like to improve; it also highlights and strengthens areas where clients already have success to aid in future times of stress and coping. However, wellness counseling can also be helpful to clients affected by trauma, addiction, depression, anxiety, and a range of issues. The reason is because wellness counseling presents a framework for client and counselor to understand the precipitating factors underlying symptomology and to devise holistic treatment plans and interventions. The relationship between environmental context—such as experiencing a lifetime of systematic racism, early childhood experiences, family dynamics, genetic predispositions, and individual brain chemistry—and the unique way we each process our lived experiences has a profound effect on the health of mind, body, spirit, emotion, and connection with others. In sum, the world needs wellness!

Wellness Is Transtheoretical and Honors the Change Process

Wellness is also versatile because it is transtheoretical. In other words, it can serve as a framework within which other theories or interventions can be used. For instance, wellness counseling can include using a model as a framework for treatment planning (e.g., Clarke et al., 2016), but the intervention selected to achieve the wellness goals can be anything from cognitive behavior therapy to acceptance and commitment therapy.

Unlike many other interventions, wellness counseling honors the stages of change (Myers & Sweeney, 2005a, 2005b). Wellness counseling recognizes that each client comes to counseling with a different level of importance, confidence, and readiness for change (Miller & Rollnick, 2012). If a counselor pursues setting a change plan with the client too quickly, the outcome is less likely to be positive. Given this reality, the wellness counselor thus focuses the intervention on what is most important to the client. The wellness model offers a framework for identifying areas of clinical relevance to the client (Myers et al., 2012), which also prevents a resistance dynamic from emerging between client and counselor (Miller & Rollnick, 2012).

It is apparent that at a crowded table of different approaches that counselors can select from, wellness counseling should hold a prominent seat. The benefits of wellness counseling described here are but the tip of the iceberg regarding the utility of this approach. There are probably several advantages to wellness counseling that you would add to this list, and we encourage you to reflect on those.

Wellness Is for Counselors Too!

Learning wellness counseling can be doubly helpful for counselors. It provides a self-care approach for the counselor that can be applied throughout one's career, and the experience of incorporating wellness into one's own life can facilitate continual improvement as a wellness counselor. Compassion fatigue and burnout have been identified as two possible enemies of counselor wellness (Lawson, 2007; Thompson, Amatea, & Thompson, 2014). The question is then, how can counselors stave off these threats? Wellness offers some answers. For example, counselors who hold favorable views of their place of employment and who are high in mindfulness and constructive coping skills report less compassion fatigue and burnout (Thompson et al., 2014). If you are in a position of leadership for a mental health site, these research findings underscore the relevance of organizational wellness. For counselors, mental wellness and holistic coping skills appear to be beneficial. These topics are covered throughout this book. Hence, as you progress through the chapters, consider how you might integrate the wellness principles and practices from this book in your own life. You may find that this expedites your learning process while enhancing your wellness as a counselor. In Chapter 15, "Wellness Counseling for Counselors," the literature on this topic is reviewed, and specific recommendations for counselor self-care are presented. To conclude this chapter, we provide a road map of this book, highlighting what you can expect from each chapter.

Conclusion

It is our intention that this book serve multiple purposes: provide meaningful information to both novice and experienced counselors, offer resources that can used with clients, and include learning materials that counselor educators can incorporate in most classes and supervision. This book is interactive; hence, there are learning activities and reflection prompts throughout. Counselors and counselor educators may find these activities and the discussion prompts useful in gaining depth of understanding and applying concepts. Beginning in Part II, wellness boosters are presented. Wellness boosters are activities that clients can do that result in increased short-term wellness in one or more domains. They represent the distillation of tenets of well-being in a given area into simple and typically brief self-help interventions that can have a high-level positive effect in a short period of time. Counselors can also engage in the boosters to enhance their own wellness. The case examples infused throughout illustrate clinical application of wellness counseling principles and practices. Resources are paired with most chapters and may be integrated into the counseling process with clients.

You may have chosen to read this book for many reasons. Perhaps your path to wellness counseling was similar to mine. You may be a counseling student in a wellness class preparing to dive into the deep waters of this philosophy and approach. You may be an experienced counselor looking to add a holistic perspective to your tool belt of interventions. You may have realized that wellness is one of the missing links in your counseling approach. Some of you have been using wellness-related approaches with your clients and want to enhance your knowledge and skill set. Regardless of your reason for picking up this book, we look forward to journeying with you toward identifying helpful ways to support our clients' well-being.

Reflection Prompts

1. Why is (or why will) wellness counseling (be) important for you in your work with clients?
2. What are the benefits of using wellness counseling? What are the challenges?

3. In what ways are you already incorporating wellness counseling into your work with clients?
4. Why do you believe that wellness is relevant to the identity of counselors?
5. How would you describe wellness counseling to a client?
6. What information about wellness counseling are you hoping to learn through this book?
7. What value-added is provided by counselors using wellness approaches to the mental health landscape?
8. What counseling theories do you use most often and interest you the most? How might these theories integrate with wellness counseling?

Learning Activities

Interview

Interview a peer or colleague. Ask him or her about:
- Ways they incorporate wellness into their work with clients
- Challenges they have faced
- The benefits of wellness counseling
- How wellness counseling fits with their identity as a counselor

Organizational Assessment

Conduct an assessment of your agency, school, or private practice regarding application of wellness in your site's policies, procedures, philosophy, and work with clients. Identify areas of strength and areas for growth.

Resources

American Counseling Association's Task Force on Counselor Wellness and Impairment

http://www.creating-joy.com/taskforce/index.htm

This website operationalizes impairment and provides links to literature, assessments, and skills for enhancing wellness to prevent impairment.

American Psychological Association, Stress in America

http://www.apa.org/news/press/releases/stress/index.aspx

A presentation of data collected by the American Psychological Association since 2007 on stress levels, underlying reasons for stress, and ways of dealing with stress.

Healthy People 2020
https://www.healthypeople.gov/
> This website contains data on a variety of variables related to wellness and national goals for improving health.

National Survey on Drug Use and Health
https://nsduhweb.rti.org/respweb/homepage.cfm
> A comprehensive and frequently cited data set on mental health and substance use outcomes across the life span.

References

American Psychological Association. (2016, March 10). *Stress in America™: The impact of discrimination.* Retrieved from http://www.apa.org/news/press/releases/stress/2015/impact-of-discrimination.pdf

Asay, T. R., & Lambert, M. J. (1999). The empirical case of the common factors in psychotherapy: Quantitative findings. In M. A. Hubble, B. L. Duncan, & S. D. Miller (Eds.), *The heart and soul of change: What works in therapy* (pp. 23–55). Washington, DC: American Psychological Association. https://doi.org/10.1037/11132001

Baicker, K., Cutler, D., & Song, Z. (2010). Workplace wellness programs can generate savings. *Health Affairs, 29,* 304–311.

Baughman, K. R., Bonfine, N., Dugan, S. E., Adams, R., Gallagher, M., Olds, R. S., . . . Ritter, C. (2016). Disease burden among individuals with severe mental illness in a community setting. *Community Mental Health Journal, 52,* 424–432.

Blanchflower, D. G., & Oswald, A. J. (2008). Is well-being U-shaped over the life cycle? *Social Science & Medicine, 66,* 1733–1749.

Center for Behavioral Health Statistics and Quality. (2016). *2015 National Survey on Drug Use and Health: Detailed tables.* Rockville, MD: Substance Abuse and Mental Health Services Administration.

Child and Adolescent Health Measurement Initiative. (2013, May). *2011–2012 National Survey of Children's Health: SAS code for data users: Child health indicator and subgroups, Version 1.0.* Retrieved from http://www.childhealthdata.org/docs/nsch-docs/sas-codebook_-2011-2012-nsch-v1_05-10-13.pdf

Clarke, P. B., Adams, J. A., Wilkerson, J., & Shaw, E. G. (2016). Wellness-based counseling for caregivers of persons with dementia. *Journal of Mental Health Counseling, 38,* 263–277.

Fiske, A., Wetherell, J. L., & Gatz, M. (2009). Depression in older adults. *Annual Review of Clinical Psychology, 5,* 363–389.

Gerrity, M. (2016, May). *Evolving models of behavioral health integration: Evidence update 2010–2015.* Retrieved from https://www.milbank.org/wp-content/uploads/2016/05/Evolving-Models-of-BHI.pdf

Gibson, D. M., Dixon, A. L., & Myers, J. E. (2012). Promoting spiritual growth through holistic wellness: Practical strategies for school counselors. *Counselling and Spirituality, 13,* 79–98.

Hooper, L. (2014). Mental health services in primary care: Implications for clinical mental health counselors and other mental health providers. *Journal of Mental Health Counseling, 36,* 95–98.

Kaplan, D. M., Tarvydas, V. M., & Gladding, S. T. (2014). 20/20: A vision for the future of counseling: The new consensus definition of counseling. *Journal of Counseling & Development, 92,* 366–372.

Kuerbis, A., Sacco, P., Blazer, D. G., & Moore, A. A. (2014). Substance abuse among older adults. *Clinics in Geriatric Medicine, 30,* 629–654.

Lai, K., Guo, S., Ijadi-Maghsoodi, R., Puffer, M., & Kataoka, S. H. (2016). Bringing wellness to schools: Opportunities for and challenges to mental health integration in school-based health centers. *Psychiatric Services, 67,* 1328–1333.

Lambert, M. J., & Barley, D. E. (2001). Research summary on the therapeutic relationship and psychotherapy outcome. *Psychotherapy: Theory, Research, Practice, Training, 38,* 357–361.

Lawson, G. (2007). Counselor wellness and impairment: A national survey. *The Journal of Humanistic Counseling, 46,* 20–34.

Leonard, N. R., Gwadz, M. V., Ritchie, A., Linick, J. L., Cleland, C. M., Elliott, L., & Grethel, M. (2015). A multi-method exploratory study of stress, coping, and substance use among high school youth in private schools. *Frontiers in Psychology, 6,* 1028.

Mattke, S., Liu, H., Caloyeras, J. P., Huang, C. Y., Van Busum, K. R., Khodyakov, D., & Shier, V. (2013). Workplace wellness programs study: Final report. *Rand Health Quarterly, 3*(2), 7.

Mattson, M., Lipari, R. N., Hays, C., & Van Horn, S. (2017). *A day in the life of older adults: Substance use facts.* Retrieved from https://www.samhsa.gov/data/sites/default/files/report_2792/Short-Report-2792.html

Miller, W. R., & Rollnick, S. (2012). *Motivational interviewing: Helping people change.* New York, NY: Guilford Press.

Myers, J. E. (1992). Wellness, prevention, development: The cornerstone of the profession. *Journal of Counseling & Development, 71,* 136–139.

Myers, J. E., Clarke, P. B., Brown, J. B., & Champion, D. A. (2012). Wellness: Theory, research, and applications for counselors. In M. B. Scholl, A. S. McGowan, & J. T. Hansen (Eds.), *Humanistic perspectives on contemporary counseling issues* (pp. 17–44). New York, NY: Routledge.

Myers, J. E., & Sweeney, T. J. (2004). The indivisible self: An evidence-based model of wellness. *Journal of Individual Psychology, 60,* 234–244.

Myers, J. E., & Sweeney, T. J. (Eds.). (2005a). Assessing wellness: Formal and informal approaches. In *Counseling for wellness: Theory, research, and practice* (pp. 39–42). Alexandria, VA: American Counseling Association.

Myers, J. E., & Sweeney, T. J. (Eds.). (2005b). Stages of change and wellness. In *Counseling for wellness: Theory, research, and practice* (pp. 169–176). Alexandria, VA: American Counseling Association.

Myers, J. E., & Sweeney, T. J. (2006). *The wellness and habit change workbook*. Greensboro, NC: Author.

Myers, J. E., Sweeney, T. J., & Witmer, J. M. (2000). The Wheel of Wellness counseling for wellness: A holistic model for treatment planning. *Journal of Counseling & Development, 78,* 251–266.

National Public Radio, Robert Wood Johnson Foundation, & Harvard School of Public Health. (2013, September). *Education and health in schools: A survey of parents: Summary.* Retrieved from https://www.npr.org/documents/2013/dec/rwjf_npr_harvard_edpoll.pdf

Razzano, L. A., Cook, J. A., Yost, C., Jonikas, J. A., Swarbrick, M. A., Carter, T. M., & Santos, A. (2015). Factors associated with co-occurring medical conditions among adults with serious mental disorders. *Schizophrenia Research, 161,* 458–464.

Saul, J., & Rodgers, R. F. (2016). Wellness, not weight: Changing the focus in children and adolescents. *Journal of the American Academy of Child & Adolescent Psychiatry, 55,* 7–9.

Scott, K. M., Lim, C., Al-Hamzawi, A., Alonso, J., Bruffaerts, R., Caldas-de-Almeida, J. M., . . . Kawakami, N. (2016). Association of mental disorders with subsequent chronic physical conditions: World mental health surveys from 17 countries. *JAMA Psychiatry, 73,* 150–158.

Semple, R. J., Droutman, V., & Reid, B. A. (2017). Mindfulness goes to school: Things learned (so far) from research and real-world experiences. *Psychology in the Schools, 54,* 29–52.

Shannonhouse, L., Myers, J., Barden, S., Clarke, P., Weimann, R., Forti, A., . . . Porter, M. (2014). Finding your new normal: Outcomes of a wellness-oriented psychoeducational support group for cancer survivors. *The Journal for Specialists in Group Work, 39,* 3–28.

Sweeney, T. J., & Myers, J. E. (2005). Counseling for wellness. In J. E. Myers & T. J. Sweeney (Eds.), *Counseling for wellness: Theory, research, and practice* (pp. 185–196). Alexandria, VA: American Counseling Association.

Thompson, I., Amatea, E., & Thompson, E. (2014). Personal and contextual predictors of mental health counselors' compassion fatigue and burnout. *Journal of Mental Health Counseling,* *36,* 58–77.

Villalba, J. A., & Myers, J. E. (2008). Effectiveness of wellness-based classroom guidance in elementary school settings: A pilot study. *Journal of School Counseling, 6,* 1–31.

Watson, J. C., & Lemon, J. C. (2011). A profile of adolescent wellness: Implications for working with a help-seeking population. *The Journal of Humanistic Counseling, 50,* 70–83.

Chapter 2

History and Background

*A people without the knowledge of their past history, origin,
and culture is like a tree without roots.*

—Marcus Garvey

• • •

Although modern conceptualizations of wellness are relatively new,
attention to wellness dates back to ancient times, and current trends
are greatly influenced by previous movements throughout Asia, Europe, and the United States. As you read later chapters in this book,
you will likely notice that many of the current wellness models and
counseling interventions share similar concepts with ancient movements. In fact, ancient healing systems include many practices that
are thought to be "new wave" in the mental health field today. After
reviewing ancient traditions more closely, it appears many current
practices have been rediscovered rather than newly developed. In
the following sections, we review some of the previous movements
that appear to have influenced our current views of wellness.

Ancient Wellness

Ayurveda

Ayurveda originated in India more than 5,000 years ago and is considered by many to be the oldest healing system known. The system
began in ancient Vedic culture and was passed down through oral
tradition. Ayurveda is a holistic system that emphasizes synchrony

among the mind, body, and spirit. Ayurveda emphasizes health maintenance and prevention through balance of body, mind, and consciousness. One's balance is achieved through diet, lifestyle, and right thinking. The system maintains that each individual is unique and has their own *constitution*. A constitution consists of an individual's energy pattern, which is a combination of emotional, mental, and physical characteristics. A variety of sources can contribute to disruption in balance for one's constitution (e.g., relationships, physical trauma, dietary choices). Through insight and understanding, individuals can understand the causes of disruption and work to reestablish their balance and order.

Ayurveda asserts that there are three energies in the body that need to be balanced to maintain optimal health. Vata is associated with movement, Pitta is associated with metabolism, and Kapha is associated with body structure (Lad, 1984). To maintain balance in one's constitution, Ayurvedic physicians emphasize a daily routine that includes attention to personal hygiene, prayer, breathing, and exercise. Additionally, diet, cleansing, yoga, and meditation are strongly emphasized within the Ayurvedic tradition. The Ayurvedic Institute, located in Albuquerque, New Mexico, is one of the leading Ayurveda schools and spas outside of India. The institute provides resources, seminars, education, and consultations. For more information, you can visit the institute website at http://www.ayurveda.com.

Traditional Chinese Medicine (TCM)

TCM dates back more than 2,000 years and stems from the ancient Chinese philosophy Taoism. In the United States today, TCM is primarily used as complementary therapy in conjunction with modern Western medicine. The four foundational principles of TCM include the following:

1. Your body is an integrated whole.
2. You are completely connected to nature.
3. You were born with a natural self-healing ability.
4. Prevention is the best cure.

The mind and body connection is strongly emphasized in TCM. A primary goal is to help individuals integrate the body, mind, and spirit to create balance, harmony, and wellness. According to TCM, our bodies interact with nature, and our bodily processes all affect each other. This concept is embedded within the Five Element Framework, which includes a depiction of the five major internal organs (i.e., liver, heart, spleen, kidney, and lungs) and their interrelationships with one another and the environment. Within TCM, the framework is used to identify imbalances among one's emotions, body, mind, and spirit. The theory suggests a reciprocal relationship between various emotions and organ functioning. For example, lung is connected to grief, spleen is connected to worry, heart is connected to joy, kidney is connected to fear, and liver is connected to anger.

Another important component of TCM is the idea that energy, known as Qi, flows throughout various channels in the body, known as meridians. Regulating the energy flow is a key aspect of understanding health and healing. A related concept is the Yin and Yang theory. Within TCM, Yin and Yang are two opposing, yet complementary, energies in the body that must be balanced for an individual to experience a sense of harmony. Practitioners of TCM use a variety of healing methods. Each of the methods is based on Qi and the notion that we have the ability to self-heal. By using a specific healing approach, we can balance our Qi, which, in turn, helps our body regain healthy functioning. The TCM focus is holistic and includes attention to diet, exercise, and spirituality. Some of the specific approaches in TCM include acupuncture, acupressure, herbal medicine, eating, qigong, and tai chi. These approaches have now become popular even within Western medical practices (https://www.tcmworld.org).

Greek and Roman Medicine

Hippocrates, known as the "father of modern medicine," introduced a focus on disease prevention rather than just treating illness. The Greek medical community believed that illness was related to diet, lifestyle, and environmental factors. Humoral theory was prominent because the belief was that individuals needed a balance among the four humors (blood, black bile, yellow bile, and phlegm) to maintain health. The patient's contribution to illness was acknowledged during this time, and the relationship between mental and physical health became an important focus (Bendick, 2002).

Ancient Romans adopted many of the philosophies from ancient Greece related to disease prevention through lifestyle choices. Additionally, ancient Rome placed an emphasis on public health and personal hygiene by creating aqueducts, developing sewage systems, and building public toilets. They also created public baths with pools, and some had gyms and massage rooms.

Modern Wellness Movements

During the 19th century, many alternative therapies emerged throughout Europe and the United States. Holistic practices that focused on prevention and self-care became popular. These approaches—including naturopathy, homeopathy, chiropractic, and osteopathy—promoted the idea that health is maintained through lifestyle choices; diet; exercise; and a balance of body, mind, and spirit. Although these practices fell out of favor in the mainstream with the advent of modern medicine, many of them have reemerged in popularity with both the general public and medical community as part of the current renewed focus on holistic well-being.

Halbert Dunn is widely acknowledged as the father of the modern wellness movement. Dunn's (1961) book titled *High-Level Wellness* included 29 of his lectures in which he described his wellness philosophy and proposed a focus on prevention of illness by promoting healthy lifestyles. Dunn's work was not initially popular; however, several scholars, including Bill Hettler, incorporated his ideas into their work in the 1970s. In 1977, Bill Hettler, in collaboration with Dennis Elsenrath and Fred Leafgren (who were faculty members at the University of Wisconsin—Stevens Point), developed the Institute for Lifestyle Improvement, which in 1985 became the National Wellness Institute.

The current global perspective on health appears to include a strong emphasis on holistic wellness. For instance, the World Health Organization (1948) provided the following definition of health: "Health is a state of complete physical, mental and social well-being and not merely the absence of disease or infirmity" (p. 1). Additionally, in the United States, there is a current trend toward integrated primary care in which mental and behavioral health concerns are addressed within the primary health care setting (Vogel, Malcore, Illes, & Kirkpatrick, 2014). This movement acknowledges the link between mental and physical health and aims to improve overall health outcomes through a holistic approach. Current trends and policies related to integrated health care are discussed in Chapter 3.

Theoretical Wellness Models in Counseling

Wellness at the Core of the Counseling Profession

The counseling profession has historically maintained a wellness perspective as part of its developmental orientation. Leaders in the Humanistic Movement, such as Abraham Maslow and Carl Rogers, have greatly influenced the training and approaches for professional counselors. Professional counselors tend to endorse strength-based and holistic approaches to treating clients. Rogers's (1951, 1961) foundational works promoted a holistic perspective with a focus on individuals' personal growth. Although counselor training includes a variety of theoretical perspectives, counselors tend to approach human functioning from a holistic perspective and to explore all aspects of a client's functioning, including emotional, mental, occupational, social, physical, and spiritual dimensions. In a recent study with 211 participants, Mellin, Hunt, and Nichols (2011) found that counselors embraced a preventive, developmental, and wellness orientation in their work. Recently, Kaplan, Tarvydas, and Gladding (2014) provided the following definition of counseling: "Counseling is a professional relationship that empowers diverse individuals, families, and groups to accomplish mental health, wellness, education, and career goals" (p. 368).

The school counseling profession initially emerged in the early 1900s with a primary focus on vocational guidance focus. However, educating the "whole" child has long been a perspective of school professionals, dating back to Dewey (1916). Currently, counselors' role in schools is closely aligned with a wellness perspective. Their focus is holistic and preventive and consists of an emphasis on students' academic, career, and social and emotional development (American School Counselor Association, 2012, 2014). School counselors are expected to conduct large-group psychoeducational guidance lessons or small-group activities to promote students' holistic development. For example, the American School Counselor Association's (2014) Mindsets and Behaviors standards, which guide desired student competencies, state that school counselors should help students develop a "belief in development of whole self, including a healthy balance of mental, social/emotional and physical well-being" (p. 2).

Although an emphasis on holistic wellness has been a central part of counseling literature throughout the profession's evolution, there is not a consensus definition within the field. Most wellness models are multidimensional and emphasize positive aspects of functioning and strengths rather than deficits. Wellness models do tend to include similar components, such as mental, emotional, spiritual, physical, social, and vocational (Witmer & Young, 1996). Roscoe (2009) conducted a review of nine popular wellness models and found that most models include social, emotional, physical, intellectual, and spiritual dimensions. A few models also included occupational wellness, whereas one model included a psychological dimension, and another included an environmental dimension. Researchers have also proposed additional dimensions, such as "EcoWellness" (Reese & Myers, 2012) and "TechnoWellness" (Kennedy & Baker, 2016). A comprehensive review of wellness models is beyond the scope of this book. However, we believe it's important to review the most common models that influence current counseling practice and research.

Hettler's Six Dimensions of Wellness Model

One of the first modern wellness models was developed by Bill Hettler in 1976. The Six Dimensions of Wellness Model is interdependent and includes occupational, physical, social, intellectual, spiritual, and emotional dimensions. The model is clear and includes practical recommendations for individuals to maintain optimal health and well-being. A major focus of the model is on personal responsibility within each of the domain. Each domain includes two tenets to be followed. A summary of the domains and the basic tenets is included in Table 2.1.

The Indivisible Self Model of Wellness (IS-Wel)

The IS-Wel (Myers & Sweeney, 2005) is likely the most well-known and researched wellness model in the counseling profession (Myers & Sweeney, 2008). The IS-Wel is empirically developed and evolved from the authors' theoretical Wheel of Wellness model, which was based on Adlerian individual psychology (Hattie, Myers, & Sweeney, 2004). The IS-Wel consists of five wellness factors (Creative Self, Coping Self, Essential Self, Physical Self, and Social Self) and 17 secondary wellness factors that are embedded within each of the five factors. The Creative Self includes areas such as thinking, emotions, control, work, and humor. The Coping Self includes leisure, stress management, self-worth, and realistic beliefs. The Social Self includes friendship and love. The Physical Self includes exercise and nutrition, and the Essential Self includes spirituality, gender identity, cultural identity, and self-care. Each of these factors is considered within the different contexts in a client's life, including their stage of development, local community (e.g., family, neighborhood), institutions (e.g., school, government), and global policies. The breakdown of factors is included in Figure 2.1.

Practitioners and researchers can use the Five Factor Wellness Inventory (Myers, Sweeney, & Witmer, 2000) to assess individuals' level of wellness. This 73-item instrument provides information about one's total wellness and the five second-order wellness factors. The

Table 2.1

Hettler's Six Dimensions of Wellness Model

Wellness Dimension	Tenets
Occupational	It is better to choose a career which is consistent with our personal values, interests, and beliefs than to select one that is unrewarding to us.
	It is better to develop functional, transferable skills through structured involvement opportunities than to remain inactive and uninvolved.
Physical	It is better to consume foods and beverages that enhance good health rather than those which impair it.
	It is better to be physically fit than out of shape.
Social	It is better to contribute to the common welfare of our community than to think only of ourselves.
	It is better to live in harmony with others and our environment than to live in conflict with them.
Intellectual	It is better to stretch and challenge our minds with intellectual and creative pursuits than to become self-satisfied and unproductive.
	It is better to identify potential problems and choose appropriate courses of action based on available information than to wait, worry, and contend with major concerns later.
Emotional	It is better to be aware of and accept our feelings than to deny them.
	It is better to be optimistic in our approach to life than pessimistic.
Spiritual	It is better to ponder the meaning of life for ourselves and to be tolerant of the beliefs of others than to close our minds and become intolerant.
	It is better to live each day in a way that is consistent with our values and beliefs than to do otherwise and feel untrue to ourselves.

Note. Adapted from "The Six Dimensions of Wellness Model," by B. Hettler, 1976. Available at https://cdn.ymaws.com/www.nationalwellness.org/resource/resmgr/pdfs/SixDimensionsFactSheet.pdf. Copyright 1976 by Bill Hettler. Adapted with permission.

Five Factor Wellness Inventory can be used by researchers to investigate how wellness relates to other aspects of individuals' development and functioning. Practitioners can use the assessment to help clients evaluate their own levels of wellness and to assist with treatment planning and goal setting (Myers et al., 2000).

Substance Abuse and Mental Health Services Administration (SAMHSA)

SAMHSA has become a leading organization in promoting and supporting holistic wellness efforts. Although the organization did not develop a unique model, SAMHSA promotes the following eight dimensions of wellness: (a) emotional, (b) environmental, (c) financial, (d) intellectual, (e) occupational, (f) physical, (g) social, and (h) spiritual. The organization is active in wellness promotion

CONTEXTS:

Local (safety)
Family
Neighborhood
Community

Institutional (policies & laws)
Education
Religion
Government
Business/Industry

Global (world events)
Politics
Culture
Global Events
Environment
Media
Community

Chronometrical (lifespan)
Perpetual
Positive
Purposeful

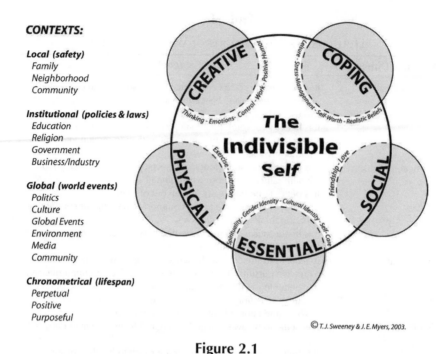

© T. J. Sweeney & J. E. Myers, 2003.

Figure 2.1

The Indivisible Self: An Evidence-Based Model of Wellness

Note. Creative = Creative Self; Coping = Coping Self; Social = Social Self; Essential = Essential Self; Physical = Physical Self. From *The Indivisible Self: An Evidence-Based Model of Wellness*, by T. J. Sweeney and J. E. Myers, 2003, Greensboro, NC: Author. Copyright 2003 by T. J. Sweeney and J. E. Myers. Reprinted with permission.

through disseminating literature about wellness strategies, providing resources on their website, developing podcasts, sponsoring a wellness week, and funding grants to develop wellness-focused programs and training.

Research

The research supporting the importance of holistic wellness has emerged from multiple disciplines, such as counseling, psychology, social work, medicine, nursing, public health, and education. We are at a point where it is undeniable that wellness is an important factor for individuals' overall quality of life and is strongly connected to mental and physical health. The wellness domains are somewhat distinct but still interrelated. Throughout each domain chapter, we provide the most current information and research related to wellness and wellness counseling. Although the research we present is from a variety of disciplines, we would be remiss to not mention

Melvin Witmer, Tom Sweeney, and Jane Myers as leaders who have contributed tremendously to the wellness literature within counseling and who have mentored countless students to continue wellness research and practice. These leaders have framed how we emphasize wellness at the core of the profession and have been the driving force behind the available models and research support for wellness counseling. Their work has played an important part in how we conceptualized this book and how we organized the topics. A collection of articles related to wellness counseling and wellness among a variety of subpopulations is available on the Chi Sigma Iota website for members (https://www.csi-net.org).

We acknowledge that counselors have a unique role in wellness promotion. Our professional perspectives and approaches are focused on strengths and holistic functioning. At the same time, we believe our clients' and students' wellness depends on our ability to (a) understand and use the research from other disciplines (e.g., health, medicine), (b) effectively collaborate with these disciplines as part of a multidisciplinary team, and (c) conduct our own research and put it into practice. Going forward, we advocate for collaborate research on the most effective approaches for wellness counseling and for developing systems that work in concert to promote wellness for individuals, groups, and families. We also hope to implement strategies to bring the research to practice. These aspects are discussed throughout this book.

Conclusion

In this book, we are not proposing a new model or theory of wellness for the counseling profession. Rather, we have organized our chapters in a way that captures the multidimensional nature of holistic wellness. Thus, we present holistic wellness through the following sections: Mind, Body, Spirit, Emotion, and Connection. As you read through the sections, you may notice some overlap. Indeed, as previous authors have noted, we believe wellness is a synergistic construct in which the various components are related and work together to promote holistic functioning.

The future of wellness is exciting and filled with innovative new approaches to help us experience the best possible lives. As we implement new strategies to maintain our wellness, it is important to not dismiss practices from previous time periods and cultures. Likewise, counselors should become familiar with more ancient practices and be aware of the potential benefits for clients.

Reflection Prompts

1. How do you believe the wellness domains are connected? Discuss how you believe each domain affects the others.
2. Have you tried any of the practices from ancient medicine? If so, what was your experience like? If not, what are your perceptions of these practices?

Learning Activities

Conduct an Internet search for local centers that offer Ayurveda or TCM.

- What are some of the services offered?
- How do these services compare with what you consider to be modern wellness activities?

Review the Substance Abuse and Mental Health Services Administration website (https://www.samhsa.gov/wellness-initiative/eight-dimensions-wellness) and filter through some of the resources.

- Which resources do you believe would be most helpful with clients?
- How can you use these resources now and in the future?

Resources

Chi Sigma Iota International Honor Society

https://www.csi-net.org

A counseling honor society focused on professional identity and wellness promotion.

Substance Abuse and Mental Health Services Administration Wellness Initiative

https://www.samhsa.gov/wellness-initiative/eight-dimensions-wellness

A wellness initiative to raise awareness and to provide resources.

References

American School Counselor Association. (2012). *The ASCA national model: A framework for school counseling programs* (3rd ed.). Alexandria, VA: Author.

American School Counselor Association. (2014). *Mindsets and behaviors for student success: K–12 college- and career-readiness standards for every student.* Retrieved from https://www.schoolcounselor.org/asca/media/asca/home/MindsetsBehaviors.pdf

Bendick, J. (2002). *Galen and the gateway to medicine.* Bathgate, ND: Bethlehem Books.

Dewey, J. (1916). *Democracy and education: An introduction to the philosophy of education.* New York, NY: Macmillan.

Dunn, H. L. (1961). *High-level wellness: A collection of twenty-nine short talks on different aspects of the theme "high-level wellness for man and society."* Arlington, VA: R.W. Beatty.

Hattie, J. A., Myers, J. E., & Sweeney, T. J. (2004). A factor structure of wellness: Theory, assessment, analysis, and practice. *Journal of Counseling & Development, 82,* 354–364.

Hettler, B. (1976). *Six dimensions of wellness.* Stevens Point, WI: University of Wisconsin, National Wellness Institute.

Kaplan, D. M., Tarvydas, V. M., & Gladding, S. T. (2014). 20/20: A vision for the future of counseling: The new consensus definition of counseling. *Journal of Counseling & Development, 92,* 366–372. https://doi.org/10.1002/j.1556-6676.2014.00164.x

Kennedy, S. D., & Baker, S. B. (2016). Using the TechnoWellness Inventory (TWI) to examine and apply a new wellness construct. *Journal of Counselor Leadership and Advocacy, 3,* 41–51. https://doi.org/10.1080/2326716X.2016.1145559

Lad, V. (1984). *Ayurveda: The science of self-healing.* Santa Fe, NM: Lotus Press.

Mellin, E. A., Hunt, B., & Nichols, L. M. (2011). Counselor professional identity: Findings and implications for counseling and interprofessional collaboration. *Journal of Counseling & Development, 89,* 140–147.

Myers, J. E., & Sweeney, T. J. (Eds.). (2005). *Wellness in counseling: Theory, research, and practice.* Alexandria, VA: American Counseling Association.

Myers, J. E., & Sweeney, T. J. (2008). Wellness counseling: The evidence base for practice. *Journal of Counseling & Development, 86,* 482–493.

Myers, J. E., Sweeney, T. J., & Witmer, M. (2000). Counseling for wellness: A holistic model for treatment planning. *Journal of Counseling & Development, 78,* 251–266.

Reese, R. F., & Myers, J. E. (2012). EcoWellness: The missing factor in holistic wellness models. *Journal of Counseling & Development, 90,* 400–406. https://doi.org/10.1002/j.1556-6676.2012.00050.x

Rogers, C. (1951). *Client-centered therapy: Its current practice, implications and theory.* London, England: Constable.

Rogers, C. (1961). *On becoming a person: A therapist's view of psychotherapy.* London, England: Constable.

Roscoe, L. J. (2009). Wellness: A review of theory and measurement for counselors. *Journal of Counseling & Development, 87,* 216–226.

Sweeney, T. J., & Myers, J. E. (2003). *The Indivisible Self: An evidence-based model of wellness.* Greensboro, NC: Author.

Vogel, M. E., Malcore, S. A., Illes, R. C., & Kirkpatrick, H. A. (2014). Integrated primary care: Why you should care and how to get started. *Journal of Mental Health Counseling, 36,* 130–144.

Witmer, J. M., & Young, M. E. (1996). Preventing counselor impairment: A wellness approach. *Journal of Humanistic Education & Development, 34,* 141–155.

World Health Organization. (1948). *Constitution of the World Health Organization.* Geneva, Switzerland: Author.

Chapter 3

Trends in Health and Wellness

Of all the forms of inequality, injustice in health care is the most shocking and inhumane.

—Martin Luther King Jr.

• • •

In the previous chapter, we explored the history of wellness specifically as it relates to individuals. The purpose of this chapter is to provide context for how wellness interacts with systems, such as health care, to affect the emerging treatment and prevention health care paradigm ushered in by the Patient Protection and Affordable Care Act of 2010 (ACA). From a public health lens, we review current trends and policies and examine the role professional counselors have in advocating for client wellness and their own professional role in preventative medicine. Furthermore, the strength-based, self-care focus, and holistic nature of wellness counseling fits well with trauma-informed care, which encourages counselors to be educated about the impact of trauma on clients. Finally, we highlight specific wellness competencies in the counseling profession, which have been proposed by Barden, Conley, and Young (2015).

Advances in Modern Medicine and Lifestyle Diseases

In the past 50 years, we have seen remarkable improvements in human health and wellness as a result of extraordinary advances in medicine. In the past 20 years alone, our understanding of neuro-logic diseases has exploded with new knowledge of the interplay between genes and the environment (a field called genomics). For example, with the development of The Cancer Genome Atlas, which complies the genomic changes in all cancers, individualized cancer treatment has revolutionized the oncology field. New drugs have emerged, such as the development of the highly active antiretroviral therapy for treatment of HIV, which has changed the HIV diagnosis for many from a death sentence to a manageable chronic disease. Improvements in medical technology, such as the widespread use of ultrasounds in emergency medicine, have facilitated rapid and ac-curate diagnoses of life-threatening conditions.

Yet, preventable chronic diseases, aptly called *lifestyle diseases*, are on the rise and more prevalent in industrialized countries than develop-ing ones. As the relationship between people and their environment is altered with modernization, health and wellness often go by the way-side. One prime example can be found in studying the epidemiology of eating disorders. The prevalence of eating disorders, which are con-centrated in industrialized Western countries, has risen in Asia over the past 40 years as a result of globalization and industrialization. A fascinating natural experiment occurred in Fiji in the 1990s, when TV first became available on the island. Becker, Burwell, Herzog, Ham-burg, and Gilman (2002) studied Fijian school-age girls in 1995, be-fore TV was available, and again 3 years later. Of the girls surveyed in 1998, 29% had high eating-disorder risk scores, compared with 13% in 1995. In addition, compared with girls who watched TV less fre-quently, girls who watched TV three nights a week or more were 1.5 times more likely to describe themselves as "too big or fat" and 1.3 times more likely to diet (Becker et al., 2002).

Through modernization, our whole relationship with food has undergone massive changes that have resulted in quite dire con-sequences. For instance, because the typical Western diet includes more meat, dairy, alcohol, sugar, and processed foods, incidence of obesity, heart disease, cardiovascular disease, Type 2 diabetes, and many types of cancer have steadily increased. As can be seen in Table 3.1, in the past decade, there has been a decrease in deaths from now-treatable conditions such as tuberculosis, flu, and diarrhea as well as a dramatic reduction in death as a result of childbirth. Com-paratively, in 2014, the top causes of death were intricately connect-ed with diet and lifestyle choices.

Researchers have suggested that lifestyle modifications (e.g., diet, physical activity) can prevent upward of 90% of Type 2 diabetes, 80%

Table 3.1

Leading Causes of Death in the United States
for Years 1914 and 2014

1914		2014	
Cause	**No. Deaths**	**Cause**	**No. Deaths**
1. Heart disease	96,428	1. Heart disease	614,348
2. Tuberculosis	86,359	2. Cancer	591,699
3. Pneumonia and influenza	80,703	3. Chronic lower respiratory disease	147,101
4. Nephritis	60,494	4. Accidents	136,053
5. Intracranial lesions of vascular origin	57,033	5. Stroke	133,103
6. Cancer	47,986	6. Alzheimer's disease	93,541
7. Diarrhea, enteritis, and ulceration of the intestines	45,811	7. Diabetes	76,488
8. Accidents excluding motor vehicle	44,831	8. Influenza and pneumonia	55,227
9. Premature birth	26,078	9. Nephritis, nephrotic syndrome, and nephrosis	48,146
10. Senility	12,233	10. Intentional self-harm	42,773

Note. All data are from the Centers for Disease Control and Prevention at https://www.cdc.gov/.

of heart disease, and 70% of stroke and colon cancer (Willet, 2002). In fact, improving diet alone has been shown to reverse chronic disease processes, such as heart disease and Type 2 diabetes, and protect against everything ranging from high cholesterol to Alzheimer's disease to mental illness. As an example, in a randomly controlled trial, researchers showed that a plant-based, vegetarian diet improved mood disturbance symptoms, depression, anxiety, and stress within just 2 weeks (Beezhold & Johnston, 2012).

Social Determinants of Health

In addition to the individual level action we can take to promote health and wellness, we must also consider the impact of systems on our access and ability to make healthy choices. *Social determinants of health* are the conditions in the environment that affect our health, well-being, and quality-of-life outcomes. The Office of Disease Prevention and Health Promotion under the U.S. Department of Health and Human Services provides science-based, national goals for improving the health of all Americans. For the past 30 years, they have released three national agendas (one every 10 years), the most recent being Healthy People 2020 (https://www.healthypeople.gov/). A new topic area in the Healthy People 2020 initiative, social determinates of health are broken into five key areas: (1) economic stability, (2) education, (3) social and community context, (4) health and health care, and (5) neighborhood and built environment. Table 3.2 gives examples of issues within each determinant that have been shown to affect mortality and morbidity, life expectancy, health care expenditures, and health status (see https://www.cdc.gov/).

Exploring wellness through this public health lens, we see that individual health problems are intricately tied to community health problems and that environment and culture not only help define community health problems but also show how those issues can be addressed and with what resources. If we simply focus on health and wellness of the individual, we ignore the interplay of social factors with biological factors that lead to negative health outcomes disproportionately experienced by minority and underserved populations. That is, *health disparities* are differing health outcomes driven by the social, economic, and environmental disadvantages experienced by certain groups of people in the conditions in which they live, learn, work, and play. Although health disparities are often thought of as specific to race and income, there are systematic barriers to accessing health care to all marginalized groups, including sexual and gender minorities, people with limited English proficiency, and people living in both rural and inner cities (Agency for Healthcare Research and Quality, 2014).

Health and Mental Health Disparities

Diversity characteristics historically linked to discrimination (e.g., race/ethnicity, gender, socioeconomic status, religion, mental health, disability, sexual orientation, immigration status) are known to influence health status and create barriers to optimal health for

Table 3.2

Healthy People 2020 Approach to Social Determinants of Health

Economic Stability	Education	Social and Community Context	Health and Health Care	Neighborhood and Built Environment
Poverty	High school graduation	Social cohesion	Access to health care	Access to healthy foods
Employment	Enrollment in higher education	Civic participation	Access to primary care	Quality of housing
Food security	Language and literacy	Discrimination	Health literacy	Crime and violence
Housing stability	Early childhood education and development	Incarceration		Environmental conditions

Note. Adapted from Centers for Disease Control and Prevention data at https://www.cdc.gov/

individuals, families, and communities (see https://www.healthy-people.gov/2020/topics-objectives/topic/social-determinants-of-health). Health disparities affect Americans in striking ways. One study showed that there is a life expectancy difference of 33 years among different groups in the United States (Murray et al., 2006). Research by the Joint Center for Political and Economic Studies showed the economic impact of health disparities by examining the combined costs of health inequalities and premature death in the United States, resulting in $1.24 trillion spent between 2003 and 2006 (LaVeist, Gaskin, & Richard, n.d.).

How exactly do social determinants of health affect people's actual physical health? One crucial way is through the deleterious impact of stress on the body. One example of the ways stress can harm people's health lies within our DNA. *Telomeres*, which are the sections of DNA that repeat over and over again, are found at the end of people's chromosomes, and their length shortens each time a cell divides. Therefore, telomeres are like the rings of a tree trunk, a cellular clock that can be measured to estimate age. Telomeres also can shorten prematurely as a result of disease and other stressors. Therefore, as people age, their telomere length naturally shortens; however, stress on the body can speed up this process. Shortened telomere length is associated with increased risk for chronic disease (such as high blood pressure and diabetes) and increased risk for mental health issues (such as depression and other mood disorders). By comparing telomere length with social determinants of health, researchers have been able to show the connection among poverty, racism, neighborhood, and other behavioral stressors and biopsychosocial processes at the cellular level (Geronimus et al., 2015; Ridout et al., 2015).

A stark example of health disparities is the alarming statistic that in the United States, Black mothers die at 3–4 times the rate of White mothers (Creanga, Syverson, Seed, & Callaghan, 2017). When specifically looking at pregnancy- or childbirth-related complications, Black women are 2–3 times more likely to die than White women who have the same condition (Tucker, Berg, Callaghan, & Hsia, 2007). This health disparity can be explained by many different factors that boil down to the same thing: the chronic and toxic stress of being both Black and a woman. The effects of discrimination in everyday life and even by medical professionals who distrust or do not take seriously pain and other symptoms wreak havoc on the body, which is most vulnerable to stress during and right after pregnancy.

Of course, chronic stress affects both mental and physical health, and health disparities persist. Racial and ethnic disparities are greater for mental health care than other types of health services. As shown in Figure 3.1, closing the gap in outcomes will require an approach that considers factors at both the intervention level (e.g., policy, medical health system, community programs) and the societal level (e.g., housing, income, discrimination; Primm et al., 2010). Simply put, mental health disparities exist for minorities and other stigmatized groups because of barriers to access, which includes access to the following:

- reliable transportation;
- services open around work time;
- clinicians who value their cultural norms and see their symptoms in the context of their environment;

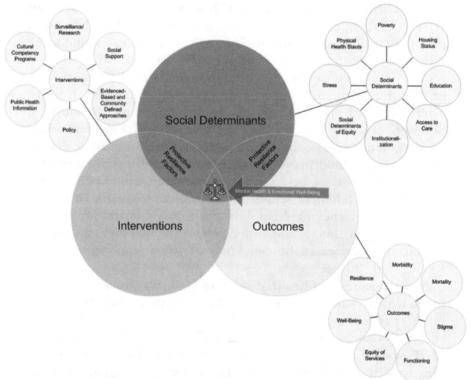

Figure 3.1

Primm et al.'s (2010) Proposed Model of Interactions Among Social Determinants, Interventions, and Outcomes to Promote Mental Health

Note. From "The Role of Public Health in Addressing Racial and Ethnic Disparities in Mental Health and Mental Illness," by A. B. Primm et al., 2010, *Preventing Chronic Disease, 7*, p. A20. Available at https://www.cdc.gov/pcd/issues/2010/jan/09_0125a.htm. Copyright 2010 by the Centers for Disease Control and Prevention.

- a community that supports seeking mental health services;
- treatment settings free from racism, bias, and discrimination;
- services in their native language; and, perhaps most influentially,
- adequate and affordable health insurance coverage.

Health Policy, Health Promotion, and Advocacy

Wellness is intricately tied to the health care system because a healthy population leads to lower health care costs, which leads to lower insurance costs, which leads to more people with access to insurance, and which leads back to where we started, with a healthier population (see Figure 3.2). As with any cycle, the reverse is also true. An unhealthy population leads to higher medical costs, higher insurance premiums, fewer people with access to insurance, and back again to an unhealthy population. In 2010, before the passage of the ACA, the United States was stuck in the downward cycle, with health care costs and the number of uninsured Americans steadily rising (Obama, 2016). Two key goals in the ACA were to increase access to health insurance and lower health care costs, and this aim was mainly accomplished through a focus on wellness and prevention. Expanding Medicaid coverage gave access to health insurance to low-income Americans, many of whom are members of marginalized communities that experience the largest health disparities. Furthermore, by including the mandate to require health insurance, the healthiest Americans (e.g., young adults) enter the health insurance market, effectively spreading the risk out, which lowers premiums

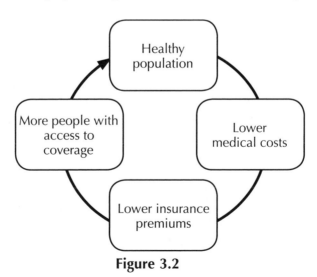

Figure 3.2

Wellness and Health Care Cycle

and makes coverage more accessible to all. The more people with health insurance, the more people will take advantage of preventative care, which lowers health care costs for everyone. An example is going to a primary care doctor covered by insurance for a well visit (primary prevention) or at the first sign of sickness (secondary prevention) rather than to the emergency room with a full-blown, and more costly, illness (tertiary prevention). To bolster this mission even further, the ACA mandated that insurance companies cover preventative services that included health and wellness issues related to behavioral health, not just physical health, such as alcohol and other drug misuse, diet and obesity issues, family planning and maternity care that includes depression screening, and domestic and interpersonal violence services. Finally, the Prevention and Public Health Fund was created by Section 4002 of the ACA and is the first mandatory funding mechanism dedicated to increasing prevention measures and improving public health.

After the passage of the ACA, the uninsured rate declined by 43%, with 49 million uninsured Americans in 2010 declining to 29 million in 2015 (Cohen, Martinez, & Zamnitti, 2016). Expanding insurance coverage created access to health and financial security for 20 million Americans, and it improved prevention services for the millions who already had insurance (Obama, 2016). Any large piece of legislation can be improved, and the ACA is no exception. The fact that our health care system is privately run means that it is left open to similar marketing influences as business—at the end of the day, more services means more money. In this paradigm, primary prevention (e.g., education and access to nutritious food) costs individuals less, but tertiary prevention (e.g., high-cholesterol medicine or cardiovascular surgery) makes many businesses (e.g., hospitals, pharmaceutical companies, the dieting economy) more. However, if the policy is simply reversed, there will be an immediate and dramatic impact on the health and well-being of millions of Americans. Given the dramatic shift in the political climate since the inception of the ACA, it is imperative that wellness counselors pay attention to the rapidly shifting policy that has such a large impact on the accessibility of prevention and health care services. At the time of writing this book, the fate of the ACA is unclear. Congress has held more than 50 votes to repeal the legislation; however, no bill has been successful in both the House and the Senate. However, the Tax Cuts and Jobs Act of 2017 included a repeal of the individual mandate (which the American Counseling Association officially opposed). This repeal does not go into effect into 2019, so the impact on the health care system is unknown. Regardless of political affiliation, advocating for expanded health care coverage, access, and prevention services is a crucial role of the wellness counselor.

Another form of advocacy is through health promotion, which empowers people with skills, education, and access to gain control over and improve their health. As a public health strategy for prevention, health promotion goes beyond the individual toward societal interventions that use education, technology, and policy. For example, as smoke-free laws have become ubiquitous in public spaces, exposure to secondhand smoke has been cut in half, dropping from 52% of the population in 1999 to 25% in 2012 (Homa et al., 2015). Human papillomavirus vaccines, first approved in 2006, are estimated to prevent up to 90% of cervical cancers (Medeiros, Rosa, da Rosa, Bozzetti, & Zanini, 2009). In 30 years, seat belt use has increased from 11% to 85%, saving hundreds of thousands of lives (National Center for Injury Prevention and Control, 2011).

Because many of the risk factors for chronic disease are behaviorally modifiable (e.g., increasing physical activity, improving diet, and not using tobacco products), the role of the wellness counselor includes advocacy to inform health promotion strategies with the context of social determinants of health to reach those people most at risk and to provide a holistic approach to care. For instance, we know the vast and damaging impact of obesity on health and well-being; however, how do you help those in poverty improve nutrition when there are no healthy food options within their community? Chronic stress is a key mechanism through which environment affects health; thus, you cannot begin to improve health without addressing all of the ways social determinants of health contribute to stress.

As a wellness counselor, there are evidence-based interventions to mitigate the adverse effects of stress. In this book, we explore the ways in which stress interferes with mind, body, spirit, emotion, and connection wellness. A crucial component of effective interventions is viewing the client in a holistic manner that considers their unique context. Exploring the impact of early childhood stress, cultural considerations, family history, trauma history, and individual characteristics and experiences that affect resilience and motivation is key. A trauma-informed approach is woven throughout this book to highlight the ways in which an individual's unique experiences with stress and coping affect their overall health and wellness, helping us hold space for our clients to explore the possibility of lasting and sustainable change.

To that end, we have included the Wellness Counseling Competencies proposed by Barden et al. (2015; see Table 3.3). Although these competencies have not been officially endorsed by the American Counseling Association, we feel they are a great starting place to

Table 3.3

Wellness Counseling Competencies

Competency	Description
Assessment	
Knowledge	a. Understand the foundation of counseling from an integrated model of biological, psychological, and social/relationship dimensions.
	b. Demonstrate comprehension and evaluation of medical terminology, medical procedures, and results of critical medical tests.
Skills	a. Conduct a comprehensive biopsychosocial interview and evaluate interactions between biological and psychological findings.
	b. Recognize and evaluate client counseling needs while integrating disabilities, illnesses, or injuries with strengths, resources and supports.
	c. Assess a client's compliance with medical and/or counseling treatments and to gauge the effect of the client's economic/social/cultural environment on the ability to engage in treatment.
	d. Help clients understand the value and purpose of medical testing.
Treatment	
Knowledge	a. Knowledge of the most current evidence-based treatments and efficacy of counseling interventions on health outcomes.
	b. Understand the causes and treatment of major medical disease categories and the interaction with mental and social/cultural stressors.
	c. Recognize environmental and social factors that interfere with client engagement in healthy or wellness behaviors.
	d. Knowledge of biological responses to pharmacology/psychotropic medications and the influence of psychotropic medications on client functioning.
	e. Knowledge of effective and ineffective complementary and alternative medicines, including meditation, herbal treatments, acupuncture, and diet.
	f. Knowledge of the most effective methods to deal with counseling issues associated with traumatic medical events and the ability to help clients deal with grief, death, and the dying process.
	g. Knowledge of the most effective methods of prevention and health promotion.
	h. Knowledge of emerging technologies to assist clients in monitoring and changing health behaviors.
Skills	a. Implement evidence-based counseling practices to improve health and wellness that take into account the client's stage of change, cultural, religious, or spiritual background attitudes and values.
	b. Demonstrate ability to work with other health care providers in a team approach.
	c. Use emerging technologies to assist clients in monitoring and changing health behavior, such as exercise, diet, and smoking.

Note. Adapted from "Integrating Health and Wellness in Mental Health Counseling: Clinical, Educational, and Policy Implications," by S. M. Barden, A. H., Conley, and M. E. Young, 2015, *Journal of Mental Health Counseling, 37*, p. 159. Copyright 2015 by the American Mental Health Counselors Association. Adapted with permission.

consider the knowledge and skills that professional counselors need to effectively integrate health and wellness into their counseling practice. Read through these competencies and keep them in mind as you move through the rest of this book. In Part II, we explore the five areas of wellness: mind, body, spirit, emotion, and connection.

Conclusion

In this chapter, we have explored the impact that a modern lifestyle has on people's health and wellness and the role that prevention plays in combating the prevalence of lifestyle diseases. The impact of environment on health and wellness was examined, not just at the individual level but also at the systems level through social determinants of health and resulting health disparities. Wellness counselors can be viewed as ambassadors of both prevention and intervention, and they must advocate at the client, professional, and community levels for access and equity in health care.

Reflection Prompts

1. What are ways that you interact with the health care system? In what ways does your privilege afford you access to health and wellness services? What barriers do you face?
2. What do you currently do as a regular preventative health and wellness measure? What could you improve?

Learning Activities

Exploring Your Social Determinants of Health

Create a genogram mapping the impact that the social determinants of health (education, neighborhood/environment, social support, finances, and health care) have had on the past three generations of your family's health. Use one color or symbol to denote a positive impact on health and another to show a negative impact.

Resources

American Counseling Association

https://www.counseling.org/government-affairs/
actioncenter?vvsrc=%2fHome

Stay up to date on the American Counseling Association's official positions on legislative issues through their government affairs initiatives and opportunities for advocacy.

American Public Health Association

https://www.apha.org/policies-and-advocacy/advocacy-for-public-health/coming-to-dc

The American Public Health Association advocates for public health issues, and this website offers great tips and strategies for advocacy, including sample e-mails to Congress and how to meet with lawmakers in Washington, DC.

Trust for America's Health

http://healthyamericans.org/health-issues/prevention-fund-state-by-state-information/

This comprehensive resource gives state-by-state fact sheets on how the Prevention and Public Health Fund is benefiting each state.

References

Agency for Healthcare Research and Quality. (2014, May). *2013 National healthcare disparities report* (AHRQ Publication No. 14-0006). Retrieved from https://www.ahrq.gov/sites/default/files/publications/files/2013nhdr.pdf

Barden, S. M., Conley, A. H., & Young, M. E. (2015). Integrating health and wellness in mental health counseling: Clinical, educational, and policy implications. *Journal of Mental Health Counseling, 37,* 152–163.

Becker, A. E., Burwell, R. A., Herzog, D. B., Hamburg, P., & Gilman, S. E. (2002). Eating behaviours and attitudes following prolonged exposure to television among ethnic Fijian adolescent girls. *The British Journal of Psychiatry, 180,* 509–514.

Beezhold, B. L., & Johnston, C. S. (2012). Restriction of meat, fish, and poultry in omnivores improves mood: A pilot randomized controlled trial. *Nutrition Journal, 11,* 9.

Cohen, R. A., Martinez, M. E., & Zammitti, E. P. (2016, May). *Early release of selected estimates based on data from the 2015 National Health Interview Survey.* Retrieved from https://www.cdc.gov/nchs/nhis/releases/released201605.htm

Creanga, A. A., Syverson, C., Seed, K., & Callaghan, W. M. (2017). Pregnancy-related mortality in the United States, 2011–2013. *Obstetrics & Gynecology, 130,* 366–373.

Geronimus, A. T., Pearson, J. A., Linnenbringer, E., Schulz, A. J., Reyes, A. G., Epel, E. S., . . . Blackburn, E. H. (2015). Race-ethnicity, poverty, urban stressors, and telomere length in a Detroit community-based sample. *Journal of Health and Social Behavior, 56,* 199–224.

Homa, D. M., Neff, L. J., King, B. A., Caraballo, R. S., Bunnell, R. E., Babb, S. D., . . . Wang, L. (2015). Vital signs: Disparities in non-smokers' exposure to secondhand smoke—United States, 1999–2012. *Morbidity and Mortality Weekly Report, 64,* 103–108.

LaVeist, T. A., Gaskin, D. J., & Richard, P. (n.d.). *The economic burden of health inequalities in the United States.* Retrieved from http://jointcenter.org/sites/default/files/Economic%20Burden%20of%20Health%20Inequalities%20Fact%20Sheet.pdf

Medeiros, L. R., Rosa, D. D., da Rosa, M. I., Bozzetti, M. C., & Zanini, R. R. (2009). Efficacy of human papillomavirus vaccines: A systematic quantitative review. *International Journal of Gynecological Cancer, 19,* 1166–1176.

Murray, C. J. L., Kulkarni, S. C., Michaud, C., Tomijima, N., Bulzacchelli, M. T., Iandiorio, T. J., & Ezzati, M. (2006). Eight Americans: Investigating mortality disparities across races, counties, and race-counties in the United States. *PLOS Medicine, 3*(12), e545.

National Center for Injury Prevention and Control. (2011). *Policy impact: Seat belts.* Retrieved from https://www.cdc.gov/motorvehiclesafety/pdf/policyimpact-seatbelts.pdf

Obama, B. (2016). United States health care reform: Progress to date and next steps. *Journal of the American Medical Association, 316,* 525–532.

Patient Protection and Affordable Care Act, Pub. L. 111-148, 42 U.S.C. §§ 18001–18121 (2010).

Primm, A. B., Vasquez, M. J., Mays, R. A., Sammons-Posey, D., McKnight-Eily, L. R., Presley-Cantrell, L. R., . . . Perry, G. S. (2010). The role of public health in addressing racial and ethnic disparities in mental health and mental illness. *Preventing Chronic Disease, 7,* A20.

Ridout, S. J., Ridout, K. K., Kao, H. T., Carpenter, L. L., Philip, N. S., Tyrka, A. R., & Price, L. H. (2015). Telomeres, early-life stress and mental illness. *Advances in Psychosomatic Medicine, 34,* 92–108.

Tax Cuts and Jobs Act, Pub. L. 115-97, 131 STAT. 2054 (2017). Retrieved from https://www.congress.gov/115/plaws/publ97/PLAW-115publ97.pdf

Tucker, M. J., Berg, C. J., Callaghan, W. M., & Hsia, J. (2007). The Black–White disparity in pregnancy-related mortality from 5 conditions: Differences in prevalence and case-fatality rates. *American Journal of Public Health, 97,* 247–251.

Willet, W. C. (2002, April 26). Balancing life-style and genomics research for disease prevention. *Science, 296,* 695–698.

Part II
The Five Domains
of Wellness

Chapter 4

Mind

Between stimulus and response there is a space.
In that space is our power to choose our response.
In our response lies our growth and our freedom.

—Viktor Frankl

• • •

If you have ever taken an introduction to psychology or cognition course, you have probably learned about Phineas Gage. In 1848, 25-year-old Phineas Gage was tasked with blowing up rocks to clear a new railway path. An unfortunate accident led to a tamping iron blowing through his left cheek, behind his eye socket, and out the top of his head. Miraculously, Gage did not die; however, the accident left much of his left frontal lobe destroyed, and his personality dramatically changed. If you are familiar with this story, you probably remember learning that Gage went from even-tempered to aggressive and profane, making it clear for the first time in history that there was absolutely a connection between the biological structure of the brain and our personality and behavior. What is less known about Gage is that although he did eventually die decades later from complications from his brain damage, his dramatic personality shift was not permanent. Just a few years after his accident, Gage regained important skills, such as planning and focus, and he was able to lead a relatively normal life. When it comes to the brain, even in the event of massive damage, healing is possible.

Wellness is not simply aspirational, and it should not be a privilege only reserved for few. Wellness counseling has something to offer every client, regardless of their presenting issue, life circumstance, or health challenge. The brain is truly amazing (what we know about it is constantly evolving!), and having a framework for how it works is a starting place to empower any client to train their mind to increase well-being. Working with clients to help them understand how the brain functions, how amazing the process of *neuroplasticity* is, and how the mind interprets what the brain is telling it can be an empowering catalyst toward making intentional movement forward in the change process. *Mind wellness* is conceptualized as the positive interaction among genes, neurobiology, experiences, thoughts, and emotions to strengthen the neural circuitry that supports wellness. In this chapter, we explore how biology and brain structure work, which lays the foundation to explore the relationship among our thoughts, behaviors, and emotions.

The Brain

Let's start with some basic brain anatomy. *Neurons* are the basic nerve cells that transmit information through electrical and chemical signals. The human brain is composed of billions of neurons, and each one contains the cell body (which includes the nucleus where genetic materials is stored), dendrites (tiny branches that receive information), and an axon (which transmits information). *Neurotransmitters* and *neuromodulators* are brain chemicals that are transmitted from the axon to the dendrites of other cells across tiny spaces called *synaptic gaps*. These connections among neurons form neural networks that are the elaborate electrical patterns that underlie our thoughts, feelings, and behavior. You have probably heard the phrase "neurons that wire together, fire together," and this basically means that as you form associations and repeat experiences, you strengthen neural networks that basically keep you on your current path, unless you set an intention not to. Our habits and patterns of thinking, behaving, and reacting are often the things that get in our way when we are working toward wellness. Therefore, you have to train your brain to set you on a new and different path—a path toward wellness.

You are probably familiar with some neurotransmitters because they tend to get a lot of press. Some examples are serotonin (affects motivation and mood and plays a role in depression and anxiety), dopamine (affects experience of enjoyment and pleasure and plays a role in addiction), and norepinephrine (affects attention and thinking and plays a role in stress response). Neurotransmitters can have either an activation effect or an inhibitory effect on the actions of the receiving neuron. This effect is not clear cut and depends on what type of receptor is present on the target cell. There are currently 53 known neurotransmitters (and the number keeps growing!), and each one can affect the genetic factory in the receiving cell nucleus differently. Therefore, neurotransmitters can modify how our genes respond, thus modifying the next signal that a neuron sends to the next one in the neural network. This concept of the intricate interplay between genes and environment, or *neuroepigenetics*, has opened up a whole new way scientists understand the impact that experience (e.g., parental behavior, stress, learning, substance use, environmental toxins, trauma) has on our neural function.

A really great way to teach basic brain anatomy to a client or student is to use the "Brain in the Palm of Your Hand" activity by Dr. Daniel Siegel (see http://www.drdansiegel.com/resources/everyday_mindsight_tools/). As depicted in Figure 4.1, in this exercise, you hold your hand up in a fist position. The wrist and palm are the *brain stem*, or the "reptilian brain." The brain stem sends messages to

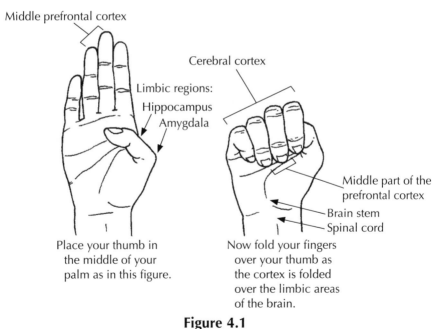

Figure 4.1

The Brain in the Palm of the Hand

Note. The hand model depicts the major regions of the brain: cerebral cortex in the fingers, limbic area in the thumb, and brain stem in the palm. The spinal cord is represented by the wrist. From Daniel J. Siegel, 2010, *Mindsight: The New Science of Personal Transformation*, p. 15. Copyright 2010 by Mind Your Brain, Inc. Reprinted with permission.

the rest of the body about basic functions related to things such as hunger, sleep, and arousal.

Next is the thumb, or the *limbic system*. Considered the "old mammalian brain," the limbic system works closely with the brain stem to create our basic drives and emotions and is composed of five major regions. The *amygdala* is our emotional response center that is responsible for perceiving danger and is the key to emotions such as fear and anxiety. When we are threatened, the amygdala sends out a distress call to the *hypothalamus*, and it initiates our fight, flight, or freeze response. The hypothalamus, which can be thought of as the command center of the brain, works with the pituitary gland to regulate hormones and the body's stress response. Next, the *hippocampus* is responsible for memories and links physical sensations, emotions, thoughts, facts, and reflections into coherent recollection. This process is called *encoding* and acts like the filing cabinet of the brain. Finally, the *cingulate cortex* regulates attention and focus and acts like the web browser of the brain. The front of the cingulate, the *anterior cingulate*, mediates what you are paying attention to, or what tabs are open on your computer screen. Looking at your hand, you will notice this part of the thumb is touching the fingers covering it and therefore acts as a gateway between this limbic region and the region represented by your other fingers, the cortex.

The second knuckle of the back of the hand represents the *cortex*, or the "new mammalian brain." This area is responsible for what we typically consider thinking, or what underlies our perception, motor skills, speech, cognition, and metacognition (or the ability to think about thinking). The cortex encompasses the frontal, occipital, parietal, and temporal lobes and visually is what most people associate with the brain. Continuing from the second knuckle of the fingers and down to the finger tips, tucked under when in the fist position, is the *prefrontal cortex/orbitofrontal cortex*. This area is the switchboard of the brain and is responsible for emotional awareness, emotional regulation, response flexibility, intuition, mindsight, self-awareness, and morality. It is this part of the brain that is credited with self-concept and self-esteem.

Now that you have the gist of the brain in the palm of your hand, a useful way to connect brain function with behavior is what Siegel refers to as "flipping your lid," or when you lose control. Imagine your hand with your thumb tucked in, but open your four fingers to face up. This depiction is the image of flipping your lid. When only your brain stem and limbic system are talking (palm, thumb), you are in essence taking the cognitive "low road." We are basically reacting to stimuli with the emotional part of the brain, so when our lid is flipped, our fight-or-flight response and our emotions connected to old memories are exposed. If we are able to keep our cool (imagine the fist position), our lid is down, protecting those reactionary parts of the brain and activating a detour through the "high road" through our cortex, which is where rational thinking takes place. This metaphor is particularly useful when working with children, couples, and families. The wellness counselor can teach clients to explore situations in which their lid is flipped and help pinpoint warning signals before it happens. Children can simply tell a parent or counselor that they feel like they are about to flip their lid to signal a need for space to calm down and take a break. Partners can learn to take this space when they feel angry to avoid doing or saying something they later regret.

Stress Response

Another important way to see all of the different parts of the brain working together is through the stress response. The stress response is evolutionary because it is what keeps us alive in the midst of danger. When we encounter a rapid, stressful circumstance, the brain stem alerts the limbic system to kick into survival mode. This process starts with the hypothalamus communicating to the pituitary gland to send quick messages to other parts of the body to act in ways beneficial to survival (e.g., telling our digestive system to save energy and slow down). The pituitary gland signals to the adrenal glands to release a combination of hormones, including adrenaline and cortisol, that give us energy to fight back, run away, or freeze. On the basis of our emotional response, the amygdala makes the decision how best to respond. However, because traumatic situations often cause pain, the adrenals might also release opiates (the body's natural pain killer) and oxytocin (which increases positive feelings and the desire to connect with others). This combination is a really powerful cocktail that is especially useful during a rare stress-inducing event. There are many stories of people in traumatic experiences who find the strength to lift something extremely heavy off of another person or run away on a broken leg thanks to these hormones.

However, there is a downside to this hormone release as well. The amygdala and hippocampus—the emotion response and encoding centers—are sensitive to hormone fluctuations. Therefore, a traumatic event often leads to challenges in the encoding and consolidation of memory. Although cortisol helps to keep you alive by keeping your blood sugar and blood pressure up to help you escape, prolonged exposure to raised levels of cortisol has been shown to decrease the number of neurons in the hippocampus by causing them to fire too frequently and literally excite to death (again affecting memory). Circuits in the prefrontal cortex (i.e., rational thought) get short circuited, so the "IF this, THEN that" mechanism of our thinking goes by the wayside. The opiates relieved blunt pain, but this can cause an extreme reaction when coupled with cortisol in which you literally freeze (as opposed to fight or flight, called *tonic immobility*) or perhaps have a blunted or flat affect in the aftermath. From an evolutionary perspective, this process is helpful for survival. If we were living in the wild, we might need to fight an animal to stay alive. However, most of the stressors we experience now are more chronic (e.g., we dread going to work, we are struggling to pay our bills on time). Therefore, although the body's natural stress response is really great at keeping people alive in rare moments of extreme stress, staying in a chronic state of stress over time has extremely deleterious effects on their health and well-being.

An important goal of wellness counseling is to always keep the impact of stress on the brain and body in mind when exploring interventions, also commonly known as a *trauma-informed approach*. We must also remember that stress is subjective. Individuals differ in what they perceive as stressful, and everyone has different stress thresholds and access to coping resources. Because the complex stress response in the brain elicits profound and important hormones, over time, this powerful cocktail causes disintegration and creates neural networks fraught with "low-road" connections between memories and painful emotions. *Memory consolidation* is the process of converting our short-term, or working, memory into long-term memory. Typically, this process can be gradual, in which our memories can flow in and out of our awareness. During a stressful or traumatic event, this process can occur instantaneously with our emotions and perceptions from all five senses imprinting onto a salient memory. This occurrence is useful, evolutionarily speaking, so we remember as many details as possible about a possible life-threatening situation to increase our chances of survival by avoiding it in the future. However, this process becomes extremely cumbersome when we are essentially reliving that traumatic experience daily with various triggers and memory activations. Therefore, the idea of memory reconsolidation is to erase the powerful neural network that connects memory with emotion. What is being removed is not autobiographical; you cannot erase what happened to you or your memory of it. However, through reconsolidation, you can take away (or decrease) the emotional charge that accompanies that memory. Therapeutic methods for accomplishing this goal include counteractive and transformative therapies. Counteractive methods work from the top down, practicing control in the neocortex (cognitive behavior therapy [CBT], mindfulness, etc.). Transformative approaches take a bottom-up approach, working with the deeper emotional centers of the brain (eye movement desensitization and reprocessing, Gestalt therapy, etc.).

Because the role of memory is so important in working through stress and trauma, a constructivist/narrative therapy approach can be particularly useful from a trauma-informed standpoint. On the one hand, memory can be amplified in many ways during trauma (picture your brain taking a screen shot, and every detail is connected to a complex emotional response); on the other hand, because the hippocampus is so affected by the stress response, the consolidation of those strong memories into a coherent narrative (i.e., episodic memory) can be severely damaged. It is common for trauma survivors to remember events in several snapshot-type memories but without a clear sense of timeline or details between pictures. Therefore, relatively standard questions to gain more information (from a well-meaning counselor to a detective)—such as "what happened next?" or "why did you do this versus this?"—become stress inducing in and of themselves, and a person's inability to answer often becomes misconstrued as resistance or suspicious.

A more trauma-informed way to help a client explore the narrative of their experience is to ask questions about sensations rather than rational thought (again, remember low-road vs. high-road activation during stress). Examples are "what could you see during the experience?" or "are there any particular smells that you remember?" By helping a client explore their memory in a way consistent with how it was encoded creates a safer way to connect back to the trauma and begin to break the problematic emotional triggers. Similarly, when working with children, art and play therapy can be particularly useful to help explore their memory without the need for complex language and descriptions. Even with adults, asking to draw a picture can be much easier than answering the question "what happened?" given the screen shot versus timeline nature of memory encoding during stress. Using narrative therapy to create a new story about the event, you can imagine you are forming new neural connections in your hippocampus that help you open a different (more positive) file when presented with a similar experience or are reminded of that memory.

Although we cannot get rid of stress in our lives, we can take small steps to become better at managing it. For some quick strategies to support mind wellness, we offer the following boosters:

1. The next time you feel stressed (traffic on the way to work, an inconsiderate neighbor, etc.), take a deep breath in and try to imagine that breath calming the emotional center of your brain, signaling to the rest of your body that this experience is something you can cope with and is actually a small blip in your day.
2. Try to notice when you give in to impulses. Without judgment, just try to notice when you decide on something on a whim, and take note whether it is occurring when you feel stressed out.
3. Practice distress tolerance on your own. The next time you are physically uncomfortable (e.g., sitting in a bad chair during a long meeting), use this as an opportunity to practice coping skills that you can apply to emotional pain. Experiment with paced breathing (breathe in and out for the same number of seconds), progressive muscle relaxation (intentionally tighten a muscle, then relax it), acceptance and perspective (lean into what you are experiencing, and know you have withstood worse), and using your five senses to self-soothe (what can you see, hear, smell, touch, etc.).

Rewiring the Brain, Retrain the Mind

As we learned from Phineas Gage, each part of the brain has an important role to play, and damage to specific areas has profound implications for brain function depending on where the damage occurs. Although mapping brain function in this way is an incredibly important feat in recent history, it is not the end of the story. The concept of *neuroplasticity*, or the ability of the adult brain to undergo dramatic change, challenges us to contemplate the role of experience in potentially reorganizing our brain function. A clear example of this is examining the brain of a patient who has suffered a severe stroke. Researchers have shown that in people who have experienced a stroke that catastrophically affected one area of the brain, often rehabilitation is possible to essentially train a different area of the brain to pick up the slack of the damaged part. We know that, in children, brain plasticity is especially salient. There are many examples of young children suffering from seizures who undergo an extreme surgery called a hemispherectomy, in which one half of their brain is removed. As long as this surgery happens before 4 years old, most children will continue to grow and develop normally. One reason scientists think that this is possible is because young brains are incredibly malleable as a result of the exorbitant number of neurons that children possess at an early age. Therefore, if many neurons are removed, children are still left with enough neurons to function normally. Through rehabilitation, the cortical real estate that is left is shaped into what is needed. Therefore, through plasticity, we see that the cortical land assignments of the brain can be rezoned from life experiences and intentional training.

One of the key researchers who has shown not just neuroplasticity but *neurogenesis* (growing, not just reorganizing, new nerve cells) in humans is Fred "Rusty" Gage (yes, that Gage—Rusty is a direct descendent) and his lab at the Salk Institute for Biological Studies (La Jolla, CA). Gage and his lab partners were able to prove that, contrary to conventional wisdom in the field of neuroscience, we are not born with all the neurons we will ever have. His research showed that neural stem cells can propagate new neurons in the hippocampus; thus, people's environment and experiences can help the brain grow, heal, and change. What this finding means for wellness counseling is that change is possible, starting at the cellular level.

Perception and Depression

Earlier, when describing the limbic system, we mentioned that the hippocampus could be thought of as the filing cabinet of your brain. As you are presented with new information, it is your hippocampus that processes experiences and stores them away into memories. Exactly how information is stored in files is an important component in how you then experience emotion connected with those memories. Let's say you go to a haunted house, and someone dressed up as a ghost jumps out at you. Your brain starts to respond to this experience, your pituitary gland likely releases some adrenalin, and you feel your heart beating; perhaps you start to sweat. As part of the stress response, your limbic system performs an appraisal. Is this stimuli harmful? Can I cope? If you are a person who enjoys haunted houses, your emotional response center, the amygdala, sends signals that you interpret as exhilarating or even fun. Therefore, your hippocampus files this experience away in a folder reserved for exciting or pleasant things. However, if you have never been to a haunted house or are a person who scares easily, when the ghost jumps out and your body floods with adrenaline, your amygdala interprets fear rather than excitement, sending signals to your body to get ready to fight, flee, or freeze. Your hippocampus would likely file this into a folder for things that are scary or negative. Therefore, although the event might be exactly the same for two different people, the file which the hippocampus puts the memory in drastically affects the story we tell about that memory.

Additionally, the hippocampus has been shown to be reduced up to 10% in size in people with depression. What is the best way to treat depression? Even though treatment regiments have changed a lot over the past few decades, and with all of the advances in neuroscience, we know that the answer is, *it's complicated.* Nearly half of all people with clinical depression fail to respond to medication, yet we know from brain research that the impact of depression on brain structure is measurable. The neurogenesis theory of depression posits that severe depression inhibits neural birth in the brain (Miller & Hen, 2015). For those for whom antidepressants work, the current theory is that most common antidepressants (selective serotonin reuptake inhibitors [SSRIs]) increase serotonin, which is a feel-good hormone. However, these drugs typically take up to a month to take effect—so what is happening in the meantime? Many researchers now think that SSRIs helps stimulate neurogenesis in the hippocampus. After a few weeks, it is the new neurons, and thus our ability to experience novelty in our lives, that have an impact on depression, not simply the addition of serotonin.

Sounds amazing, right? Well, what about the other half of people who do not respond to medication? Is there a way to change your brain and combat the effects of depression medicationfree? The good news is, *absolutely.* The bad news is, *it's complicated.* We say this not because it is hard to do but because there is no one-size-fits-all way to get your brain working the way you want it to. What we do know is that depression is influenced by several factors, including genetic predisposition, early childhood experiences, stress, and social support. How much or how little each of these factors plays into depression completely depends on the individual; thus, there is no easy fix. However, there are lots of little things you can do to change the course of your brain function exactly because the system is so complicated. Think of traffic in a large city during rush hour. One small change (a fender bender, a traffic light going out, an abandoned car interfering with one lane of traffic) can have a massive impact on the whole system. For better or for worse, the same is true with the brain.

In social psychology, Heider's (1944) attribution theory gives a framework for how we explain the world around us. Attributions are explanations we tell ourselves for outcomes that affect our thoughts about event and behavior on future events. Attributions can be internal or external (it is your doing, or it is the doing of some outside source), stable or unstable (it is set in stone, or it is something that can change). For example, let's say you are driving to work, and you get pulled over for speeding. The potential attribution combination responses can be seen in Table 4.1.

The key here is that the event is the same in every scenario—getting a speeding ticket. However, the difference in explanation for why that event happened likely has a large impact on your mood and your experience of how your day went. People with depression often view positive outcomes as external (i.e., luck) and negative outcomes as internal (i.e., personal flaw). The internal stable combination becomes particularly harmful when the explanation for negative events becomes a part of the story you tell about yourself ("Of course this bad thing happened, bad things always happen to me"). Thus, when exploring behavior change with someone who is depressed, attribution theory has a big impact on self-esteem and motivation to change. If you are viewing events in your life as internal stable, what is the point of putting effort into change? However, if you challenge yourself to consider a negative event from an alternate framework of an unstable (or external) attribution, there is potential for a different outcome—there is hope.

Neurogenesis and Trauma

As we mentioned earlier, the stress response has a profound impact on the brain, which, in turn, has important implications for people's thoughts, behaviors, and emotions. Another piece of people's evolutionary survival instinct is that the mind has an implicit negativity bias. If you hear a rustle in the bushes, your mind expects a bear, and thus the stress response starts. However, chances are what you actually hear is a rabbit; therefore, although your mind can process that the threat is not real, your brain and body are already paying the price. The repeated exposure to stress, particularly in early childhood, can change the structure of the brain, leading to challenges

Table 4.1

Attribution Examples for Getting a Speeding Ticket

Attribution	Explanation 1	Explanation 2
Internal–Stable	It's a part of me.	I'm a bad driver.
Internal–Unstable	It's something I did, but it can change.	I wasn't paying attention.
External–Stable	It's not me, and it is not likely to change.	That spot is a speed trap.
External–Unstable	It's not me, and it can change.	The cop was in a bad mood.

throughout life. A growing body of research has explored the impact of chronic stress, trauma, and other adverse childhood experiences (ACEs) on the developing brain (e.g., see Anda et al., 2006). It is clear that the perpetual stress response includes disruptions to the hippocampus, hypothalamic–pituitary–adrenal (HPA) axis, and glucocorticoid response to stress. As we just discussed, smaller hippocampal volume (fewer neurons available to fire) is found among a clinical population of adults with early abuse and related psychiatric disorders (e.g., posttraumatic stress disorder, depression, borderline personality disorder) but not in children with posttraumatic stress disorder. This finding suggests that it is not a single ACE that stunts brain growth but a persistent exposure to ACEs plus chronic stress that lead to decreased brain function over time and mental health concerns into adulthood.

Cortisol is the main corticosteroid regulated by the HPA axis, and it is the most commonly known stress hormone. The main job of cortisol in the body is actually to restore homeostasis after exposure to stress, yet prolonged release of cortisol results in anything but the body functioning at status quo. Cortisol increases blood sugar, weakens the immune system, and atrophies the hippocampus; moreover, as a result of chronic stress, cortisol is thought to initiate an inhibitory feedback loop that leads to the continued release of cortisol, fueling the perpetual stress response cycle.

A key finding from the original ACEs study (Felitti et al., 1998) was just how common these experiences are. This is a great place to start when approaching wellness counseling with a trauma-informed lens—by understanding the ubiquitous nature of stress and the far too common experience of trauma, we can begin to view symptoms as normal reactions to abnormal experiences rather than pathologizing the behavior. Common responses that increase during times of stress are actually positively correlated with cortisol secretion (e.g., sleep deprivation, caffeine, and alcohol), compounding the impact of stress on the body. Collecting a trauma history, as well as resilience indicators, on all clients is an important practice that should be included in wellness counseling.

Trauma-informed wellness counseling uses interventions with a neurobiological basis to target first the nervous system regulation and then the mind (cognitions and emotions). An important component of well-being is self-regulation. By understanding our biological stress response, we can first focus on our immediate sensations and reactions to learn to modulate our reactivity. This then sets the stage for more successful regulation of our secondary reactions of thoughts, emotions, and behaviors. Leitch (2017) talked about the resilient zone as the place where neuroplasticity and neurogenesis can happen. Self-regulation skills can be taught to clients who use their strengths to create small successes, leading to a greater sense of mastery and self-efficacy. By teaching and practicing more constructive ways to respond to stress, you "utilize neuroplasticity to wire-in greater resilience and decrease the power of stressors to trigger reactivity" (Leitch, 2017, p. 8). Mindfulness meditation is one such practice that also serves as a bridge between mind wellness and the other wellness domains.

Neurobiology of Mindfulness

Meditation, or the practice of training the mind, is a range of practices that includes a focus on awareness, self-regulation of attention, mental stillness or silence, relaxation, connection, and compassion. Meditation has seen a resurgence in the past few decades, with research on the benefits of meditation in general, and most often mindfulness, specifically, touting an expansive list of benefits. We say "resurgence" because meditation is certainly not new, and the benefits have been known by ancient mystics, sages, and Eastern philosophers for centuries. However, in the last few decades, we have seen a resurgence of the utility of meditation in fields such as medicine, education, coaching, and business. With the rapidly growing field of neuroscience and the ability to map brain function, researchers have shown that meditation is effective in increasing relaxation (Kabat-Zinn, 1990); increasing happiness and emotional health (Greschwind, Peeters, Drukker, van Os, & Wichers, 2011); altering the startle response and fight, flight, or freeze response (Levenson, Elkman, & Ricad, 2012); decreasing anxiety, addiction, anger, chronic pain, insomnia, phobias, blood pressure, and stress (Ospina et al., 2007); improving the stress recovery response (Goleman, 1976); and altering or extinguishing negative cognitions as well as increasing emotional regulation (Hayes, Luoma, Bond, Masuda, & Lillis, 2006; Segal, Williams, & Teasdale, 2002).

For years, neuroscience researchers used brain imaging technology to determine how the brain responds to stimuli. You put a person in the scanner, play a sound or ask them to do a cognitive test, and then see which areas of the brain light up. However, in the mid-90s, a graduate student at the time, Bharat Biswal, was curious about what the brain was doing when a person was simply at rest. His research showed that the brain structure and organization of neural connections known to work together do so even in the absence of a specific job or task, a concept known as *resting-state connectivity* (Biswal, Yetkin, Haughton, & Hyde, 1995). Neuroscientists have taken this idea and expanded the research to show correlated neural activity in many different known networks. One interesting network includes the areas of the brain that are important for complex cognitive processes such as self-awareness, emotional processing, and recalling memories: the *default mode network*. The default mode network is active when you are resting and experience your mind wandering. When you become aware that you have lost focus (perhaps you have experienced this phenomenon while reading this chapter!), often you have been thinking about yourself, others, remembering the past, or planning the future. These different functions are all correlated when the mind is seemingly at rest. It is this neural network that has been shown to be altered by mindfulness meditation, which has significant implications for emotional regulation, stress resilience, and stress-related health outcomes (Creswell et al., 2016).

Another interesting body of research comes from looking at the brains of Buddhist monks who are, of course, experts at meditation. Scientists—such as Richard Davidson, founder of the Center for Healthy Minds at the University of Wisconsin–Madison, Brian Knutson from Stanford, and Zoran Josipovic from New York University— have used magnetic resonance imaging to watch the brains of experienced Buddhist monks while they meditate to try to understand how their practice affects their neurobiology. By and large, what they have found is that the brains of experienced meditators show more resilience and plasticity (Davidson & Lutz, 2008), are more connected to their body through stronger immune functioning (Davidson et al., 2003), have stronger neural circuitry related to attention and processing speed (Lutz, Slagter, Dunne, & Davidson, 2008), and are strengthened through generosity and compassion (Lutz, Greischar, Rawlings, Ricard, & Davidson, 2004).

Biology, Cognition, and Behavior Change

Cognition refers to the mental act of knowing or acquiring knowledge from one's perceptions, attitudes, and beliefs. When people talk about a mind–body separation, they are typically referring to the idea that the mind (or cognitive function) is somehow separate from the biological being. This idea of separation breaks down when we start to consider the complicated interplay between the body and mental well-being.

One way to consider the way the body and mind are connected is to look at the brain changes that occur in developmentally predictable ways. For example, the brain undergoes changes during puberty, pregnancy, and as a result of aging. To illustrate this point, consider the adolescent brain. We know that the brain is still forming during adolescence, which helps explains roller-coaster emotions and irrational choices. Decades ago, it was largely believed that the brain was fully developed by 12 years old. More recent research indicates that the brain is not truly mature until 25 years old. Consider the controversy in our criminal justice system regarding when to try a person as an adult. Unfortunately, many states are trying offenders at younger and younger ages as adults, whereas research moves in the direction of delaying the time period of adulthood. In fact, research shows that the teenage brain and adult brain operate in functionally different ways. Regions in the back of the brain (the brain stem and limbic system) that mediate direct contact with the environment by controlling such sensory functions as vision, hearing, touch, and spatial processing mature the earliest. Between 6 and 12 years old, neuron growth increases with the thickening of neurons, and their branchlike dendrites peak when girls are about 11 years old and boys are 12½ years old. As the brain switches from proliferating to pruning, the body comes under the hormonal assault of puberty. The orbitofrontal cortex (remember that this is the home of the executive functions—planning, setting priorities, organizing thoughts, suppressing impulses, weighing the consequences of one's actions) is the last part of the brain to be pruned and shaped to its adult dimension.

Young adolescents rely heavily on the amygdala (emotion and gut reactions), whereas adults rely more on the frontal lobe (planning and judgment). Therefore, adolescents are highly emotional and impulsive, whereas adults (relatively speaking) are highly rational. From a cognition standpoint, adults and adolescents literally think differently. Adolescents also have less activity in the nucleus accumbens, a region in the frontal cortex that directs motivation to seek rewards (connected to laughter, pleasure, pain, fear, and addiction). This finding makes sense when we consider the extreme risk taking that is a hallmark of the adolescent period. Dopamine, the brain chemical involved in motivation and in reinforcing behavior, is more abundant in adolescents. Furthermore, rapid changes in dopamine-rich areas of the brain may be an additional factor in making teens vulnerable to the stimulating and addictive effects of alcohol and other drugs. Obviously, there are huge implications for school discipline, criminal justice system, and so forth when considering how to treat adolescents who have made mistakes.

Counseling Interventions

Moving from the biological underpinnings of our cognitions, the complex interplay among our emotions, behaviors, and thoughts has an immense impact on our well-being. In counseling and psychology, theories of behavior change can be categorized into three waves.

First-Wave Interventions

Starting in the 1950s, behaviorism was gaining traction in reaction to Freud's psychoanalytic theory. The hallmark principles of this first wave were classical and operant conditioning. You have likely learned about classical conditioning and the famous experiments on Pavlov's dog. Although you are certainly not going to work with your clients to salivate when they hear a bell, the modern-day equivalent might be mindlessly eating snacks while watching TV or sweating when called on to give a presentation. S*timulus control* is learning which cues can either trigger an undesired behavior or promote a desired one and exploring these automatic behaviors related to areas for change identified by the client can be helpful.

Operant conditioning, and the work of B. F. Skinner, provided the notion that behavior is a result of learning and that we learn through reinforcement or punishment. In operant conditioning terms, a *reinforcement* is anything that increases the likelihood of a behavior, and a *punishment* is anything that decreases it. *Positive* refers to the presentation of a stimulus, and *negative* refers to the removal of a stimulus. (In pop culture, the term "negative reinforcement" is almost always used incorrectly. Negative reinforcement is simply taking away a stimulus to increase a certain behavior, but because of assumed connotations of the words, this term is often used to describe things such as spanking or detention, which are both actually *positive punishment*). Reinforcement is typically more effective than punishment because you are focusing on the behavior you want versus the one you do not. Therefore, if rewards are motivating to a client, they can set up their own operant condition system that capitalize on their strengths in other wellness domains to help make small behavior changes. For example, if clients want to start incorporating regular physical activity (*body wellness*) into their week, and they are motivated by spending time with friends (*connection wellness*), they could create a plan in which they reward themselves with a coffee date with a friend (positive—adding stimulus) on days that they go to the gym (reinforcement—increase desired behavior).

Second-Wave Interventions

The second wave added cognitive dimensions to behaviorism, with CBT as the most ubiquitous approach used by a variety of helping professionals. One intervention that ties mind wellness into other parts of the integrated whole is the CBT concept of the cognitive triangle. The cognitive triangle visually depicts that thoughts, feelings, and behaviors are interconnected. The wellness triangle in Figure 4.2 situates wellness at the heart of the cognitive triangle with the intention to show that all the domains are interrelated and have a reciprocal relationship with wellness. The wellness counselor can show the figure to explain this concept and ask the client to think of examples from their own life to aid with their understanding. The client's presenting concern can then be filtered through this cognitive wellness triangle to facilitate both consciousness raising and intervention.

The following is a case example. A wellness counselor is working with a client with an addiction to alcohol and prescription pills and a co-occurring anxiety disorder. The client's preferred anxiety medication was discontinued by the psychiatrist because of the client's risk of abusing it. The client has felt insecure and stressed about coping with cravings and anxiety without the pills. Counselor and client viewed a recent related overwhelming experience through the triangle. The counselor used thoughts as a starting point; however, the wellness cognitive triangle can start at whichever point is most

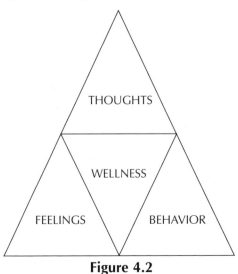

Figure 4.2

Wellness Triangle

salient for the client, whether thought, behavior, or feeling. "What was going through your mind when you were feeling stressed at this time?" The counselor made sure the client identified specific cognitions. "I can't deal with stress without my pills," and "This is unfair that my pills are not being given to me." The counselor then asked, "What feelings arose alongside the stress?" The counselor is careful to ensure that the client states specific feelings. The client noted that the cognitions led to feelings of "anxiety, discouragement, anger, and stuckness." The thoughts and feelings influenced the client's behaviors of defensiveness toward treatment staff, initially planning to meet friends to drink (although he did not go and did not relapse) and stopping attendance at 12-Step meetings.

The counselor then handed the client a copy of a wellness model to refer to and asked, "How have this and similar experiences affected your overall well-being?" The client acknowledged that connection wellness was affected because lack of 12-Step attendance disconnected him from a sober support network, emotion wellness was affected because these experiences made him feel like a "failure," and body wellness was affected because of visceral cravings when planning to drink with his friends. An equally powerful role of the wellness cognitive triangle would be in ascertaining the coping thoughts, feelings, and behaviors that occurred that prevented him from relapsing in spite of taking some steps toward doing so. The positive impact on the client's wellness can then be de-constructed.

Third-Wave Interventions

Building on these first two generations, the third wave of treatment approaches prioritizes promoting well-being versus reducing symptoms. Informed by neuroscience, a key component of third-wave interventions is mindfulness. Therapeutic approaches based on mindfulness have been shown to be efficacious in both healthy and clinical populations and can be practiced in preschools to retirement homes. Examples of therapeutic approaches to mindfulness include mindfulness-based stress reduction (Kabat-Zinn, 1990), mindfulness-based cognitive therapy (Segal et al., 2002), mindfulness-based relapse prevention (Bowen, Chawla, & Marlatt, 2010), dialectical behavior therapy (Linehan, 1993), and acceptance and commitment therapy (Hayes et al., 2006). In addition to helping clients, mindfulness has also been shown to increase self-efficacy in beginning counselors (Greason & Cashwell, 2009).

Mindfulness-based stress reduction (MBSR) is a secular mindfulness curriculum that involves teaching and experiential practices.

MBSR activities generally include formal meditation practice, informal mindfulness practice of bringing awareness to everyday life (e.g., mindful eating, mindful walking), and mindful inquiry training in which you practice being present, without judgment, in your own subjective experiences. Practitioner Spotlight 4.1 highlights one such activity: *distress tolerance.*

On the basis of the research we have reviewed, we have the following general recommendations for incorporating mind wellness in counseling:

- Teach the client the basics of the brain to cultivate a sense of control over one's mind;
- Help the client develop flexible and realistic beliefs and goals (cognitive and behavioral strategies);
- Affirm positive thinking and coping mechanisms;
- Support self-efficacy;
- Encourage insight, awareness, self-monitoring, regulation, and metacognition; and
- Help the client develop and practice coping strategies.

Conclusion

Using a neurobiological lens that amplifies how the mind and body are wired to respond to stress and fear facilitates an important shift away from viewing your clients' symptoms and behaviors as checklists to diagnose to viewing them as clues on how to bring their whole selves back into balance. By including neurobiologically based, trauma-informed interventions, counselors can support all clients across culture, race, class, and so forth because the hard wiring in brains is the same. What is important to keep at the forefront of treatment is that what is considered stressful or a threat is based on the individual's lived experience, which is highly informed by their culture, race, class, and so forth. Mind wellness is intricately connected to the other domains of wellness and is an important place to start when working with clients.

Reflection Prompts

1. How could you incorporate mindfulness into your work with clients? Have you engaged in any intentional mindfulness work personally? How did it go?
2. *Brain plasticity*, the ability to change one's brain (for better or for worse) throughout life, is truly incredible. What is something you would like to train your brain to do? Respond differently to stress? Approach time management differently? Learn a foreign language?

Practitioner Spotlight 4.1
Integrating Yoga in Counseling

Jacy Rader

I am a licensed professional counselor and registered yoga teacher working in private practice. I specialize in treating clients with anxiety through a mind, body, and spirit approach. I integrate psychotherapy and yoga, which includes breathing and meditation as well as physical yoga postures. When working with clients with anxiety, I focus on helping them decrease their arousal response, gain control over their nervous system, identify and confront fears, and develop new coping skills.

In the first few sessions, I teach clients different breathing techniques, such as using the diaphragm to deepen the inhale and extend the exhale. Clients with anxiety often come into my office unaware of their diaphragm, which means they often use short, shallow breaths that send a direct message to the nervous system to fight, flee, or freeze. Ordinarily, I see an immediate change in clients, as evidenced by their fullness of breath, pace of speech, and relaxation of muscle tension.

I also teach meditation exercises to clients as a way to focus their attention on present experiences. This practice allows them to break unhelpful thinking patterns and increases their distress tolerance, or ability to experience an uncomfortable emotion or experience. Meditation can be as simple as concentrating on the breath for beginners. In later sessions, I guide clients through meditations to help them become aware of their thoughts or emotions without becoming fixated or attached to them. By bringing awareness inward, clients can develop an observer perspective, meaning they can create space and distance from a challenge to be able to choose how they respond, as opposed to unhelpful reflex reactions.

Yoga poses are another tool that can help clients build their emotional distress tolerance and learn new coping skills to manage anxiety. It is common for anxiety or other challenging emotions to arise while holding a difficult pose. In these moments of temporary distress, clients learn to withstand their anxiety, hold the pose, relax unnecessary tension, and breathe through the discomfort. Clients who are anxious typically feel a sense of urgency, believing their emotions will overwhelm them or will last indefinitely. Yoga can teach them that they are strong enough to breathe through challenging feelings and that feelings are temporary.

Through the integration of talk therapy, yoga, breathing, and meditation, I notice a deep sense of healing and transformation in my clients. Clients develop tools to be in the present moment, relax their nervous system, tolerate overwhelming emotions, and grow the ability to problem solve. Learning and cultivating change by way of mind, body, and spirit has been a powerful dynamic for clients in my practice.

• • •

3. Think back on a time when you handled stress well. How did you cope? What did you do that helped the situation? What can you take from that experience to help you the next time a stressful situation arises?

Learning Activities

Brain in the Palm of Your Hand Exercise

Talking through the brain in the palm of your hand metaphor takes practice, and you will have to tailor it to the particular age group of your client. Identify the population that you plan to work with, and consider what brain terminology and information are appropriate for that age group. Pair up with a partner and practice explaining the brain to each other, acting as if you are talking with someone from your future client population. Give each other feedback, and try again!

Helpful Hint: There are plenty of examples of counselors doing this activity on YouTube, in addition to Dr. Daniel Siegel himself. It is always helpful to see how someone else might do it to get ideas for yourself!

Mindfulness Activity: Practice Mindfulness in the Moment

This week, take 3–4 hours of your time and do something that you truly enjoy. The time may be spent with family members, intimate partners, or close friends, or it may be spent alone. Pay close attention to what is going on during this time. Try to notice the little things that you may not always think about. Reflect on the time and be mindful of what is going on.

- What is it that you truly appreciate about the moments?
- If you are with others, what is it that you appreciate about them?
- What are the feelings that arise for you?
- What are you grateful for?

Resources

Authentic Happiness

https://www.authentichappiness.sas.upenn.edu/

Founded by Dr. Martin Seligman and his work on Positive Psychology, this website offers free resources and assessments on happiness and well-being.

Center for Mindfulness in Medicine, Health Care, and Society

https://www.umassmed.edu/cfm/

The home of Jon Kabat-Zinn's mindfulness-based stress reduction research, the University of Massachusetts Medical School houses mindfulness trainings as well as free resources on mindfulness.

Dr. Dan Siegel's Website
http://www.drdansiegel.com/resources/
> There are many free resources (as well as useful books to buy)
> on his website.

References

Anda, R. F., Felitti, V. J., Walker, J., Whitfield, C. L., Bremner, J. D.,
Perry, B. D., . . . Giles, W. H. (2006). The enduring effects of abuse
and related adverse experiences in childhood: A convergence of
evidence from neurobiology and epidemiology. *European Archives
of Psychiatry and Clinical Neuroscience, 56,* 174–186.

Biswal, B., Yetkin, F. Z., Haughton, V. M., & Hyde, J. S. (1995). Functional connectivity in the motor cortex of resting human brain using echo-planar MRI. *Magnetic Resonance in Medicine, 34,* 537–541.

Bowen, S., Chawla, N., & Marlatt, G. A. (2010). *Mindfulness-based relapse prevention for addictive behaviors: A clinical's guide.* New York,
NY: Guilford Press.

Creswell, J. D., Taren, A. A., Lindsay, E. K., Greco, C. M., Gianaros, P. J.,
Fairgrieve, A., . . . Ferris, J. L. (2016). Alterations in resting-state functional connectivity link mindfulness meditation with reduced inter-
leukin-6: A randomized controlled trial. *Biological Psychiatry, 80,* 53–61.

Davidson, R. J., Kabat-Zinn, J., Schumacher, J., Rosenkranz, M., Muller,
D., Santorelli, S. F., . . . Sheridan, J. F. (2003). Alterations in brain
and immune function produced by mindfulness meditation. *Psychosomatic Medicine, 65,* 564–570.

Davidson, R. J., & Lutz, A. (2008). Buddha's brain: Neuroplasticity and
meditation. *IEEE Signal Processing Magazine, 25,* 174–176.

Felitti, V. J., Anda, R. F., Nordenberg, D., Williamson, D. F., Spitz, A.,
Edwards, V., . . . Marks, J. S. (1998). Relationship of childhood abuse
and household dysfunction to many of the leading causes of death
in adults. *American Journal of Preventive Medicine, 14,* 245–258.

Goleman, D. (1976). Meditation and consciousness: An Asian approach to mental health. *American Journal of Psychotherapy, 30,*
41–54.

Greason, P. B., & Cashwell, C. S. (2009). Mindfulness and counseling
self-efficacy: The mediating role of attention and empathy. *Counselor Education and Supervision, 49,* 2–19.

Greschwind, N., Peeters, F., Drukker, M., van Os, J., & Wichers, M.
(2011). Mindfulness training increases momentary positive emotions and reward experience in adults vulnerable to depression:
A randomized controlled trial. *Journal of Consulting and Clinical
Psychology, 79,* 618–628.

Hayes, S. C., Luoma, J., Bond, F., Masuda, A., & Lillis, J. (2006). Acceptance and commitment therapy: Model, processes, and outcomes. *Behaviour Research and Therapy, 44,* 1–25.

Heider, F. (1944). Social perception and phenomenal causality. *Psychological Review, 51,* 358–374.

Kabat-Zinn, J. (1990). *Full catastrophe living: How to cope with stress, pain and illness using mindfulness meditation.* New York, NY: Bantam Dell.

Leitch, L. (2017). Action steps using ACEs and trauma-informed care: A resilience model. *Health & Justice, 5*(5). https://doi.org/10.1186/s40352-017-0050-5

Levenson, R. W., Elkman, P., & Ricad, M. (2012). Meditation and the startle response: A case study. *Emotion, 12,* 650–658.

Linehan, M. M. (1993). *Cognitive-behavioral therapy of borderline personality disorder.* New York, NY: Guilford Press.

Lutz, A., Greischar, L. L., Rawlings, N. B., Ricard, M., & Davidson, R. J. (2004). Long-term meditators self-induce high-amplitude gamma synchrony during mental practice. *Proceedings of the National Academy of Sciences of the United States of America, 101,* 16369–16373.

Lutz, A., Slagter, H. A., Dunne, J. D., & Davidson, R. J. (2008). Attention regulation and monitoring in meditation. *Trends in Cognitive Sciences, 12,* 163–169.

Miller, B., & Hen, R. (2015). The current state of the neurogenic theory of depression and anxiety. *Current Opinion in Neurobiology, 30,* 51–58. https://doi.org/10.1016/j.conb.2014.08.012

Ospina, M. B., Bond, K., Karkhaneh, M., Tiosvold, L., Vandermeer, B., Liang, Y., . . . Klassen, T. P. (2007). Meditation practices for health: State of the research. *Evidence Report/Technology Assessment, 155,* 1–263.

Segal, Z. V., Williams, J. M., & Teasdale, J. D. (2002). *Mindfulness-based cognitive therapy for depression: A new approach to prevention relapse.* New York, NY: Guilford Press.

Siegel, D. J. (2010). *Mindsight: The new science of personal transformation.* New York, NY: Bantam Books.

Chapter 5

Body

The best six doctors anywhere and no one can deny it are
sunshine, water, rest, air, exercise, and diet.

—Wayne Fields

• • •

Physical wellness is crucial to our bodies' optimal health and functioning, and it encompasses external areas of physical health and
nutrition and the internal area of body image. In this chapter, we
explore *body wellness*, which we have conceptualized as growth toward
intentional behaviors and thought processes related to integrating
how you nourish, move, and express gratitude toward your body.
The relationship among physical health, mental health, and wellness
is explored as we consider how to work with the whole person.

Physical Activity and Health

Physical health is an important component of body wellness. When
you think about physical health and wellness, what is the first thing
that comes to mind? For many of us, it is a picture of a gym buzzing
with people lifting weights and running on a treadmill. Although the
gym is certainly a component of physical wellness, it is important to
differentiate between *physical activity* and *exercise*. Physical activity is
really any bodily movement that uses your muscles and expends energy. Exercise, however, is structured physical activity for the express
purpose of sustaining or improving health and fitness. Exercise is a

type of physical activity, and in terms of wellness, it is physical activity in general that we want to focus on because it is accessible, value neutral, and (to some degree) an already existing part of everyday life.

There are many benefits of physical activity on health and wellness. Moving your body reduces the risk of cardiovascular disease, Type 2 diabetes, and many cancer and other disease processes. It strengthens your bones and muscles, increases longevity, and helps maintain a healthy weight. Perhaps most noticeably, physical activity affects mental health through positively affecting sleep, mood, self-esteem, life satisfaction, and cognitive function as well as decreasing stress, depression, and anxiety (Biddle & Asare, 2011; Bize, Johnson, & Plotnikoff, 2007). What is so powerful about physical activity is that all of these improvements are interrelated and contribute to a positive-feedback loop, helping you stick with it if you can just get over the initial motivation hump.

For example, if you are feeling depressed, you are likely either sleeping too much or too little, and even if you stay in bed all day, you constantly feel drained and lethargic, finding it difficult to concentrate. Under these circumstances, the idea of hitting the gym or running a 5K probably seems impossible. However, maybe it is a nice day, and you decide you are going to walk to your mailbox to get your mail. You step outside and feel the sun on your face, and a cool breeze moves across your body. As you are walking down your driveway, you stretch your back out and roll your shoulders down, releasing tension you did not even realize you were carrying. When you get back into your house you feel refreshed, even if just by a small increment, and maybe you sit down to accomplish a task rather than turn the TV back on. Maybe this moment of clarity and attention just lasts for 5 minutes. However, if you take note of it, the next day you might feel motivated to get the mail again, and the next day walk down your street, and in a week walk around the block a few times.

As you incorporate more physical activity into your day, you notice that your sleep is improving; at the end of the day, you fall asleep more easily and wake up actually feeling refreshed. With better sleep under your belt, you are more productive at work and feel a sense of accomplishment when you leave for the day. All of these small changes are setting up new neural pathways in your brain that are shifting your thoughts and emotions by lifting the depressed lens you are viewing the world through. Neuroscientist Alex Korb (2015) referred to this chain of reactions as "the upward spiral"—because your brain is such a complex system, one small action sets in motion another, and so on. Viewing depression in this way, healing begins to feel attainable because you just need to take one small step to get the ball rolling (or, in this case, the body moving).

In fact, researchers have shown that physical activity actually stimulates neurogenesis in the hippocampus (Leasure & Jones, 2008), which (as discussed in Chapter 4) is smaller in people with depression. Neuroscientists (e.g., Boecker et al., 2008; Rovio et al., 2010; Winter et al., 2007) have found that physical activity increases serotonin (mood), norepinephrine (concentration), dopamine (energy), and endorphins (pain killers). These neurotransmitters are important for overall mental health, and many depression and anxiety medications target these same chemicals. Studies from Duke University have consistently shown that physical activity is comparable with antidepressants for treating mild to moderate depression; regardless of treatment group (medication or exercise), those who continue to engage in exercise 10 months later reporting lower depressive symptoms than nonexercisers (Babyak et al., 2000). Therefore, whether medication, physical activity, or a combination of both is used to treat depression, engaging in regular physical activity is a useful way to prevent relapse and maintain wellness.

We know that physical activity has a positive impact on well-being—both physical and mental—at the cellular level. However, what about the psychosocial component (Lubans et al., 2016), which is so important for motivation? To answer that question, we can look at sources of motivation found at the *interconnection* between body wellness and other wellness domains:

- Mind wellness—Physical activity provides you an opportunity for mastery experiences that increase your feelings of accomplishment and self-efficacy.
- Body wellness—Physical activity helps you connect to your body and improves your self-perception, or body image.
- Sprit wellness—Physical activity often involves connecting with yourself and with nature. Being in nature can increase the enjoyment that comes from an activity (e.g., running on a trail vs. indoors on a treadmill).
- Connection wellness—Physical activity can improve mood, distract from negative emotions, and decrease stress, and it provides an opportunity to connect with others, both for support and healthy competition.

Looking at this list, which motivation hypothesis fits you the best? If you want to start a habit of going on a run before work, are you more likely to stick with it if you plan it with a friend or alone on a favorite trail? Do you need to set small goals for yourself or continually up your challenge to feel accomplished, or do you just like the way you feel afterward? Perhaps it is a combination. Finding out which psychosocial mechanism is most motivating for your clients, and how it relates to other wellness domains, is an important part of treatment planning and helps set people up for success.

When working with a client on body wellness and physical activity, it is always important to refer the client to their primary care physician for a physical to approve a change in activity level. It is also important to have a baseline idea of how much activity is a good goal. The Centers for Disease Control and Prevention recommended that children and adolescents engage in 60 minutes or more of physical activity each day (U.S. Department of Health and Human Services, 2008). This regimen includes both aerobic activity and muscle strengthening, each at least 3 days per week. Adults should engage in 2½ hours of moderate-intensity aerobic activity each week or 75 minutes of vigorous-intensity aerobic activity each week and 2 or more days per week of muscle-strengthening activities. It is important to consider your client's abilities and desire in terms of the intensity of activity. Although we know there are many benefits to physical activity, overdoing it can actually lead to more negative affect for some individuals. This outcome is especially true for individuals who are new to a physical activity routine. When working with a client to find ways to increase physical activity, it helps to learn about what they enjoy. If the activity involves choice, is voluntary, and is considered leisure (vs. chores or compulsory activity), research has shown that the mental health benefits are amplified (Leasure & Jones, 2008). Think back to your childhood—did you play outside until you were called in for dinner? Was there a neighborhood game that ruled your summer? What did you enjoy doing before physical activity became tainted with all the social expectations and pressures that come along with formal exercise? See Practitioner Spotlight 5.1 for a discussion of wellness interventions for men experiencing homelessness.

Following is a list of practical considerations when incorporating physical health and activity in wellness counseling:

- Evaluate the client's intentions (e.g., seeking physical health counseling or general counseling);
- Ensure that the client has been evaluated by a physician;
- Collaborate with, and refer to, fitness professionals;
- Determine the client's level of readiness and intervene at their stage of readiness;

Practitioner Spotlight 5.1

Wellness Interventions for Men Experiencing Homelessness

Michael D. Brubaker

Physical exercise is a well-known intervention for clients with substance use disorders because it can lessen withdrawal symptoms, reduce anxiety and depression, and support greater abstinence rates (Wang, Wang, Wang, Li, & Zhou, 2014). While serving as the program coordinator of a residential recovery center for men experiencing homelessness, I helped to implement a series of exercise activities as part of a comprehensive wellness program addressing physical fitness, nutrition, mental health, and spiritual well-being. Many of our clients were highly capable individuals who had lost their sense of purpose through a life of alcohol, crack, and opioid addictions. Exercise was one of the most immediate ways for them to build in a manageable routine, regain their natural production of endorphins, and attain concrete physical goals.

In a community-based intervention such as this one, it was essential that we developed a culture of change and positive attitudes toward physical fitness. To this end, we solicited the aid of our clients, many of whom were former athletes, to lead morning workouts and encourage one another to pursue greater wellness. Because clients have different abilities, it was essential that clients met with our medical health partners and were given permission to participate at appropriate levels. Agency volunteers were also involved in activities, including a basketball tournament, which raised much excitement among clients as they built new relationships with supportive community members.

Over time, as this wellness culture permeated the center, the management team realized the need for a track for clients to walk or run on as part of their daily routines. In collaboration with our volunteers and clients, we developed a walkathon for the track, which successfully raised the necessary funds to pave a circular track on the premises, which was frequently used by clients. This positive, community-based effort became a physical sign of our collective commitment to health and well-being, and the power of a realizing a vision, all of which brought inspiration to clients and clinicians alike. Much credit goes to Dr. James Bass, the Director of Men's Services, and our many clients who provided leadership for this effort.

• • •

- Educate clients about the benefits of physical activity;
- Assess financial/environmental barriers and brainstorm solutions;
- Explore clients' goals and interests and discover pleasurable activities;
- Collaboratively develop realistic goals;

- Incorporate physical activity as part of the holistic wellness plan; and
- Support clients' self-efficacy.

Nutrition

Hippocrates, who is traditionally regarded as the father of medicine, famously said, "Let food be thy medicine and medicine be thy food"; yet, the divide between what people put in their bodies and how they feel persists. Although medical technology continues to advance rapidly, lifestyle diseases continue to rise. People's diets are high in sugar, saturated fats, and processed food; as a result, more people are taking prescription drugs to combat the damage done by these foods. Two out of every three Americans are overweight, and rates of Type 2 diabetes continue to rise—most notably among kids.

The connection between what people eat and their physical and mental health cannot be overstated. Yet, many counselors are hesitant to discuss nutrition with clients. Although giving diet advice and creating nutritional treatment plans are beyond the expertise of most counselors, understanding the impact between what people eat and how they feel is a crucial piece of wellness counseling. By understanding the basic science behind food and body wellness, we can educate and empower clients to rethink their relationship with food.

Nutrition and Health

You cannot turn on the television or glance at social media without being bombarded with the latest diet trend. The amount of information out there on what not to eat can be overwhelming, and often contradictory. From a high-protein diet to a vegan juice cleanse and everything in between, wading through the miracle cures and quick fixes filling up your news feed is a daunting task. We think the best approach for your own wellness and when working with clients is to gain a foundational understanding of how food contributes to health. When you focus on what foods are bad for you, guilt and shame can quickly hijack your brain, signaling you to shut down and change the topic. Instead, cultivating an understanding of how food can enrich your health and nourish your body can lead to positive associations with food through fulfillment, gratitude, and motivation.

One ubiquitous nutrition recommendation is to eat a plentiful amount of fruits and vegetables, with a focus on a variety of colors (U.S. Department of Agriculture, Center for Nutrition Policy and

Promotion, n.d.). In addition to being a high-fiber/low-calorie food source, fruits and vegetables are full of phytonutrients or phytochemicals. "Phyto" means from plants; thus, phytonutrients are chemical compounds found in fruits, vegetables, grains, nuts, teas, spices, and legumes and are what give these foods their rich color (obvious exceptions are foods such as cauliflower and onions, which are white but are still high in phytonutrients). Table 5.1, adapted from the Osher Center for Integrative Medicine (n.d.), summarizes the known health benefits from many phytonutrients.

As can be seen from this table, there are many different phytonutrients that enrich the health of people's bodies in some really amazing ways. The mechanisms of how these phytonutrients benefit health include the antiviral, anti-inflammatory, antibacterial, and antioxidant properties of these chemicals. Looking at just one of these in detail provides a great example of how to incorporate nutrition in body wellness.

Cancer and Antioxidants

If you think back to your high school chemistry class, you might remember that an atom is made up of protons, neutrons, and electrons. The center of the atom is the nucleus, which houses protons and neutrons, and the electrons fly around the nucleus. The proton has a positive charge, and the electron has a negative charge. Normal,

Table 5.1

Benefits of Foods by Color

Color	Food	Phytonutrient	Possible Health Actions
Red	Tomatoes, cranberries, watermelons, radishes	Lycopene, vitamin C	Support breast, prostate, and urinary tract health; reduce inflammation
Orange	Sweet potatoes, carrots, mangos, pumpkins	Beta-carotene	Supports immune system and vision
Yellow	Oranges, lemons, bell peppers, peaches	Vitamin C, flavonoids	Inhibit tumor growth, detoxify system
Green	Kale, collard greens, broccoli, brussel sprouts	Folate, indoles, lutein	Support healthy cells, eyes, arteries, lungs, and liver
Green/white	Garlic, onions, asparagus	Allyl sulfides	Support immune system, reduce cell division
Blue/purple	Acai berries, blueberries, purple grapes, plums	Anthocyanins, resveratrol	Destroys free radicals, reduce inflammation, support cardiovascular health
Brown	Whole grains, legumes, ginger	Fiber, isoflavones, gingerol	Lower cholesterol and inflammation; support breast, bone, and joint health

Note. Adapted from "Healthy Dietary Approaches for Cancer Patients," by the Osher Center for Integrative Medicine (n.d.).

or neutral, atoms have an equal number of protons and electrons, so they balance each other out. When certain chemicals in your body gain or lose an electron, they form *free radicals*. These out-of-balance molecules roam around your body looking for other molecules to connect with. This process can be a good thing when they connect to bacteria in immune cells, but it can be extremely problematic when they connect to DNA or other important cells, causing damage and instability—a mechanism that is thought to be behind the development of cancer cells (Valko et al., 2007). You have probably already heard of free radicals, and many skin care or health products market their products as protecting against free radicals. Environmental toxins (such as ultraviolet rays from the sun) and internal processes (such as inflammation) contribute to abnormally high concentrations of free radicals. The most common free radicals in your body are ones that contain oxygen, which is why breathing in toxins is so harmful (e.g., second-hand smoke).

How can you rid your body of harmful free radicals? The answer is *antioxidants*—something you have certainly heard many times as the star ingredient in "super foods." Foods high in antioxidants include berries, sweet potatoes, dark chocolate, and pecans. Drinks high in antioxidants include green tea, coffee, and red wine (however, excess alcohol causes free radicals, so it is best to limit to one glass). The reason antioxidants are so amazing is because they act as free-radical scavengers in our body, roving around donating electrons to neutralize free radicals, preventing them from causing damage to other cells that leave them vulnerable to cancer cells (Kim & Park, 2008).

I (Abigail) like to imagine antioxidants as little Pac-Men, scouring my body looking for free radicals to "eat up." In the morning, when I make my smoothie, I enjoy putting in kale and blueberries because I picture releasing those antioxidant Pac-Men with each sip. The knowledge of why antioxidants are a super food, and understanding how they interact with free radicals, motivates me to seek them out; the indirect result is that I make better food choices—not because I am limiting what I can eat or counting calories but because I am excited to nourish my body.

An important note here is that the exact relationship between food and disease (i.e., cancer) is complex and is explored through the field of *nutrigenetics*. That is, we know that nutrients in certain foods have anticarcinogenic properties that stimulate certain cancer-fighting pathways (either killing cancer cells or preventing new cancer cells from growing). However, the exact mechanisms that stimulate those pathways can vary in intensity depending on specific genetic factors. Thus, like so many things in life, the exact outcome depends on the person. Therefore, we would certainly not recommend diet as a singular cure for disease; however, focusing on good nutrition gives people's bodies the best shot at fighting disease and preventing it in the first place.

As a wellness counselor, you do not have to be an expert on everything, and nutrition is no exception. However, as the previous example shows, depending on where a client's focus is regarding their health, it can be empowering to research how something you can control (i.e., what you eat) can work to heal, nourish, and prevent disease.

Following is a list of practical considerations when incorporating nutrition in wellness counseling:

- When nutrition is an issue, ensure that the client is up to date on physicals.
- Collaborate with, or refer to, a nutritionist.
- Assess readiness and importance of nutrition to the client.
- Assess for food insecurity and financial/environmental barriers to accessing healthy food.
- Educate about nutrition and wellness.
- Develop realistic goals and plans.
- Promote self-monitoring.

Body Image

So far, we have been discussing the external components of how we move and what we eat, but it is impossible to talk about body wellness without discussing the internal connection to *mind wellness.* Body wellness is more than what you do; it includes how you think and feel about your body, because these cognitions and emotions have an enormous impact on your behavior. The idea that mind and body are somehow two disconnected entities is a philosophical argument dating back to Descartes in the 1600s. However, to fully discuss what wellness in the body domain entails, we must explore the concept of body image that is, of course, connected to the physical body but rooted in the mind. When you close your eyes and imagine what you look like, what do you see? What do you think other people see when they look at you? This mental representation of your physical appearance is your body image, and it may or may not actually be accurate. How you view yourself is based not just on your mirror image but also on your experiences, emotions, messages you receive from others, and what you see in the media. Thus, your body image is vulnerable to distortions and the related mental health concerns that come with a negative body image, such as anxiety, depression, and disordered eating.

Looking at disordered eating specifically, it is important to note that there is a complex relationship between mind and body wellness for those struggling. Unlike other addictions, food is not something you can abstain from in any healthy, meaningful way; yet, it is one of the most basic things people can control in terms of their own bodies. Take the connection between physical activity and disordered eating. Physical activity has positive effects on self-esteem, mood, and body image that reduce the risk of eating pathologies. Furthermore, the psychological effects of exercise (more than the physical benefits) can help prevent and treat eating disorders (Hausenblas & Fallon, 2007). However, it is crucial to assess your client before recommending physical activity, because a subgroup of eating pathologies includes those who binge in the form of compulsive exercise. As this example shows, disordered eating and eating pathologies are a complex issue that requires advanced clinical skills and training. We recommend referring clients to eating disorder specialists if their eating behaviors cross the line from an unhealthy relationship to food to a diagnosable eating pathology.

An important place for prevention related to body image and the development of eating disorders is with kids, as young as you can get them. Researchers have shown that kids as young as 3–6 years old may express dissatisfaction with their bodies (Davidson & Birch, 2001), hold negative attitudes toward bigger body sizes (Spiel, Paxton, & Yager, 2012), and worry about fat or dislike something about their appearance (Hayes & Tantleff-Dunn, 2010). As you might imagine with all the changes that happen developmentally (physically, emotionally, socially, and identity-wise) during childhood and adolescence, often body image does not stabilize until the late 20s or 30s (Gillen & Lefkowitz, 2012). However, although kids and teens who are right in the middle of identity development are the most vulnerable to forming a negative body image, there are many factors that affect your body image throughout your lifetime. Internal processes—such as self-esteem, negative self-talk, internalized constructs of femininity and masculinity, and an unrealistic image of the "thin ideal"—affect the discrepancy between what you see in the mirror and what you think you should see in the mirror. People's body image is also affected by their family and peer pressure from social groups, cultural trends, the dieting industry, and exposure to media.

What other factors have affected your body image? Can you think of a time in your life when you struggled with a negative body image? What contributed to a time in your life in which you felt satisfied with your body image?

Counseling Interventions

When working with clients on cultivating a healthy body image and embracing themselves as they are, cognitive behavior therapy and solution-focused interventions provide a useful framework for learning to challenge negative thoughts and creating concrete strategies to move forward rather than compare with others or dwell on hurtful interactions. A strength-based approach is crucial to progress toward loving and respecting your body for what it can do for you versus simply what it looks like. A goal is to help clients name specific feelings to amplify the root cause of body negativity. Think of a time when you have been in a dressing room trying on clothes that just did not fit the way you thought they would when you saw them on the hanger. In that moment, if asked how you feel, a common response might be "fat." Body image guru and veteran school counselor Julia V. Taylor (highlighted later in Practitioner Spotlight 5.2) always says "fat isn't a feeling." What is really going on for you in that moment, and what emotions are you experiencing? Maybe you have had a baby, and even though it has been over a year, you are feeling overwhelmed with the realization that your life in every possible way (not just your shape) will never go back to the way it was before. Maybe you just noticed that someone who you think is smaller than you grabbed the same shirt to try on, and you feel embarrassed to come out wearing it because you have decided that she will look better in it. Or maybe you struggle with feeling too small, and you feel disappointed when your body does not fill out your shirt even though you have begun lifting weights. One helpful intervention is a cognitive behavior therapy thought record to explore the emotions that accompany events and situations in which you feel most vulnerable to thoughts that perpetuate a negative body image.

Another useful theoretical counseling framework to support healthy body image work is feminist therapy. A feminist wellness counselor is mindful to praise efforts opposed to outcomes, celebrates size variety along with other more traditional forms of diversity, and empowers clients to create goals for themselves rather than leading them to culturally popular or stereotypically gendered physical goals (such as losing weight or reaching a certain size). Additionally, from a trauma-informed perspective, it is important to

Practitioner Spotlight 5.2

Interview

Julia V. Taylor

Question: What do you think counselors need to know about wellness counseling as it relates to body image in young women?

Answer: There are two misconceptions I often hear about body image: (1) that body image is solely related to weight and (2) that people who have a healthy body image always feel great about their body. Body image is a complex term and is, generally speaking, how you feel about your body, most of the time. People with a healthy body image have a clear and true perception of what they look like and do not judge their bodies on the basis of how they look. It is also true that people with a healthy body image have days when they do not feel great about how they look. However, those days are limited, and there is not constant judgment about their physical appearance.

Obtaining a healthy body image is difficult for young women. Their bodies are constantly changing, there is intense pressure to fit in with peers, and they are bombarded with unhealthy media messages. Our society is saturated with inconsistent, unrealistic expectations about beauty and weight. It is difficult for young men and is inescapable for young women. Most beauty products that young women purchase contain an overarching message of "there is something wrong with your body, and our product (food, diet, makeup, lotion, cleanser, acne cream, "skinny jeans," teeth whitener, etc.) will "fix it." The dieting industry makes billions of dollars but has an incredibly high failure rate, yet we continue to fuel it.

Lastly, teens are exposed to thousands of images on social media that fuel unhealthy comparisons. Not too long ago, Photoshop was an expensive computer program that easily crashed your hard drive. Now, all it takes is a few clicks on your cell phone to alter an image to the societal and socially constructed view of perfection. I believe that prevention and advocacy are key to wellness counseling with this vulnerable population. We have to teach young women about media literacy and self-care. This goal can be achieved by exposing the media industry and teaching students to advocate against what is being sold and told to them. They deserve to know that the fitness models they see on social media are not real. They need to be exposed to diverse, female role models who strive to make a difference, not achieve a particular body type. A former graduate student presented about self-care at a conference and started off her presentation by asking her audience, "Do you get up at 5 a.m. to work out because you are taking care of your body, or do you get up at 5 a.m. to work out because you hate your body?" It silenced the room and was quite possibly the most powerful message I have heard about self-care. Young women need to be taught that wellness and health are based on the individual and look different for everyone.

(continued)

Interview *(continued)*

Question: What are some key considerations for counselors when incorporating a wellness counseling approach with young women?

Answer: Understand the realm of body image. You can be direct and ask, "How do you feel about your body?" With wellness counseling and body image, there are a lot of psychoeducational components. Be prepared to teach. Avoid minimizing feelings. Do not tell a young women who believes she is ugly how beautiful she is or another who is upset about her acne that "It's not that bad, I hardly noticed." Instead, dig underneath the surface and find out what is there. Sometimes, I say something along the lines of, "I disagree with what you are saying, but I do hear you, say more about . . . ." This way, I am not agreeing with, discounting, or minimizing what they are saying.

Avoid the term "diet." I think diet is the worst four-letter word, and it represents deprivation and something temporary. Instead, teach young women about making healthy choices when possible and fueling their bodies in a manner that works for them and helps them to feel good.

There is not a means to an end when it comes to exercise. Too many people start and stop exercise programs because they do not meet their weight-related goals, and too many people exercise solely to burn calories. Help young women find movement they enjoy, and teach them the multitude of health benefits associated with exercise and movement. Exercise does not have to involve a gym membership or even sweat. It can be dancing, gardening, walking with a friend, or yoga/meditation. Exercise is a gracious act of self-care when it truly is about self-care.

Know, and check, your privilege. Many people do not have access to organic foods or a gym. Some of your clients may not feel safe walking or running alone in their neighborhoods. Know who you are working with, and be careful not to suggest something that is not feasible.

Size is not a reflection of health, and this needs to be constantly reflected in how you treat and approach your clients. As counselors, we need to create a safe, nonjudgmental environment for all youths to feel valued and appreciated. In my experience, teens intuitively know who is safe and who is not.

Nobody makes long-term changes when shamed. I am often asked "What about obesity?" when I discuss body image and youths. Yes, we have an obesity epidemic. However, I am not a medical doctor or dietician, although I do know this: We have to teach young people to love and accept their bodies, as they are. If they desire to, or are advised by a medical professional to make a weight-related change, it always starts with self-love and acceptance.

• • •

note that experiencing childhood adverse childhood experiences is correlated with low self-esteem and adulthood obesity (Williamson, Thompson, Anda, Dietz, & Felitti, 2002). Experiencing trauma, particularly sexual trauma, is the ultimate message that your body does not have value. How you feel in your own skin has important implications for how you feel when physically intimate with another person. Helping clients to honor, appreciate, and value their bodies can have a profound impact on how they expect others to respect their bodies.

Because body image is so transformed during childhood and adolescence, if you are going to be working with these ages groups, it is important to consider how wellness counseling extends to parents and caregivers. Encourage parents to talk to their children about puberty, their changing bodies and desires, and active consent. Perhaps work with the school nurse to create information that models how to have these conversations. Challenge parents and caregivers to examine their own habits that might interfere with a healthy body image, such as constantly being on a diet, verbalizing negative self-talk (and therefore modeling it), shrugging off compliments, and sending negative messages about the size or sexual behaviors of others. Brainstorm ways to compliment someone that are not about their looks, and model that whenever you can. It is important for kids to hear that they are kind, brave, intelligent, good problem solvers, leaders, and friends—not just that they are cute or have value based on how their bodies look.

Media Literacy

We have already mentioned that exposure to media is a factor that affects body image. An important task of the wellness counselor is to help clients gain media literacy skills to challenge the harmful messages that bombard them daily. The National Association for Media Literacy Education (n.d.) defined media literacy as "the ability to access, analyze, evaluate, create, and act using all forms of communication" (para. 1). This association has highlighted the inevitability of media exposure in our fast-paced, all-consuming media age and has suggested that media literacy expertise is needed to be a productive student or worker, a responsible citizen, and a competent consumer given the highly sophisticated way media targets us on a multisensory level. Try exploring the ways in which media affects your wellness—influencing your thoughts, feelings, and behavior. By learning media literacy skills, you empower your client to become an active, rather than a passive, consumer of media.

A hallmark of media literacy is asking questions. Ask clients to bring in magazine ads that stand out to them, or find some together online and practice asking questions together. Why was this advertisement made and by whom? Who is this ad speaking to? Who is it ignoring? How might this ad be interpreted differently by different people? How do you know whether the information is true? Who is benefiting and who is being harmed by this ad? If you are working with kids, this can become a fun game where once you start noticing the sell behind the message, you start to notice it everywhere. If you are able to work with a group, make an activity out of unpacking confusing or conflicting messages and challenge the sexism, racism, sizeism, classicism, homophobia, and so forth inherent in the message. Like anything else, once you start to peer behind the curtain, you began to take power away from external authority and find it in yourself.

Barriers to Body Wellness

Body wellness encompasses a vast landscape—from how you think about your body, to how you move your body, to how you fuel your body. Thus, there are many barriers to consider when working with a client. Internally, the script of negative automatic thoughts that bolster self-doubt, low self-esteem and efficacy, and harmful stereotypes are modeled for them on a daily basis from advertisements, peers, and even their own families. Their minds are easily led down a road of irrational generalizations—such as "I can't," "I don't have time," or "I don't deserve"—that trap them in a circle. Quick fixes to soothe their anxious brains, such as sugar and alcohol, binging and purging, as well as TV and the Internet, offer temporary relief to long-term habits that squash motivation to change and wire them to need more.

When people are under stress, their bodies pay the price. When a person's brain activates the stress response, their body gets signals to prepare for danger. The musculoskeletal system becomes on guard, tensing muscles to be ready to move and buffer injury and pain. The respiratory system becomes overactive, and breathing becomes rapid and shallow. In the cardiovascular system, the stress hormones released cause the heart rate to go up and blood vessels to dilate to speed up the blood delivery system. This process causes blood pressure to go up, and in a prolonged state, it increases risk for hypertension, heart attack, or stroke. The endocrine system is the main delivery system of stress hormones signaled to be released by the brain. Cortisol and epinephrine are great for energy for fight or flight; however, the result is increased blood sugar, leaving the body vulnerable to Type 2 diabetes. The gastrointestinal system slows down to divert energy to more pressing needs, causing food to move slower through your body and your intestines to absorb less nutrients. Stomach aches, nausea, and heartburn are common. Moreover, prolonged exposure to elevated stress hormones reduces libido and affects both the male and female reproductive system.

As discussed in Chapter 3, the result of chronic stress and all of these negative impacts on the body systems is profound. Minorities and other marginalized groups experience chronic stress that leads to marked health disparities and, ultimately, early death. A key piece of wellness counseling is working with every client on decreasing stress and increasing coping strategies to mitigate the impact of stress on their body. Life is stressful, and no one is immune. However, you can learn to soothe your stress response to allow your body to reset more often and more efficiently. From a trauma-informed approach, learning to self-regulate an overactive stress response is crucial and an empowering step toward healing.

Externally, the most clear and persistent barrier to body wellness is access: access to role models who hold up a mirror to teach you to see yourself the way they see you, access to time and safe places to move your body freely and without fear, and access to food that you can afford that nourishes your health. Think back to Chapter 3 and the social determinants of health; The environment we live in and the access that we have to healthy food, safe communities, and education are critical to positive health outcomes and body wellness.

Barriers to body wellness can seem overwhelming at times; therefore, we wanted to offer a few ideas for body wellness boosters—that is, simple interventions that can be enacted by the client in a short period of time that bolster wellness in the body domain:

1. As you take a daily walk to your mailbox, or to your office, bring all your awareness to the act of walking. Feel your feet move across the ground, your muscles contract and release with each step, and the sounds and sensations around you. When you get to where you are going, take a deep cleansing breath in, breath out any stress you are feeling, and set an intention for the day.
2. Pay attention to your food! For at least one meal a day, turn off the TV, put your phone down, and close your computer. As

you eat each bite, see whether you can notice distinct flavors and whether they change as you chew. Bring your awareness to the process of swallowing, and pay attention to how your level of hunger changes as you approach satiation. Chances are, your food will taste better, and you will feel full sooner than you think!

3. During your morning routine, instead of focusing on how your clothes fit, what kind of hair day you are having, or what the scale says, think about one thing your body is going to do for you today. Are your legs going to carry you to where you need to go? Will your hands take care of a loved one or an animal? Will your ears facilitate connection with others as you listen to their needs? Take a moment to express gratitude toward your body and all that it does for you.

4. Clean up your social media! As you scroll through your news feed or Instagram stories, unfollow anyone or any page that is sending negative messages or contributing to your stress. Unfriend to create space for positive images, messages, and motivation.

Conclusion

When working with a client on body wellness, remember that change comes from loving and respecting your body, not shaming it. Coping skills training that integrates the body with other wellness domains, such as cognitive restructuring interventions and mindfulness exercises, grounds clients in their bodies and begins the process of feeling peace in their own skin.

Reflection Prompts

1. What do you believe are some current challenges to maintaining a healthy diet?
2. What are some presenting problems/concerns for clients that might relate to nutrition, diet, and weight?
3. How might you incorporate aspects of nutrition in your clinical practice?
4. What makes engaging in sufficient physical activity challenging?
5. How might you incorporate the topic of physical activity in your clinical practice?
6. When you are stressed out, where do you feel it in your body? What are some physical indicators to yourself that stress is weighing you down?

Learning Activities

Food Log

Keep a food log for 4 days. You can do it by writing it down, or you can download an app to help you track your consumption. If possible, include 2 weekend days and 2 weekdays. Record as much information as possible about each meal. Include the food items, serving sizes, brand, restaurant (if you went out to eat), and preparation method. Record the nutritional value of each meal. If it is not readily available on the packaging, conduct a quick Internet search to get information that is as accurate as possible. Conduct an informal comparison of your intake with the recommended intake by the U.S. dietary guidelines and assess your diet:

http://www.choosemyplate.gov/food-groups/

http://www.cnpp.usda.gov/Publications/DietaryGuidelines/2010/
  PolicyDoc/ExecSumm.pdf

Next, do a basic Internet search to see whether you can find any information on the effects of food that you have eaten on mood or well-being. For example, if you ate a steak, you may want to Google "steak and mood." Try several of these combinations and see whether you find any information.

Body Image Activities for Teens

Try conducting the following body image activities for teens
(adapted from Julia V. Taylor):

- *Comparisons.* Teenagers are comparing creatures. This activity teaches kindness and acceptance by taking the "than me" out of comparisons. Have your clients list the people they compare themselves with and why. You might get, "she's prettier than me," "she's much faster than me swimming," or "he is so much stronger than me." Next, have them drop the comparison and make a new list—for example, "she's pretty," "she's a fast swimmer," or "he is strong." Discuss how unhealthy and unproductive comparisons are and how to show kindness and compassion toward other people.

- *What's left?* Have your clients each bring in a popular teen or health magazine and teach them about the advertising industry—the notion of "there is something wrong with your body, and our product is going to change that." For example, if you use this shampoo, you will have silky smooth hair. If you use this mascara, you will have long, curly lashes. Or if you buy this acne product, your face will clear up within days. Next, have them go through the magazine and fold down the pages that contain an advertisement that makes those types of claims. When they are done, notice what is left and discuss.

(continued)

Body Image Activities for Teens *(continued)*
- *Wellness challenges.* Instead of goals, try giving teenagers weekly wellness challenges. This way, they are working on one small thing, and often a challenge feels less daunting to a teenager than a goal. Here are a few examples: Unfollow one person on social media who makes you feel badly about yourself or your body, look in the mirror each morning and say "good morning" (this act can progress to other positive, kind words), say "no" to one thing that your gut tells you to say "no" to, and put your phone on airplane mode for 1 week when you go to sleep (yes, the alarm will still work!). Make sure you write down their challenges and follow up with them.

Resources

Academy of Nutrition and Dietetics
http://www.eatright.org/resources/food/nutrition

This website provides resources on all things nutrition and health, including food, supplements, and fitness.

Forks Over Knives
https://www.forksoverknives.com/

This organization, which made the compelling documentary of the same name, houses many plant-based diet resources and recipes.

Mindful Schools
https://www.mindfulschools.org/personal-practice/walking/

This post provides a mindful walking guide.

National Association for Media Literacy Education
https://namleboard.files.wordpress.com/2017/10/parent_guide_final.pdf

This document serves as a parent's guide to media literacy.

References

Babyak, M., Blumenthal, J. A., Herman, S., Khatri, P., Doraiswamy, M., Moore, K., . . . Krishnan, K. R. (2000). Exercise treatment for major depression: Maintenance of therapeutic benefit at 10 months. *Psychosomatic Medicine, 62,* 633–638.

Biddle, S. J. H., & Asare, M. (2011). Physical activity and mental health in children and adolescents: A review of reviews. *British Journal of Sports Medicine, 45,* 886–895. http://dx.doi.org/10.1136/bjsports-2011-090185

Bize, R., Johnson, J. A., & Plotnikoff, R. C. (2007). Physical activity level and health-related quality of life in the general adult population: A systematic review. *Preventative Medicine, 45,* 401–415. http://dx.doi.org/10.1016/j.ypmed.2007.07.017

Boecker, H., Sprenger, T., Spilker, M. E., Henriksen, G., Koppenjoefer, M., Wagner, K. J., . . . Tolle, T. R. (2008). The runner's high: Opioidergic mechanisms in the human brain. *Cerebral Cortex, 18,* 2523–2521.

Davidson, K. K., & Birch, L. L. (2001). Childhood overweight: A contextual model and recommendations for future research. *Obesity Reviews, 2,* 159–171.

Gillen, M. M., & Lefkowitz, E. S. (2012). Gender and racial/ethnic differences in body image development among college students. *Body Image, 9,* 126–130.

Hausenblas, H. A., & Fallon, E. A. (2007). Exercise and body image: A meta-analysis. *Journal of Psychology and Health, 21,* 33–47.

Hayes, S., & Tantleff-Dunn, S. (2010). Am I too fat to be a princess? Examining the effects of popular children's media on young girls' body image. *The British Journal of Developmental Psychology, 28,* 413–426.

Kim, M. K., & Park, J. H. (2008). Cruciferous vegetable intake and the risk of human cancer: Epidemiological evidence. *Proceedings of the Nutrition Society, 68,* 103–110. https://doi.org/10.1017/S0029665108008884

Korb, A. (2015). *The upward spiral: Using neuroscience to reverse the course of depression, one small change at a time.* Oakland, CA: New Harbinger Publications.

Leasure, J. L., & Jones, M. (2008). Forced and voluntary exercise differentially affect brain and behavior. *Neuroscience, 156,* 456–465.

Lubans, D., Richards, J., Hillman, C., Faulkner, G., Beauchamp, M., Nilsson, M., . . . Biddle, S. (2016). Physical activity for cognitive and mental health in youth: A systematic review of mechanisms. *Pediatrics, 138,* e20161642. https://doi.org/10.1542/peds.2016-1642

National Association for Media Literacy Education. (n.d.). *Media literacy defined.* Retrieved from https://namle.net/publications/media-literacy-definitions/

Osher Center for Integrative Medicine. (n.d.). *Healthy dietary approaches for cancer patients.* Retrieved from https://www.osher.ucsf.edu/patient-care/self-care-resources/cancer-and-nutrition/dietary-guidelines/

Rovio, S., Spulber, G., Nieminen, L. J., Niskanesn, E., Winblad, B., Tuomilehto, J., . . . Kivipelto, M. (2010). The effect of midlife physical activity on structural brain changes in the elderly. *Neurobiology of Aging, 31,* 1927–1936.

Spiel, E. C., Paxton, S. J., & Yager, Z. (2012). Weight attitudes in 3- to 5-year-old children: Age differences and cross-sectional predictors. *Body Image, 9,* 524–527.

U.S. Department of Agriculture, Center for Nutrition Policy and Promotion. (n.d.). *Dietary guidelines.* Retrieved from https://www.cnpp.usda.gov/dietary-guidelines

U.S. Department of Health and Human Services. (2008). *2008 physical activity guidelines for Americans.* Retrieved from https://health.gov/paguidelines/pdf/paguide.pdf

Valko, M., Leibfritz, D., Moncol, J., Cronin, M. T., Mazur, M., & Telser, J. (2007). Free radicals and antioxidants in normal physiological functions and human disease. *International Journal of Biochemistry & Cell Biology, 39,* 44–84.

Wang, D., Wang, Y., Wang, Y., Li, R., & Zhou, C. (2014). Impact of physical exercise on substance use disorders: A meta-analysis. *PLoS ONE, 9,* e110728. https://doi.org/10.1371/journal.pone.0110728

Williamson, D. F., Thompson, T. J., Anda, R. F., Dietz, W. H., & Felitti, V. (2002). Body weight and obesity in adults and self-reported abuse in childhood. *International Journal of Obesity, 26,* 1075–1082.

Winter, B., Breitenstein, C., Mooren, F. C., Voelker, K., Fobker, M., Lechtermann, A., . . . Knecht, S. (2007). High impact running improves learning. *Neurobiology of Learning and Memory, 87,* 597–609.

Chapter 6

Spirit

When you discover something that nourishes your soul and
brings joy, care enough to make room for it in your life.
—Jean Shinoda Bolen

• • •

This chapter addresses the internal lives of clients and the role of
faith and meaning in wellness. Spirituality, values, ethics, and mor-
als are delineated as they relate to meaning making and the role of
self as it affects others. The spirit domain offers a useful framework
for broaching the topic of clients' religious and spiritual selves—an
area that counselors often report as challenging and uncomfortable.
We address the practical applications of exploring faith, meaning,
purpose, and spiritual development as an essential component of
the human condition. *Spirit wellness* is conceptualized as the process
of feeling connected to, and searching for, meaning, purpose, and
awe-inspired relationships with self, others, and the world around us.

Spirituality

Many scholars have suggested that spirituality is actually at the
core of wellness—the glue that connects all other domains or
perhaps the common thread woven among each other domain
(e.g., Witmer & Sweeney, 1992). A broad body of research has
shown that strong spiritual or religious beliefs are connected to
lower stress levels and higher immune function during times of

illness (*body wellness*; Koenig & Cohen, 2002); lower levels of anxiety, depression, and addiction and higher levels of self-esteem and well-being (*emotion wellness*; Cashwell & Young, 2011; Pargament, Koeing, & Perez, 2002); the ability to sustain intention and attention through contemplative practice and mindfulness (*mind wellness*; Begley, 2007); and protective factors such as social support and community building (*connection wellness*; Hill & Pargament, 2003).

However, for many individuals (including counselors), this domain is the most difficult to talk about or feel comfortable exploring. Each semester, I (Abigail) send my wellness counseling students the Five Factor Wellness Inventory (Myers & Sweeney, 2005) to take before class starts so that we can have a baseline to start the conversation. Each semester, most students report that their spiritual wellness is their lowest domain (usually right along with social wellness because graduate students are busy!). This finding is in line with national trends that show a steady gradual decline in faith beliefs of American adults (Gallup, 2016; Pew Research Center, 2015). However, an important distinction to make at this point is between the terms "religion" and "spirituality."

Religion is a belief in a higher power, usually a god or gods, organized by a system of beliefs shared by others. Religions are creedal, dogmatic, and governed by institutional rules of worship. Using the Religious Landscape Survey, the Pew Research Center (2015) found that most Americans identify with a religion (a little more than 75%; see Table 6.1).

Although it is certainly true that most Americans identify with a particular religion, there is a growing trend among Americans who more accurately describe themselves as "spiritual but not religious." In another survey, the Pew Research Center (2017) found that al-

Table 6.1

Religious Affiliation in the United States (2015)

Religion	%
Christian	70.0
Jewish	1.9
Muslim	0.9
Buddhist	0.7
Hindu	0.7
Other non-Christian faiths	1.8
Agnostic	4.0
No affiliation	15.8
Atheist	3.1

though only 54% of Americans consider themselves religious (a figure that is steadily declining), 75% identify as spiritual. This category of people who identify as spiritual but not religious is growing among all demographics—age, race, gender, religious affiliation (or not), education level, and political party affiliation. Although this trend is seen across all groups of Americans, it does skew toward younger, more educated people who have lower levels of religious observance (e.g., regularly attend a worship service).

What does all of this mean? Well, for starters, it helps us understand the diversity among Americans in terms of both religious affiliation and the role religiosity might play (or not) in their lives. However, it also gives us a window into a more nuanced look at spirituality as the larger umbrella, under which religion is one part. Cashwell, Bentley, and Bigbee (2007) have offered a really wonderful definition of spirituality:

> *Spirituality* is a developmental process that is both active and passive wherein beliefs, disciplined practice, and experiences are grounded and integrated to result in increased *mindfulness* (nonjudgemental awareness of present experiences), *heartfulness* (experiences of compassion and love), and *soulfulness* (connections beyond ourselves). (p. 67)

Spirituality is developmental in nature, meaning that it is a shared experience among all people that grows and changes over time. With this in mind, it is useful to explore what that developmental process looks like.

Spiritual Development Theory

James Fowler (1981) was the first theorist to address spirituality or faith from a developmental perspective. According to Fowler, "faith is a person's way of seeing him or herself in relation to others against a background of shared meaning and purpose" (p. 4). Faith is not necessarily religious in content but rather is a universal experience in the journey of human development. Similar to other identity development theories you might be familiar with, Fowler proposed seven stages (one prestage and six stages) that drew from the models of development proposed by Kohlberg (1963) and Piaget (1932/1960).

The developmental model starts with a prestage called *Primal Faith*; it occurs in the first, preverbal year of life and provides a foundation for the following stages. Stage 1, *Intuitive-Projective Faith*, is typically experienced from 2 to 7 years old. Powerful narratives characterize this stage, where a child may think of a supreme being as a superhero or magic. The child's imagination is unrestrained, and they are experiencing self-awareness for the first time. They may be powerfully influenced by examples, tone, actions, and stories of the visible beliefs of close adults. Conflict may arise from negative or destructive images or messages, and the child's ability to understand what is real and what is imaginary marks the transition to the next stage.

Stage 2, *Mythic-Literal Faith*, occurs in grade school. This stage is marked by the development of the ability to think logically. Stories and symbols become important ways for the child to belong to their community. Transition to the next stage occurs when a conflict arises between the stories one has been told and reality. For example, if a child is being raised within a Christian tradition, they may begin to question the story of Genesis as they learns about evolution.

Stage 3, *Synthetic-Conventional Faith*, often occurs in adolescence. This stage is characterized by conformity, and the authority is external. A person's beliefs and values are solidified into identity, and often they has not spent much time examining or challenging these beliefs. They may not even realize that their belief system is just one of many, so conflict can occur when those beliefs are called into question. Transition into the next stage occurs when there are contradictions between authority sources, and one begins to critically reflect on their beliefs. For example, a teenager might wrestle with the concept of why bad things happen to good people and vice versa. Many people actually stay in this stage permanently, particularly if they surround themselves with only like-minded people into adulthood.

If development continues, Stage 4, *Individuative-Reflective Faith*, often occurs in the mid-20s to late 30s. This stage is characterized by angst and struggle as the individual begins to see him- or herself as the authority of their own beliefs. The person begins to take responsibility for their own values, beliefs, and lifestyle. Transition into the next stage occurs when the person begins to "press on toward a more dialectical and multileveled approach to life truth" (Fowler, 1981, p. 183). If raised within a religious tradition, this stage is often about much more than that religion, and the role that religion in general plays into a wider social justice framework is often explored.

Stage 5, *Conjunctive Faith*, usually comes in midlife and often brings a more reflective recognition of multiple forms of knowing. In this stage, symbols regain power, and the person recognizes the power of their culture, ritual, and privilege. In this stage, the person is able to find meaning in their own truth while comprehending its relative nature. Transition to the next stage rarely occurs.

Finally, Stage 6, *Universalizing Faith*, is characterized by a movement toward inclusiveness while still maintaining firm commitments to values of universal love and justice. This stage is rare and occurs when people "embody in radical ways this leaning into the future of God for all beings" (Fowler, 1981, p. 211). Fowler considered historical figures such as Martin Luther King Jr. and Mother Teresa to have achieved this stage.

Looking at these stages, you may have noticed that there is a pretty big jump developmentally between Stages 3 and 4. Building on Fowler's (1981) work, scholar Sharon Parks (2000) further explored the application of spiritual development theory to the young adult population and included an additional "Young Adult" stage in between the adolescent stage (Stage 3) and the tested adult stage (Stage 4). She stated that in considering the young adult stage, "we may recognize with new strength how young adults and their mentors serve to fuel the power and promise of cultural renewal, seeding the imagination of a worthy adulthood and the promise of our common future" (p. 13). Many people in this young adult phase are in higher education (you might be yourself!), and you could argue that one goal of higher education is to cultivate inquiry, reflection, and knowledge in the young adult life and encourage this growth in human development that requires asking the big questions of meaning and purpose during the pivotal time of the college years. Parks, like Fowler, understood faith "in its broadest, most inclusive form as *the activity of meaning* that all human beings share" (p. xi).

In both theories, you will notice that age approximations are offered; however, stage progression does not automatically happen as you age. Progression through the stages is not inevitable but rather is a result of individual experiences that deepen reflective complexity of cognitive, affective, and relational aspects of spirituality. Adults can be considered stabilized at any time during Stages 2–6. Reading through the various stages, where do you see yourself? Do you have friends and family who you think might be at different stages of spiritual development? Have you adapted and put your own spin on beliefs that you were raised with? Can you think of a memory or defining moment in your life that categorically changed the way you viewed your connection to others and your place in the world?

When considering cultural applicability, spiritual development theory is rooted in the assumption that this form of identity development occurs in all populations. Spirituality, faith, or meaning making is "so *fundamental* that none of us can live well for very long without it, so *universal* that when we move beneath the symbols, rituals and

ethical patterns that express it, faith is recognizably the same phenomenon" (Fowler, 1981, p. xiii). Furthermore, spirituality is not
necessarily religious in context or content. Although religion can
often be a compartmentalized aspect of life, spirituality is an orientation or worldview that is not a separate dimension of one's being.
Fowler (1981) helped us understand that spirituality is a relational
enterprise. The Primal Faith prestage assumes that we all start on
our spiritual development in the womb through infancy relating and
learning to have faith in our parents or caregivers. As with other
aspects of our identity, spirituality continues to be shaped by our
experiences and relationships with others (Fowler, 1981). Thus, our
spiritual beliefs are often intricately tied with our family of origin,
culture, and community.

Taken together, these two theories of spiritual development lay the
foundation for exploring religious and spiritual issues with counseling students and clients. Following the assumptions that spirituality
is an essential component of the human experience and that young
adults particularly are struggling with their spiritual development, to
not explore such issues with students and clients would ignore a crucial piece of their identity development. In essence, not incorporating these issues into counseling would ignore a fundamental aspect
of the client's well-being.

Spiritual Struggles

Given the developmental nature of spirituality, which depends on
crises or challenges to move forward in the stage progression, a common component of spiritual development is experiencing a spiritual
struggle. Pargament, Murray-Swank, Magyar, and Ano (2005) defined a spiritual struggle as "efforts to conserve or transform a spirituality that has been threatened or harmed" (p. 247). Ellison and
Lee (2010) categorized events into three types of spiritual struggles:
(1) an interpersonal struggle experienced as a result of negative interactions among individuals in the same belief system (e.g., "You
want me to believe what now?"), (2) a divine struggle experienced
between an individual and their understanding of a higher power
(e.g., "Why do you let bad things happen to good people?"), and (3)
an intrapsychic struggle between a person and their own personal
belief system (e.g., "What's the point, what does this all mean?").

The key here is that spiritual struggles are normal and are what
help us move through our own spiritual identity development—understanding that different types exist will help normalize what you
or your client or students are experiencing. It is important to note

that spiritual struggles are more common in underrepresented groups, including women (Bryant, 2007), religious minorities (Bryant & Astin, 2008), and sexual minorities (Love, Bock, Jannarone, & Richardson, 2005). Particularly if a person adheres to a fundamental religious belief system that espouses a more rigid and patriarchal structure, just deciding to live a more authentic life could put a person in position to be countering strong positions within their group. Therefore, understanding where a client might be both developmentally and in relationship to their spiritual identity and community is a crucial piece of a wellness assessment. Although we know spiritual struggles are common, researchers also have shown that there are many positive outcomes of moving through a spiritual struggle, such as an increase in acceptance of others of different faiths (Bryant & Astin, 2008), positive health outcomes (Nelms, Hutchins, Hutchins, & Pursley, 2007), increased equanimity (Astin & Keen, 2006), and socially responsible leadership (Gehrke, 2008). See Practitioner Spotlight 6.1 for a discussion of treating a client experiencing grief and loss.

Meaning Making

In psychological terms, only challenge and adversity create growth. As we just saw in spiritual development theory, a common component of all human development theories is challenge, crisis, or dissonance propelling us forward into the next stage of development. Can you think of a time when you found something positive in the midst of hardship? If the answer is yes, you might not be surprised to know that people who have experienced some adversity are often happier and more resilient than those who have not (Croft, Dunn, & Quoidbach, 2013; Seery, Holman, & Silver, 2010). Happiness is undoubtedly important, and we explore this emotion more in the next chapter. The heart of spirit wellness is to look beyond happiness—to look deeper into the space where we find peace, meaning, and purpose. When asked what makes life worth living, people often answer with what gives their life meaning—not what makes them feel happy. The key is meaning making, because making sense of our lives, particularly challenges in our lives, helps to shape our identity and sense of self, increase resilience, cope better with stress, and have perspective that includes optimism for the future (Park, 2010). Powerful ways to help your clients make meaning in their lives include cultivating gratitude, finding purpose through vocation or service, and connecting with something bigger than themselves such as nature.

Practitioner Spotlight 6.1

A Case Example of Grief and Loss: Jenna

J. Robert Nations

Wellness counseling can easily incorporate spirituality as a vital component for assisting a client's improved level of functioning and quality of life. This case study demonstrates how to incorporate spirituality in wellness counseling.

Jenna was a 35-year-old, Caucasian female who was referred to counseling because of grief complications. Her husband of 10 years died unexpectedly 6 months prior to the initial appointment. She is now a single mother of two children, an 8-year-old boy and a 6-year-old girl. She came to address complications related to acute sadness, increased isolation, and loss of interest in parenting and work. She is motivated to improve and seek a way to move forward as a healthy person and parent.

My approach to complications with grief and loss is to listen for the unique way clients understand and find meaning in their loss. While asking some initial intake questions about her religious and spiritual life, Jenna disclosed religious rituals and connection to a faith community as sources of support following the death of her husband. This identification of religion as a source of support, rather than a source of discomfort, indicated that Jenna would benefit from integrating spirituality into wellness counseling. During our counseling sessions that followed, I used the wellness wheel and holistic wellness model to inform my approach to address meaning and purpose for all areas of her life. Her primary loss was her husband's death. Her belief in an afterlife and the funeral ritual were meaningful for her. She was supported in finding comfort and meaning in his life and from the faith community and funeral rituals provided. Important secondary losses for Jenna were loss of companionship, a parenting partner, and someone to share the joys of life. She spoke of understanding herself now as a widow and single mother. A new role of relating to others in family, in community, and with work colleagues was discussed.

Her sense of self was enhanced by her spiritual life. She felt accepted by her faith community and found a new connection with her religious community along with her children. She reconnected with her religious community by continuing to worship and participate in children's programs with her children. Because rituals were valued, we identified spiritual rituals of remembering her husband with the children. Celebrating his life and what meaning his life meant to her and her children was important from a spiritual perspective. Her isolation began to decrease, and a sense of self-worth and acceptance began to improve. Her religious community offered a grief support group that I recommended as adjunct to our sessions. Through acknowledging her spirituality

(continued)

A Case Example of Grief and Loss: Jenna *(continued)*

in grief counseling, Jenna found meaning in connection with her community, family, culture, and herself. By finding gradual improvement in emotional, mental, and spiritual strength, she also reported returning to work with an increased level of functioning. Wellness counseling with attention to healthy spirituality enabled Jenna to conceptualize her grief and recovery with hopefulness.

Although this case study identifies some spiritual interventions in working with grief and loss, wellness counseling can effectively use many spiritual interventions that are unique to our clients. I may identify a religious or spiritual topic through initial assessments or through a client's self-disclosure of spiritual meaning or understanding related to their presenting problem. If spirituality is important to clients, I help them talk about this as a way to improve optimal levels of functioning and promotion of wellness. Spiritual interventions may be offered as forms of rituals to practice, mindfulness and contemplative practice, prayer, readings from their holy texts, connection with religious communities, forgiveness of self and others, and encouraging conversations with religious leaders and clergy of their faith. Spirituality, like grief and loss, is unique and personal with each client. If a healthy spirituality is embodied by our clients, then it will provide meaning to all aspects of their life. Wellness counseling is enhanced when spiritual interventions are effectively used.

● ● ●

Gratitude

Gratitude is the act of bringing awareness to, and appreciation for, the things you have in your life—people, experiences, things, needs that are met, and so forth. Cultivating a practice of gratitude is one of the easiest ways to affect wellness because it does not depend on your life circumstances to have it; as long as you are still breathing, there is something to be grateful for. Gratitude helps us find peace and contentment in our own lives as well as feel closer to those around us. Try this—take a deep breath in, and as the air fills you up completely, pause and say to yourself "In this moment, I am grateful for this breath," and then exhale slowly. Do you notice anything different in how you feel? Gratitude is actually an amazing and powerful antidote to negativity in life. Recent studies have shown that gratitude can improve sleep; lower stress; and decrease depression, anxiety, and even suicidal thoughts (Korb, 2015). Sounds too good to be true, right? Well, one reason gratitude is so powerful is that it actually appears to have the largest impact on people who need it the most. The exact neural mechanisms of gratitude are still unknown, but the science we have gives us clues to how gratitude works. It seems that gratitude acts as a booster, allowing positive emotions to be more easily accessible and last longer. The practice of gratitude increases both dopamine and serotonin, which, you might remember from Chapter 4, are important for mood, motivation, and enjoyment.

When you make a conscious effort to notice and appreciate the good around you, you are calming the emotional center of your brain and allowing your focus to rest on the present rather than ruminate on the past or worry about the future. When you express gratitude to others, an important feedback loop of positivity and social connection is set in motion—you feel good and more connected, and the other person feels appreciated and more aware of blessing in their own life. Long-time practices that are more prevalent than ever in the age of social media—such as "paying it forward" or "random acts of kindness"—have a powerful butterfly effect rooted in giving and accepting gratitude. The next time you are having a rough day, search "random acts of kindness" on YouTube.com for a quick boost of feel-good neurotransmitters.

Career Development and Service

A hallmark of career development theory is the notion that finding a vocation that fits your passion, talent, and needs contributes to your overall well-being. This concept is certainly true in regard to mental and emotional health, and more recently this idea has been examined in relationship to spiritual health. Finding meaning and connection in the work that you do, and a shared mission with the people whom you work with, improves job satisfaction, productivity, and workplace culture (Garcia-Zamor, 2003). Viewing career development from a wellness lens, there is a cyclical relationship between spirituality and work. Spirituality is the guiding force that shapes our values and ethics, which has a profound impact on our behavior in school and at work. Finding meaning and purpose through your work (which, aside from sleeping, is what you spend the majority of your time doing) has a profound impact on your spiritual development. Working with a client to explore their vocation or calling through activities that clarify values and skills is an important component of wellness counseling.

It is important to note that many people do not have the luxury of finding a job based on criteria that bring meaning and purpose and feed their soul. When you have mouths to feed and a family to support, a job that provides financial stability is prioritized over one that provides spiritual stability. However, it is useful to explore meaning and purpose in any role, even if it is not a client's ultimate calling. Monica Worline, a researcher at Stanford's Center for Compassion and Altruism Research, studies compassion in the workplace and compassionate leadership. Her research suggests that no matter the work, feeling connected to others in the workplace has positive implications for employee burnout and engagement. She suggests approaching coworkers as people worthy of compassion and with empathic concern. She also points to the importance of viewing your role with a bigger-than-self lens, rather than a self-focus, to find positive motivation (Worline & Dutton, 2017).

Still, for many people, it is through service—rather than work—that they find meaning, connection, and purpose. Whether that is through volunteering your time or your talents with those in need or serving in a leadership role with a community organization or church, serving others is a form of spiritual wellness that can have a profound impact on your health. In fact, volunteering can lower your blood pressure, increase your life span, and lower your risk for depression later in life (Corporation for National and Community Service, Office of Research and Policy Development, 2007). Giving your time and your talents through service provides a sense of purpose, accomplishment, and life satisfaction that deepen your spiritual wellness and serve as a buffer from stress, depression, and isolation. Even among people with chronic pain and disease, volunteering has been shown to decrease pain levels, feelings of despair, and level of disability. The greatest gains from volunteering have been found among older populations, probably because there is often a degree of obligation involved the younger you are (Sneed & Cohen, 2013). However, there is no age too early to start fostering habits of service to empower people to find meaning through service to people, animals, and nature in their community and abroad.

EcoWellness

For some, a deep sense of meaning and purpose comes from connection with nature rather than, or in addition to, a connection with a higher power. *EcoWellness* is "a sense of appreciation, respect for, and awe of nature that results in feelings of connectedness with a natural environment and the enhancement of holistic wellness" (Reese & Myers, 2012, p. 400). EcoWellness is composed of three dimensions: access to nature, environmental identity, and transcendence in nature. The third dimension, transcendence in nature, is described by both spiritual well-being and community connectedness. Spending time in nature is awe inspiring and cultivates feelings of respect and responsibility to both the natural world and those around us. For many people, being in nature helps bring clarity and perspective that are so easily distorted in our fast-paced, tech-centered world.

To facilitate quick and frequent strategies to deepen the practice of meaning making, we offer the following spirit wellness boosters:

1. Be open to moments of awe. As you are walking on a regular route, even if you are only outside and walking from the parking lot to your office door, try to notice one thing outside that is an example of how much bigger the world is than yourself.
2. End your day with gratitude. Before you go to bed, come up with at least one thing you are grateful for that happened to you that day. Write them down to see whether you have a gratitude pattern and how that relates to your overall wellness.
3. Think back on your childhood and try to remember the first time you felt connected to others or a larger power. What is a small way you can recreate that feeling each morning when you wake up?
4. The next time you feel frustrated with a partner or loved one, try taking a deep breath and repeating the following phrase silently: "May you live with ease, may you be happy, may you be free from pain."

Barriers to Spirit Wellness

Although the vast majority of research on the intersection of religion and spirituality and well-being indicates positive outcomes, a person's spirituality or religiousness can also negatively affect their mental health. For example, the relationship one feels with a higher power can function as any other relationship in their life—for better or for worse. An insecure or anxious attachment with the divine (e.g., viewing them as distant, remote, cruel, or punishing) can lead to anxiety, depression, or perceived lower levels of emotional and social support (Bradshaw, Ellison, & Marcum, 2010; Rowatt & Kirkpatrick, 2002). Therefore, if relevant to clients, exploring their relationship with a higher power through their image of the divine and the attachment and closeness they feel in that relationship is useful.

Additionally, individuals may experience negative effects of their spirituality or religiousness if they endure what Ward (2011) described as religious or spiritual abuse. Types of religious or spiritual abuse include the following: strict or harmful dogma from religious leadership that is delivered as literal word of a higher power, spiritual bullying, pressure to behave in strict ways for fear of retribution from the religious or spiritual community, spiritual neglect by community when in emotional or physical pain, pressure to conform to strict group identity, and physical or psychological repercussion from these experiences. Those most at risk for suffering religious or spiritual abuse are individuals who feel rejected, ostracized, or punished by their religious or spiritual communities as a result of their lifestyle and identity choices, such as members of gender and sexual minorities (Wood & Conley, 2014). See Practitioner Spotlight 6.2. for a discussion of treating a college student experiencing depression and anxiety.

Another barrier to spirit wellness could be the way in which individuals use their spiritual or religious beliefs to avoid some aspect of themselves in their life in general as well as specifically in the counseling session. This concept, known as *spiritual bypass*, occurs when a person is hyperfocused on their spiritual or religious beliefs to the detriment of working through undesirable aspects of him- or herself, such as insecurity or unresolved pain (Cashwell, Glosoff, & Hammonds, 2010). Cashwell and Young (2011) have offered symptoms of spiritual bypass that include social isolation, emotional repression, spiritual narcissism, spiritual obsession, blind faith in charismatic leaders, spiritual materialism, and abdication of personal responsibility. Spiritual bypass is largely unconscious and manifested as psychological avoidance; therefore, motivational interviewing techniques are recommended (Cashwell & Young, 2011).

Finally, counselors themselves can serve as a barrier to addressing issues related to spirit wellness. Spirituality is one of the many areas of individual difference, diversity, and multiculturalism that should be addressed in counseling and counseling training, yet religious and spiritual diversity is often not thought of as important or appropriate to discuss as other types of diversity, such as race, ethnicity, or gender (Hage, Hopson, Siegel, Payton, & DeFanti, 2006). Clients' spiritual or religious values and practices are intricately intertwined with their ethnic and cultural experiences; clients and counselors alike need to develop language through which to identify and communicate the spiritual dimensions of wellness. Wellness counselors should carefully examine their values, beliefs, attitudes, and prejudices regarding their own and other's spiritual or religious orientations (or lack thereof). Assessment of the client's spirit wellness should be gathered during the intake process so that the counselor can begin to understand whether and how the spiritual views of the client affect issues in counseling and how they can be helpful

Practitioner Spotlight 6.2

Case Example

Hannah Bayne

A client's spiritual and religious identity is often directly linked to overall wellness. Quite a bit of research demonstrates that spirituality and religion can be a potent resource for coping, recovery, and prevention in maintaining overall perspective in the face of challenging situations. These practices and perspectives are vast and can include anything from formal religious membership to prayer to a Higher Power, to meditative practices, to finding sacred moments in nature. Because of the wide array of practices as well as the personal nature of spiritual and religious identity, some counselors may feel ill prepared to incorporate or address these factors in the counseling setting. However, it can be helpful to consider integration of religion and spirituality as a practice of fully understanding the client's reality and ways of being as well as an ethically responsible way to use the client's greatest resources for optimal outcomes. Viewed from this framework, integration involves similar counseling skills of active listening, empathic understanding, and allowing the client to explore how best to apply their own value system to tackle the issue at hand. In addition to using spirituality and religion as a source of strength and comfort, however, there may also be occasions when a client's spiritual or religious identity is a source of conflict in their life. In this case, it is also important for a counselor to help the client navigate conflicting beliefs and values.

Noel is an African American college sophomore who presents to counseling with concerns of depression and anxiety. She states that she has been suicidal and states, "I hate myself. I wake up and just feel disgusted with who I am, but I can't seem to get rid of the thoughts I've been having." When asked to clarify, Noel averts her eyes and softly states that she has been having thoughts about other women. She says she has struggled with thoughts like this since as early as she can remember. She feels lonely and sees her friends entering into romantic relationships, yet she has dated some men recently and feels that she would not be happy in a relationship with any of them. Recently, two of the women on her lacrosse team announced that they were dating. Noel states she has been envious of them and wishes she could have the freedom to date who she wants to date. When asked what is holding her back, Noel becomes tearful and states, "Because I have prayed so hard that God would take this away. It's sinful, I know it is, and I have tried so hard to figure out what I can do to control it. I feel so broken and unworthy." Noel states she has always been active in church, and her strongest support system is currently her campus ministry group. She states that she feels she is "living a lie" and is constantly in fear that someone will "figure out my secret." Noel states she is "losing the hope that I will ever be happy."

(continued)

Case Example *(continued)*

After screening for suicidal severity, a core part of counseling for Noel was to first unpack all of the messages that she has received regarding faith and sexuality. We discussed the messages that she had received from her church, the Bible, family and friends, and her African American community. Her history was full of messages of judgment and condemnation. Noel recounted how her gay cousin had been essentially cut off from the family as a result of his decision to come out, and she feared the same for herself. She remembered fervent prayer sessions in church when her Bible study group would pray for the sinfulness of other gay and lesbian people they knew. Noel also assessed her own images of God, independent of and also influenced by external messages. She viewed God both as a loving provider and as a stern judger. She desired to please God, and much of her depression and anxiety was tied to the fear that she would never be acceptable to Him.

In the next phase of counseling, after I was certain I understood Noel's cultural, religious, and spiritual context, we moved to allowing her to critically examine her own beliefs. This step took support and patience because many of her beliefs were well rooted, and full acceptance of religious teachings was a core part of her faith. I provided her with some resources, such as books and webpages, that provided historical context for Biblical passages as well as alternate interpretations of passages that are traditionally seen as against homosexuality. She found some freedom in being able to read these passages in context and to explore which conclusions she wanted to draw. We then progressed to a narrative approach, allowing her to tell the story of her faith and sexuality in the past, to externalize the problem as a social and cultural issue rather than as something inherently wrong within her, and to then restory her narrative into one where she could envision herself both as a lesbian and a committed person of faith. Providing her with resources to gay Christian online support groups as well as affirming churches in her area also helped with this transition. Slowly but surely, through this work, Noel was able to better understand and accept herself both as a person of faith and as a lesbian woman. She struggled with some lost relationships but overall felt much more sure of herself and experienced a marked decrease in depression and anxiety symptoms. She was eventually able to reclaim her faith as a positive part of her wellness and coping rather than as a source of conflict.

• • •

in developing the client's self-understanding. By adding a spiritual dimension in the beginning of the therapeutic relationship, the client receives the message that talking about spirituality is not only an acceptable part of the counseling process but also a core component of their holistic wellness.

In 2009, the Association for Spiritual, Ethical, and Religious Values in Counseling—a division of the American Counseling Association—published the *Competencies for Addressing Spiritual and Religious Issues in Counseling*. These 14 competencies, found in Figure 6.1, offer guidelines for counselors to grow in their own spiritual development in addition to working effectively with clients' diverse religious and spiritual issues.

Counseling Interventions

Wellness counseling offers a framework for addressing spiritual struggles. Bringing a wellness model into the session such as the one presented in this book or one of your choice elicits conversation about the different domains of wellness. This practice facilitates the counselor directly asking the client about their spiritual wellness. In focusing on spiritual wellness, the counselor can process with the client ways in which their "spiritual beliefs and practices" are fulfilling and ways in which they have been stressful for the client (Clarke, Giordano, Cashwell, & Lewis, 2013, p. 89). The counselor models the connection of spirit wellness to the whole person by asking about the positive impacts of the client's spirituality on the other wellness domains as well as negative effects. If the client is willing, the counselor and client can co-construct counseling goals for how other domains of the client's wellness can be mobilized to address the spiritual issue. For example, if a spiritual bypass concern is identified by the client, Clarke et al. (2013) stated that "possible resources include establishing a culture of support, using self-soothing strategies, and reducing shame through normalization and validation" (p. 89).

Many clients may want to focus on religious or spiritual concerns as a primary focus of counseling. Other clients may hope to integrate spiritual practices into their holistic wellness plans. Walsh (1999) summarized the spiritual practices that are common to the world's religions. Ohrt and Young (2012) provided some suggested approaches for counselors when addressing spiritual practices in counseling. Table 6.2 includes a summary of the practices, the primary components of the practices, and exercises that counselors can consider when developing interventions.

Conclusion

As the plurality of religious life in the United States continues to increase, so will the diversity of religious and spiritual strengths and struggles that clients will bring into session. Wellness counseling is a space for self-exploration, and it is essential that counselors are ready to work with a diverse clientele with a broad range of spiritual and religious backgrounds that are questioning and exploring issues of faith, meaning, and purpose.

Preamble

The Competencies for Addressing Spiritual and Religious Issues in Counseling are guidelines that complement, not supersede, the values and standards espoused in the *ACA Code of Ethics*. Consistent with the *ACA Code of Ethics* (2014), the purpose of the ASERVIC Competencies is to "recognize diversity and embrace a cross-cultural approach in support of the worth, dignity, potential, and uniqueness of people within their social and cultural contexts" (p. 3). These Competencies are intended to be used in conjunction with counseling approaches that are evidence-based and that align with best practices in counseling.

Culture and Worldview

1. The professional counselor can describe the similarities and differences between spirituality and religion, including the basic beliefs of various spiritual systems, major world religions, agnosticism, and atheism.
2. The professional counselor recognizes that the client's beliefs (or absence of beliefs) about spirituality and/or religion are central to his or her worldview and can influence psychosocial functioning.

Counselor Self-Awareness

3. The professional counselor actively explores his or her own attitudes, beliefs, and values about spirituality and/or religion.
4. The professional counselor continuously evaluates the influence of his or her own spiritual and/or religious beliefs and values on the client and the counseling process.
5. The professional counselor can identify the limits of his or her understanding of the client's spiritual and/or religious perspective and is acquainted with religious and spiritual resources, including leaders, who can be avenues for consultation and to whom the counselor can refer.

Human and Spiritual Development

6. The professional counselor can describe and apply various models of spiritual and/or religious development and their relationship to human development.

Communication

7. The professional counselor responds to client communications about spirituality and/or religion with acceptance and sensitivity.
8. The professional counselor uses spiritual and/or religious concepts that are consistent with the client's spiritual and/or religious perspectives and that are acceptable to the client.
9. The professional counselor can recognize spiritual and/or religious themes in client communication and is able to address these with the client when they are therapeutically relevant.

Assessment

10. During the intake and assessment processes, the professional counselor strives to understand a client's spiritual and/or religious perspective by gathering information from the client and/or other sources.

Diagnosis and Treatment

11. When making a diagnosis, the professional counselor recognizes that the client's spiritual and/or religious perspectives can a) enhance well-being; b) contribute to client problems; and/or c) exacerbate symptoms.
12. The professional counselor sets goals with the client that are consistent with the client's spiritual and/or religious perspectives.
13. The professional counselor is able to a) modify therapeutic techniques to include a client's spiritual and/or religious perspectives, and b) utilize spiritual and/or religious practices as techniques when appropriate and acceptable to a client's viewpoint.
14. The professional counselor can therapeutically apply theory and current research supporting the inclusion of a client's spiritual and/or religious perspectives and practices.

Figure 6.1

ASERVIC Competencies for Addressing Spiritual and Religious Issues in Counseling

Note. From *Addressing Spiritual and Religious Issues in Counseling,* by the Association for Spiritual, Ethical, and Religious Values in Counseling (ASERVIC). Retrieved from http://www.aservic.org/resources/spiritual-competencies/. Copyright 2009 by ASERVIC. Reprinted with permission.

Table 6.2

Spiritual Practices and Exercises

Spiritual Practice and Components	Exercises
Transform motivation • Recognizing beliefs about happiness • Relinquishing attachments • Recognizing what fosters happiness	• Values clarification • Identify underlying thoughts • Reduce craving and addictions
Cultivate emotional wisdom • Reduce painful feelings • Foster gratitude and generosity • Cultivate positive emotions	• Meditation • Forgiveness • Gratitude • Prayer
Live ethically • Live a life that consists of kindness, compassion, and trust	• Kind acts • Developing compassion • Apology • Empathy
Concentrate and calm your mind • Develop a focused and peaceful mind	• Yoga • Meditation • Relaxation • Concentration • Breathing
Awaken your spiritual vision • Present-moment awareness • Living life with intention	• Mindfulness meditation • Mindful eating and living • Awareness activities
Cultivate spiritual intelligence • Develop wisdom and understanding of life • Gain insight into one's self	• Self-reflection • Imagery and visualization • Spiritual reading
Express spirit in action • Engage in service and generosity • Good works • Altruism	• Service • Volunteerism • Unselfish acts • Caring

Note. Adapted from Walsh (1999) and Ohrt and Young (2012).

Reflection Prompts

1. Think of a time when you faced adversity (challenging or negative circumstances). What was going on during that time? Think about how you made it through that time. Why did you persist rather than "give up"? What helped you to make it through that time?

2. Make a list of what you have done during the past five Saturday nights. Looking over this list, do you think how you choose to spend your free time is representative of how you want to spend your time more generally?

Learning Activities

Remembering What We Have Lost

Make a list of things you once believed in but no longer believe in (e.g., Superman, Tooth Fairy, political/religious/moral belief).

- Reviewing your list, what stands out to you?
- Can you remember when you lost belief in those things and why?
- What emotions are connected with that loss?
- Could you imagine ever believing it again, perhaps in another form?

Tree of Life

On a sheet of paper, draw a tree to symbolize the timeline of your life. On the tree, draw the trunk to indicate when life remained the same or moving in the expected direction. Draw branches to represent when there is a major life change, decision, or event. Now look back at your key moments of change.

- What guided those moments—Context? Necessity? Yourself? Others?
- Do you believe there was a greater purpose or something bigger than yourself in any of these moments?
- Did any of those moments lead to greater connectedness in your life?

Role Redesign

Think about your current job (or, if you are a full-time student, the internship or position that you are working toward). For a moment, consider how the job description for your position would read—job duties, skills required, focus of the position. Next, take a mental step back and think about what *you personally* give to your position. Coming from a bigger-than-self perspective, describe your job description.

Reflect on the following questions to help you get started:

1. How are the people you work with and the people you may serve better off because of the work you do?
2. How would your colleagues describe the impact of the work you do?
3. How does your work support the shared values of your company or community?

Resources

Center for Compassion and Altruism Research and Education
http://ccare.stanford.edu/

> Stanford Medicine's home for research and resources on cultivating compassion and promoting altruism.

On Being Podcast With Krista Tippett
https://onbeing.org/

> Explore hundreds of episodes that investigate ways to connect our outer and inner lives.

References

Association for Spiritual, Ethical, and Religious Values in Counseling. (2009). *Competencies for addressing spiritual and religious issues in counseling.* Retrieved from http://www.aservic.org/resources/spiritual-competencies/

Astin, A. W., & Keen, J. P. (2006). Equanimity and spirituality. *Religion & Education, 33,* 1–8.

Begley, S. (2007). *Train your mind, change your brain.* New York, NY: Ballantine Books.

Bradshaw, M., Ellison, C. G., & Marcum, J. P. (2010). Attachment to God, images of God, and psychological distress in a nationwide sample of Presbyterians. *International Journal for the Psychology of Religion, 20,* 130–147.

Bryant, A. N. (2007). Gender differences in spiritual development during the college years. *Sex Roles, 56,* 835–846.

Bryant, A. N., & Astin, H. A. (2008). The correlates of spiritual struggle during the college years. *The Journal of Higher Education, 79,* 1–27.

Cashwell, C. S., Bentley, D. P., & Bigbee, A. (2007). Spirituality and counselor wellness. *The Journal of Humanistic Counseling, 46,* 66–81.

Cashwell, C. S., Glosoff, H. L., & Hammonds, C. (2010). Spiritual bypass: A preliminary investigation. *Counseling and Values, 54,* 162–174.

Cashwell, C. S., & Young, J. S. (2011). *Integrating spirituality and religion into counseling.* Alexandria, VA: American Counseling Association.

Clarke, P. B., Giordano, A. L., Cashwell, C. S., & Lewis, T. F. (2013). The straight path to healing: Using motivational interviewing to address spiritual bypass. *Journal of Counseling & Development, 91,* 87–94.

Corporation for National and Community Service, Office of Research and Policy Development. (2007). *The health benefits of volunteering: A review of recent research.* Retrieved from https://www.nationalservice.gov/sites/default/files/documents/07_0506_hbr.pdf

Croft, A., Dunn, E. W., & Quoidbach, J. (2013). From tribulations to appreciation: Experiencing adversity in the past predicts greater savoring in the present. *Social Psychological and Personality Science, 5,* 511–516.

Ellison, C. G., & Lee, J. (2010). Spiritual struggles and psychological distress: Is there a dark side of religion? *Social Indicators Research, 98,* 501–517.

Fowler, J. W. (1981). *Stages of faith: The psychology of human development and the quest for meaning.* San Francisco, CA: Harper and Row.

Gallup. (2016, December). *Five key findings on religion in the U.S.* Retrieved from http://news.gallup.com/poll/200186/five-key-findings-religion.aspx

Garcia-Zamor, J. (2003). Workplace spirituality and organizational performance. *Public Administration Review, 63,* 355–363.

Gehrke, S. J. (2008). Leadership through meaning-making: An empirical exploration of spirituality and leadership in college students. *Journal of College Student Development, 49,* 351–359.

Hage, S. M., Hopson, A., Siegel, M., Payton, G., & DeFanti, E. (2006). Multicultural training in spirituality: An interdisciplinary review. *Counseling and Values, 50,* 217–234.

Hill, P. C., & Pargament, K. (2003). Advances in the conceptualization and measurement of religion and spirituality: Implications for physical and mental health research. *American Psychologist, 58,* 64–74.

Koenig, H. G., & Cohen, H. J. (2002). *The link between religion and health.* London, England: Oxford University Press.

Kohlberg, L. (1963). Moral development and identification. In H. W. Stevenson (Ed.), *Child psychology: The 62nd yearbook of the National Society for the Study of Education* (pp. 277–332). Chicago, IL: University of Chicago Press.

Korb, A. (2015). *The upward spiral: Using neuroscience to reverse the course of depression, one small change at a time.* Oakland, CA: New Harbinger Publications.

Love, P. G., Bock, M., Jannarone, A., & Richardson, P. (2005). Identity interaction: Exploring the spiritual experiences of lesbian and gay college students. *Journal of College Student Development, 46,* 193–209.

Myers, J. E., & Sweeney, T. J. (2005). *Counseling for wellness: Theory, research, and practice.* Alexandria, VA: American Counseling Association.

Nelms, L. W., Hutchins, E., Hutchins, D., & Pursley, R. (2007). Spirituality and the health of college students. *Journal of Religion and Health, 46,* 249–265.

Ohrt, J. H., & Young, T. L. (2012, June). *Empirical support for spirituality: Implications for integrating spiritual practices in counseling.* Paper presented at the Biennial Conference of the Association for Spiritual, Ethical, and Religious Values in Counseling, Santa Fe, NM.

Pargament, K. I., Koeing, H. G., & Perez, L. M. (2002). The many methods of religious coping: Development and initial validation of the RCOPE. *Journal of Clinical Psychology, 56,* 519–543.

Pargament, K. I., Murray-Swank, N., Magyar, G. M., & Ano, G. G. (2005). Spiritual struggle: A phenomenon of interest to psychology and religion. In W. R. Miller & H. D. Delaney (Eds.), *Judeo-Christian perspectives on psychology: Human nature, motivation, and change* (pp. 245–268). Washington, DC: American Psychological Association.

Park, C. L. (2010). Making sense of the meaning literature: An integrative review of meaning making and its effects on adjustment to stressful life events. *Psychological Bulletin, 136,* 257–301.

Parks, S. D. (2000). *Big questions, worthy dreams: Mentoring young adults in their search for meaning, purpose, and faith.* San Francisco, CA: Jossey-Bass.

Pew Research Center. (2015). *2015 Religious Landscape Survey.* Washington, DC: Pew Forum on Religion & Public Life.

Pew Research Center. (2017). *2017 Religious landscape survey.* Washington, DC: Pew Forum on Religion & Public Life.

Piaget, J. (1960). *The moral judgment of the child* (M. Gabain, Trans.). Glencoe, IL: Free Press. (Original work published 1932)

Reese, R. F., & Myers, J. E. (2012). EcoWellness: The missing factor in holistic wellness models. *Journal of Counseling & Development, 90,* 400–406.

Rowatt, W., & Kirkpatrick, L. A. (2002). Two dimensions of attachment to God and their relation to affect, religiosity, and personality constructs. *Journal for the Scientific Study of Religion, 41,* 637–651.

Seery, M. D., Holman, E. A., & Silver, R. C. (2010). Whatever does not kill us: Cumulative lifetime adversity, vulnerability, and resilience. *Journal of Personality and Social Psychology, 99,* 1025–1041.

Sneed, R. S., & Cohen, S. (2013). A prospective study of volunteerism and hypertension risk in older adults. *Psychology and Aging, 28,* 578–586.

Walsh, R. (1999). *Essential spirituality: The seven central practices to awaken heart and mind.* New York, NY: Wiley.

Ward, D. J. (2011). The lived experience of spiritual abuse. *Mental Health, Religion & Culture, 14,* 899–915.

Witmer, J. M., & Sweeney, T. J. (1992). A holistic model for wellness and prevention over the life span. *Journal of Counseling & Development, 71,* 140–148.

Wood, A. W., & Conley, A. H. (2014). Loss of religious or spiritual identities among the LGBT population. *Counseling and Values, 59,* 95–111.

Worline, M. C., & Dutton, J. E. (2017). *Awakening compassion at work.* Oakland, CA: Berrett-Koehler.

Chapter 7

Emotion

Your intellect may be confused,
but your emotions will never lie to you.

—Roger Ebert

• • •

You are giving a big presentation, and as you step up to the podium, your mind goes completely blank; despite your rehearsals, you cannot seem to remember your opening line, and you are filled with fear as you look out into the crowd. You just had the best first date you have had in a long time, maybe ever; happiness overwhelms you, and you cannot stop smiling as you get ready for bed. *Emotions* are defined as feelings that emerge in response to an internal or external event. *Emotional wellness* encompasses individuals' identification, regulation, expression, and cultivation of emotions in self and others.

Individuals experience a range of emotions every day, and emotional responses to situations are unique for each individual. For example, some individuals might experience anger when presented with constructive feedback at work. Others in the same situation may experience disappointment, embarrassment, or guilt. Previous authors have included emotions as an important feature in their wellness models. For example, Hettler (1976) included emotions as one of the six primary dimensions in his wellness model. He stressed the importance of being aware of and accepting of a wide range of emotions that we experience, and he emphasized the benefits of being optimistic and enthusiastic about life. Myers and Sweeney (2005) emphasized emotional wellness within the Creative Self factor of their wellness model and included healthy emotional expression, positive humor, and sense of control as key aspects related to emotions.

The ability to effectively identify, monitor, and regulate emotions is an essential component of mental health. Although many individuals proceed throughout the day without thinking about their emotions, managing emotions is an active process that requires insight and action. Helping clients effectively identify and regulate their emotions are important change processes that are emphasized within many theories of counseling.

In this chapter, we discuss how emotions relate to overall wellness. For example, counselors across theoretical orientations help clients lower or raise their emotional arousal to promote well-being (Young, 2017). Additionally, researchers have identified emotion regulation skills and the ability to cultivate positive emotions as highly related to individual well-being. We discuss key components of heart wellness, including emotions, emotion regulation, and how to cultivate positive emotions. Furthermore, we recommend a learning activity, suggest discussion prompts, and provide helpful resources for working toward healthy emotions.

Emotional Intelligence (EI)

Counselors are expected to identify clients' emotions through empathic listening and responding. Likewise, counselors often help their clients identify, express, and manage their own emotions. One theory of emotion processing that has implications for counselors is EI. There are various definitions and theoretical models of EI. Zeidner, Roberts, and Matthews (2002) described EI as a group of competencies for identifying, processing, and regulating emotions for self as well as others. Additionally, Mayer and Salovey (1997) defined EI as:

> [T]he ability to perceive accurately, appraise and express emotion; the ability to access and/or generate feelings when they facilitate thought; the ability to understand emotion and emotional knowledge; and the ability to regulate emotions to promote emotional and intellectual growth. (p. 10)

Mayer, Salovey, and Caruso (2004) later conceptualized EI from a concise four-branch model that includes an individual's ability to (a) perceive emotion, (b) facilitate thought through emotions, (c) understand emotion, and (d) effectively manage emotions. An individual's skills in each branch range from basic to sophisticated. Similarly, researchers have conceptualized EI as a trait that is part of one's personality or an ability that is a form of intelligence (Zeidner, Matthews, & Roberts, 2009). Each form of EI may contribute to mental health in significant, but unique, ways. Although the research is still emerging, EI is linked with greater well-being and lower levels of stress (Zeidner, Matthews, & Roberts, 2012). EI may also be related to health-enhancing behaviors (Schutte, Malouff, Thorsteinsson, Bhullar, & Rooke, 2007).

Emotion Regulation

Our emotions influence how we think, feel, and interact with others in the world. Our ability to regulate our emotions has implications for our mental and physical health as well as our relationships. Although identifying and expressing our genuine emotions are generally considered to be healthy behaviors, we must also be able to regulate or modify our emotions to navigate the world in a socially acceptable way. When was the last time you found yourself in a situation where you experienced a strong emotional reaction? Maybe you experienced a negative interaction at work, had a disagreement with a partner, or engaged in a heated debate with a close friend or family member. To maintain relationships and avoid unhealthy conflicts, you have had to use strategies to regulate the emotions you experience in response to various situations. These regulation strategies influence your thoughts, behaviors, and physiological arousal related to emotional experiences (Gross, 2015).

Gross and John (2003) classified emotion-regulation strategies as *antecedent-focused* or *response-focused strategies*. Antecedent-focused strategies include actions we take prior to experiencing an emotional response, whereas response-focused strategies are implemented after we start to experience an emotion. Gross (2001) proposed a process model of regulation in which he described five potential points of regulation throughout an emotional experience. The five sequential regulation points include (a) situation selection, (b) situation modification, (c) attention deployment, (d) cognitive change, and (e) response modulation. The first three regulation points are antecedent focused, whereas the last two are response focused. *Situation selection* refers to strategies one would use to make it more or less likely that one would be in a specific situation that may result in undesirable or desirable emotions. For example, an individual who becomes frustrated in rush-hour traffic may avoid driving during the busy times by setting a different work schedule. *Situation modification* is a process by which an individual changes something about the situation to alter the emotional impact. In the previous example, the individual may not be able to alter work times, so he takes back roads to work to decrease his frustration related to driving in heavy traffic. *Attention deployment* includes strategies to divert one's attention to influence an emotional response. The driver may not be able to avoid driving to work in heavy traffic during rush hour, so he listens to his favorite sports talk radio to distract himself and diverts his focus away from sitting in traffic. Obtaining and using these regulation skills is important in relation to mental health. For example, those lacking emotion regulation skills have higher levels of anxious arousal and worry (Kashdan, Zvolensky, & McLeish, 2008).

Two specific regulation strategies that have been widely studied include *cognitive reappraisal* and *expressive suppression* (Gross & John, 2003). Cognitive reappraisal is a way of reframing how we think about a situation to modify the emotional response we experience and is a form of antecedent-focused regulation. For example, a student could view receiving constructive feedback on a paper as an opportunity to learn about writing rather than a harsh evaluation of her ability. Expressive suppression is a way of inhibiting behaviors that are related to emotional expression and is a form of response-focused regulation. For instance, an award winner may avoid clapping or cheering too loud when standing next to the other nominees. Research tends to support reappraisal as a more effective regulation strategy because suppression is linked to higher levels of depression, less satisfaction with life, and less optimism than those who use reappraisal (Gross & John, 2003). However, De France and Hollenstein (2017) emphasized the importance of context when using emotion-regulation strategies. The authors explained that it is more important for an individual to have a repertoire of emotion-regulation strategies to use in various situations. For example, positively reframing a negative situation may actually be counterproductive if the individual would benefit from altering the precipitating event. Additionally, suppression may be an adaptive strategy in many instances. For example, suppressing anger you feel toward your friend's child who broke your window playing baseball is likely to help you maintain a harmonious friendship. The ability to make judgments about the most appropriate emotion-regulation strategy likely requires an individual to have a high level of EI. In our previous example, you would need to identify your emotional reaction of excitement when winning an award but also be aware of and sensitive to the runner-ups' potential feelings of disappointment and envy. Many counseling interventions are focused on helping clients identify and regulate their emotions. Anger management and stress management groups are two examples of interventions that are primarily designed to address emotion regulation.

Linking Emotions to Health

The types of emotions we experience and how we manage our emotional experiences appear to have a significant impact on our physical health. Have you ever reached for a carton of Ben & Jerry's after a break-up? Or gone out for happy hour after a stressful day at work? Most of the time, engaging in these types of stress-reducing behaviors is harmless. However, those who report negative emotions actually do tend to consume more alcohol and saturated fat (Anton & Miller, 2005). Certainly, it is okay to indulge once in a while, but it can become problematic when negative emotions and unhealthy behaviors become automatic, making strong neural connections between emotionally charged events and dopamine-releasing quick fixes.

There is also support for other direct links between emotions and physical health. Are you someone who experiences road rage easily? There is good reason to work on your mindfulness while driving: Anger, aggression, and hostility are risk factors for heart disease (Smith, Glazer, Ruiz, & Gallo, 2004). Have you ever responded with "I'm fine" when a partner asks what's wrong when you are clearly upset? Suppressing emotions is linked to bodily stress and increased blood pressure for some individuals, suggesting that you really should never go to bed angry or upset (Butler, Lee, & Gross, 2007). From a positive perspective, feelings of hope are negatively correlated with illness (Richman et al., 2005), and aspects of subjective well-being (e.g., positive affect) contribute to longevity and health (Diener & Chan, 2011). Given what we know about the interconnected nature of wellness, this information should not surprise you. The research in this area is compelling and warrants strong attention to emotions as part of an overall approach to physical and mental health.

Emotional Expression/Positivity

In addition to identifying and regulating emotions, expressing emotions is also related to individuals' wellness. When helping clients with social skills, communication patterns, or relationships, counselors often focus on their ability to outwardly express the emotions they are feeling. Sometimes this process is facilitated through a structured-feedback exercise during which the individual uses the stem, "I feel _____ when _____ ." With children, we may ask them to select from pictures of faces portraying various feelings (e.g., angry, lonely, happy) to help them identify and express their emotions. We often think about and discuss emotional expression as a form of verbal communication. This method is typically the case, but we can also convey emotions through other formats such as writing, art, and music. Although there are times when it is socially appropriate to suppress emotional expression, it is typically more helpful to express emotions than suppress them. Engaging in emotional expression appears to have benefits for physical and mental health. Openly expressing emotions may actually be connected to experiencing more positive emotions (Kashdan & Breen, 2008). Conversely, suppressing emotions can lead to more negative emotions (Campbell-Sills, Barlow, Brown, & Hofmann, 2006).

Although it is ideal to experience and express more positive emotions, it is better to express genuine emotions even if the emotions are more negative (e.g., sadness, anger; Tuck, Adams, & Consedine, 2017). In counseling, we tend to agree that expressing emotions is most helpful. When a client lets out their emotions, we refer to it as a cathartic experience (i.e., expressing pent-up feelings). This process can often lead to breakthroughs for the client, including greater insight and relief from the negative feelings. In Practitioner Spotlight 7.1, Jessie Guest (a licensed professional counselor) discusses how she helps children with emotional regulations and expression.

Specific Emotional Processes Related to Wellness

Happiness

In attempting to deconstruct the word *happiness*, the father of the positive psychology movement Martin Seligman (2011) described three different routes that lead to happiness: (1) positive emotion and pleasures, (2) engagement, and (3) meaning. Seligman found that people differ in which "happiness route" they orient their lives toward and that the most reliable to way sustain happiness is to pursue all three with greater importance on the last two. Research posits that happy people are healthier overall, with lower rates of cardiovascular disease; have better immunity; heal faster after injuries; and live longer (Lyubomirsky, King, & Diener, 2005). In addition to feeling good in one's own body, the other two routes to happiness involve others and are undoubtedly linked to connection wellness. Happy

Practitioner Spotlight 7.1

Working With Emotions With Children

Jessie Guest

The ability to regulate and appropriately process and express emotions are important aspects of healthy development and often are a key focus in counseling, especially when counseling children and adolescents. My clinical work primarily focuses on working with children and adolescents, typically using play and creative arts therapy. Children express themselves differently than adults because of differing developmental stages. For example, children may use physical behaviors or yelling to express emotions or communicate needs. In my experience, I notice that children and adolescents often struggle with identifying emotions and finding the words to communicate, but they are experts at expressing emotions. As a therapist or a counselor, it is of the utmost importance to meet the client where they are—thus, seeking to understand what the child's/adolescent's behaviors are actually saying. By understanding the emotion or message behind the behaviors, the counselor can then begin to help the clients to identity emotions.

Identification of emotions is often the first place I start when working with clients. Coming from a more nondirective, client-centered approach to counseling, I often use reflection, mainly focused on identifying an action/behavior or facial expression expressed by a client and then connecting that behavior to the appropriate emotion. This method provides the child client with the feeling word that is described by what they are portraying in that moment. For example, often I see children who may throw toys or rip up paper and look angry during an activity; however, they rarely verbally express, "I am mad!" In this case, I would reflect something like, "Wow! You must be very mad to throw that toy across the room!" This prompt provides them with a word that they can use later to express this feeling as well as connecting this word to a behavior; therefore, when they want to express that they are angry, they will use the word "mad" instead of throwing things right away. This reflection is continual and repeated throughout sessions, providing the children with a new vocabulary for identifying emotions.

After the child client is able to identify feelings and use feeling words in session and at home/school, processing and appropriately expressing emotions become the focus of sessions; however, this step can be done simultaneously with identification of emotions, depending on the client. For example, in addition to reflection, if the child/adolescent chooses a way of expressing emotions that is harmful in session (e.g., throwing hard, damaging toys against the wall or at the counselor), I will reflect the feelings of anger and then redirect the client to a way of expressing emotions that is safer and more appropriate ("Wow! You are mad!

(continued)

Working With Emotions With Children *(continued)*

Toys aren't for throwing, but you can throw this softball or pillow against the ground when you are mad"). By doing this, I am first focusing on the message that the child is trying to express (anger) and then transforming the current inappropriate behavior to a more helpful coping skill or expression of emotion. If I were to focus directly on the behavior, this approach only creates more frustration for the client, because I did not reflect the emotion and missed the "true message" that the client was trying to express and focused on what I wanted to focus on, which was the poor behavior. We as counselors and caregivers to children need to ensure that the child feels heard before any change can occur.

In addition to reflection and redirection, I often use concrete coloring activities to assist the client in identifying the emotions they feel in various circumstances. For example, I often use a coloring activity that is an outline of a person (similar to a gingerbread man cutout) or a picture of a heart and explain that this picture represents the client at home, at school, or at dad's or mom's house—whichever area the child is most struggling in regarding emotional expression or processing. Then we identify five feeling words and assign each feeling a color; the client then colors the amount of that feeling that they experience in that situation in the picture. After the picture is filled with the different colors, the client names reasons and things that happen in that environment that make him or her feel that way. This activity provides information for the counselor and aids the client in talking about feelings related to something specific.

Although there are many concrete, directive interventions that can be used to assist clients with emotional regulation, practicing from a more nondirective approach, I prefer to use nondirective play therapy to guide the client in processing emotions. Providing the space and toys for the client to manipulate and concretely play out various life scenarios greatly influences the child's ability to process the emotions in ways that are safe. Nondirective play therapy or child-centered play therapy enhances accountability and provides appropriate avenues to express and process emotions. For example, a previous client of mine was struggling with a bully at school and was beginning to dislike school and to exhibit aggressive behaviors as well as signs of low self-esteem at home and school. He was 5 years old at the time of therapy. I took a nondirective approach with this client and used reflection and provided some positive feedback and self-talk examples throughout the session. The child created a sand tray scene with various cars in the playroom. His play scene consisted of about 15 cars that he would bury in the sand and one large truck. The client spent a good portion of the session burying the little cars, and then the large truck would dig each car up and throw them across the room. This play scene took about 40 minutes each session. During the fourth session, the client continued with this same scene; however, as the

(continued)

Working With Emotions With Children *(continued)*

big truck was throwing the little cars out of the sand, one little car remained. The little car talked to the big truck about his feelings, and those two cars became friends. The client brought all the little cars back without having to hide in the sand. This episode was the last time the client did this scene. After checking in with his parents, his aggression had ceased; he was using the positive self-talk he heard in session, and he no longer disliked school.

● ● ●

people tend to have deep relationships, be productive at their jobs, volunteer often, donate to charity, and be creative problem solvers.

Taken together, happy people tend to have the opposite of the chronic stress profile. Happiness is only minimally related to demographic factors such as age, race, gender, and education level. Happiness is not about having things. Of course, it would be challenging to be happy without a roof over your head or knowing where your next meal is coming from; however, after a certain minimum caloric intake and physical security are reached, increases in material wealth do not have a large impact on happiness. The problem with depending on external sources for happiness is that we constantly need more to maintain those positive feelings. Neurochemically, this is what is happening when we use alcohol and other drugs. People struggling with addiction are caught in a vicious cycle of needing more to maintain their high. Dopamine is the neurotransmitter the floods the brain's reward center. Consumer culture is based on this idea. Have you or has someone you know stood in line to get a new iPhone when the current iPhone is still working perfectly (albeit slightly slower—thanks, Apple)?

Optimism and Hope

When an individual is optimistic, it means that they anticipate that good things will happen in the future. One might argue that this concept relates more to cognitive processes than emotional responses; indeed, it could also be considered a form of spiritual wellness because having faith that goodness prevails is certainly a meaning-making framework that shapes experience. We acknowledge the interconnected nature of thinking good things will happen, finding peace in the belief that good things do happen, and feeling optimistic about the future. Focusing on the emotion dimension, optimism can help people stay positive even during stressful and challenging times. Being optimistic is also related to other positive outcomes such as psychological well-being, life satisfaction, and positive affect

(Chang, 2009). Individuals who are optimistic are also less likely to report depressive symptoms (Carver, Scheier, & Segerstrom, 2010). Additionally, optimism relates positively to better social connections, persistence in the face of challenges, goal pursuits, and some health outcomes (Carver & Scheier, 2014). There are clear benefits to being optimistic, but an important question is whether we can foster optimism in individuals. The research on specific interventions to promote optimism is limited thus far. Meevissen, Peters, and Alberts (2011) did find increased optimism through a 2-week intervention during which individuals spent 5 minutes each day imaging their best possible self. It is also likely that counselors working from a variety of theoretical approaches address optimism with clients through various change processes.

Hope is related to optimism but is a distinct disposition. Whereas optimistic people may believe in a positive future for a variety of reasons (e.g., belief in their abilities, someone will help them, the odds are in their favor), people who are hopeful believe in their own ability to set and reach goals to create positive outcomes in the future (Chang, Yu, & Hirsch, 2013). Like optimism, hopefulness is related to wellness factors such as life satisfaction and subjective well-being (O'Sullivan, 2011) and is also negatively related to depression (Chang et al., 2013). Hopefulness can also serve as a protective disposition when children and youths experience a negative event in their life (Valle, Huebner, & Suldo, 2006). Optimism and hope appear to be important dispositions that are related to a variety of wellness factors. In counseling, we emphasize these concepts because positive expectations are especially important for treatment outcomes. Hope and expectancy factors may account for up to 15% of the outcome variance in counseling treatment outcomes (Lambert & Barley, 2002). Certainly, we want to build on and promote these dispositions to increase the chance of clients successfully achieving wellness.

Forgiveness

Forgiveness is a conscious, deliberate decision to release feelings of resentment or vengeance toward a person or group who has harmed us, regardless of whether we believe they deserve our forgiveness. Worthington (2006) described forgiveness as a process of replacing unforgiving emotions that tend to be negative (e.g., anger, bitterness) toward someone with more positive emotions (e.g., empathy, sympathy, compassion). The forgiveness process is related to positive mental health and physical health outcomes through increased positive affect, decreased negative affect, and reduced stress (Green,

DeCourville, & Sadava, 2012). Although there appear to be many psychological, physical, and spiritual benefits to engaging in forgiveness, counselors must be sensitive to the client's experiences and readiness to consider the forgiveness process. As you might imagine, this process may be challenging for individuals, especially those who have experienced severe wrongdoing. Worthington (2003) developed a structured intervention titled REACH to help clients through the forgiveness process. The intervention consists of five steps: R = Recall the Hurt, E = Empathize with the Offender, A = Give an Altruistic Act, C = Commit to the Forgiveness Experience, and H = Hold on to Forgiveness When Doubt Occurs. The curriculum lasts 6 hours and can be delivered in a variety of formats, such as individual, group, or with couples.

Although much of the focus has been on the forgiveness process related to forgiving others for previous wrongdoings, an emerging area of attention is self-forgiveness. Self-forgiveness is a coping strategy that entails increasing positive and decreasing negative thoughts, feelings, behaviors, and motivations about oneself. Some scholars caution that too strong of a focus on self-forgiveness has the potential to be counterproductive. For example, some believe that promoting self-forgiveness for offenders may prematurely alleviate their feelings of distress that may be necessary for them to change their behaviors. There is a concern that the offender may fail to take responsibility for their actions and could shift blame to others. These considerations are important for counselors to consider when working with clients. However, clients who have committed minor or inadvertent offenses, or who experience shame, guilt, or regret for reasons unrelated to an offense, may benefit greatly from a self-forgiveness exercise. Self-forgiveness can be a powerful practice, particularly in the areas we have discussed as important for wellness, such as negative thoughts and body image, food and physical activity choices, and behaviors that may have exacerbated disconnect from one's values and loved ones.

Cultivating Positive Emotions and Counselor Interventions

At this point, you may be wondering what we can do if an individual consistently experiences negative emotions. Is it enough for one to be aware of negative emotions and to be able to express them to others? Certainly, having emotional awareness can be helpful. However, there are mental and physical benefits to experiencing positive emotions, and there are steps we can take to cultivate them. To be clear, we are not suggesting that individuals should simply avoid negative feelings and just focus on the positive; however, putting mindful attention into finding and experiencing positive emotional awareness can be transformative.

Emotion-Focused Therapy (EFT)

Although most theories of counseling require counselors to address emotions in some form, EFT (Greenberg, 2002) includes emotional experiences as the central features related to individuals' functioning. EFT acknowledges the importance of cognitive and interpersonal factors in client maladjustment; however, emotional processing is the primary mechanism for change. Counselors working from an EFT perspective help clients develop EI, which consists of an ability to identify their own emotions and others' emotions and to regulate their emotions through affective, cognitive, and behavioral approaches. EFT counselors also help clients to modify their emotional memories and responses. The counselor's role is that of an emotional coach who helps clients become more aware of their feelings, better cope with their feelings, regulate their emotions, and adapt emotional responses to be more effective.

Social and Emotional Learning (SEL) Programs

There is significant recent research showing that students' success in school is heavily influenced by their social and emotional skills in addition to their academic aptitude. As a result, school counselors, school psychologists, and teachers have started to develop proactive curriculums and programs to implement school-wide and within-classroom instruction to help students develop SEL. School counselors facilitate students' SEL competence through large-group psychoeducation and small-group counseling. One example of an SEL program is Merrell's Strong Teens curriculum (Carrizales, Feuerborn, Gueldner, & Tran, 2016). The curriculum includes 12 structured lessons focused on topics such as understanding emotions of self and others, identifying maladaptive thoughts, living positively, managing anger, resolving conflicts, and setting goals. The program can be implemented in a small-group or classroom setting. There are many other examples of available SEL programs. The Collaborative for Academic, Social, and Emotional Learning (CASEL) database (https://casel.org/) is a helpful resource that provides reviews and information about the effectiveness of various SEL programs. We encourage practitioners to review the CASEL database when looking for SEL programs to implement with clients.

The following are some basic considerations for counselors when selecting interventions to use with clients when incorporating emotion wellness in counseling:

- Help clients identify triggers (situations that result in negative emotions).
- Help clients develop insight and awareness of emotions.
- Work on concentration and cultivation of positive emotions.
- Facilitate reappraisal or reframing (i.e., looking at the situation another way).
- Teach and develop coping strategies and alternative behaviors.
- Promote communication to help with emotional expression.

In addition, to facilitate quick and frequent strategies when incorporating emotion wellness in counseling, we offer the following emotion wellness boosters:

1. At the end of the day, make a list of some of the things that made you happy that day. It can be helpful to reflect on the list, and the process of making it can be equally helpful.
2. Find a friend or family member who has time to listen and have a conversation with him or her. Make sure to honestly express how you are currently feeling about various areas of your life. Be open about positive as well as negative feelings. This openness can help with emotional expression.
3. Think about some situations in your life that you believe are causing frustration, anger, or disappointment. Take a few minutes and reflect on what you are learning about yourself in these situations. Consider letting go of the negative feeling and forgiving the person who is contributing to the feelings if it applies. This method can be a helpful way of reframing your experiences.
4. Download a gratitude app on your phone and record things you are grateful for once or more a week. Read over what you wrote when you are feeling a little down.
5. Find an inspirational story or book to read. Consider asking someone to read it with you and then discuss the takeaway messages.

Conclusion

As you likely have realized while reading this chapter, there is a strong interplay among individuals' emotional wellness and other aspects of their functioning. When using emotion-regulation strategies, there are cognitive and behavioral processes involved. Our emotional experiences can also evoke physiological responses and have implications for our short- and long-term physical health. Our ability to recognize and appropriately regulate and express our emotions as well as attend to others' emotions affects our relationships in the various roles we play in life. Finally, many of our emotional experiences are a result of, or are driven by, our spiritual beliefs, personal values, and culture. When working with clients on emotional wellness, it is important to keep in mind the ripple effect that emotions may have in other areas of their lives. It is imperative to conduct thorough and holistic assessments and implement interventions that attend to all aspects of functioning.

Reflection Prompts

1. Brainstorm some situations in your life that typically evoke negative emotions for you. What are some of the emotions you feel? Try to identify what specifically about the situations causes the emotions.
2. Think about someone in your life who seems to be especially attuned to others' emotions and whom you believe has a high level of EI. How do they convey that they understand others' emotions? How do they adapt their behaviors and verbal responses to help facilitate a positive social interaction?
3. Review the regulation model described by Gross (2001). Identify some strategies you use from several of the regulation points. Are the strategies helpful? Why or why not?
4. Think of some scenarios during which it would be helpful for a client to engage in cognitive reappraisal. Describe the situation and discuss how it could be reframed.
5. Describe some scenarios when it would be detrimental for a client to suppress emotions. Think of some scenarios when it would be helpful for a client to suppress emotions. Describe some strategies you might use to help the client develop contextual awareness of when to use suppression as a regulation strategy.

Learning Activities

Forgiveness Exercises

Identify someone (or yourself) whom you feel anger toward because you believe they have wronged you in some way. Think about the things that have made you angry or hurt you.

- Write down the things that have hurt you or made you angry.
- What would you like to say to this person who hurt you? Describe the things that made you angry in an honest but gentle way.

After you have completed the statement, think about exactly what this person has done. Has there ever been a time when you have acted similarly? Think about how you felt when you acted that way. Next, think about any other possible explanations for the person's behavior. Could their intentions have been different from what you initially thought?

Finally, reflect on the anger or negative feelings you have toward this person.

- When the angry feelings arise, what are you thinking about?
- What are your physiological responses?
- What are the costs of continuing to feel this way?
- What intellectual, emotional, or physical energy does it take to keep these feelings?
- What will it take for you to forgive this person?
- How can you let it go?

Sense of Control Activity

One emotion regulation strategy we discussed in the chapter is *cognitive reappraisal*. This is an antecedent-focused regulation strategy. This activity is called "sense of control." The idea is to reassess a situation and determine what aspects are within one's control to reduce feelings of stress or frustration that may arise.

Materials: Paper plates, paper (construction, notebook), pens, or markers.

Prompt: Think of a stressful situation that is going on in your life (with clients, they may have already identified something that you would like to address with them). Think about the situation and all the things that are contributing to the stress. There may be other people involved, special circumstances, or aspects of the situation that are frustrating. Take a moment to think about these things that are contributing to the situation. What is the situation? Who is involved? How is it affecting your life? Write on separate sheets of paper as many aspects of the situation that you can think of. Provide the client with an example, if needed.

(continued)

Sense of Control Activity *(continued)*

Activity: Ask the client to place all of the sheets on the plate. Go through each of the aspects and process whether the aspect is within the client's control. If it is within their control, leave the sheet on the plate. If the aspect is not within the client's control, leave the sheet off the plate or crumple it up. It may be difficult for the client to admit that certain things cannot be controlled, so processing may need to take place here as well. After reviewing the aspects that are left, discuss with the client how to work on (or change) each aspect of the stressful situation. Make a plan (specific, etc.) of when and how the work will take place.

Process: What is it like to relinquish control over these aspects? How manageable does the situation appear now?

Feedback Using "I" Statements

One strategy that is commonly used to assist individuals in expressing emotions is through a structured-feedback exercise. The following exercise can be used to help individuals learn how to express emotions in a constructive way.

Factors Affecting Feedback

Sequence: Positive and negative feedback must be heard for feedback to be effective. A positive/negative-feedback sequence increases the acceptance of negative feedback.

Focus: Feedback based on concrete, observable behaviors.

Use "I" statements rather than "you" statements to convey your feelings about a topic.

I feel _____ when _____. I would really like it if _____.

Combine with positive feedback to increase the probability that feedback is heard.

I know that you are a hard worker, and I appreciate that you provide for the family. I feel ignored when you bring work home every night. I would really like it if we could set aside a couple of nights a week for alone time.

Resources

Collaborative for Academic, Social, and Emotional Learning
https://www.casel.org

An organization with information and resources for integrating social and emotional learning into education.

Emotion-Focused Therapy Clinic
http://www.emotionfocusedclinic.org/

A clinic that provides training in emotion-focused therapy and supervision.

Forgiveness
http://www.evworthington-forgiveness.com
A website with resources for working with forgiveness.

Handbook of Emotion Regulation
http://www.niu.edu/emotionreg/aboutemotionregulation/index.
shtml
A research lab focused on emotion, emotion regulation, and temperament in children.

References

Anton, S. D., & Miller, P. M. (2005). Do negative emotions predict alcohol consumption, saturated fat intake, and physical activity in older adults? *Behavior Modification, 29,* 677–688. https://doi.org/10.1177/0145445503261164

Butler, E. A., Lee, T. L., & Gross, J. J. (2009). Does expressing your emotions raise or lower your blood pressure? The answer depends on cultural context. *Journal of Cross-Cultural Psychology, 40,* 510–517. https://doi.org/10.1177/0022022109332845

Campbell-Sills, L., Barlow, D. H., Brown, T. A., & Hofmann, S. G. (2006). Acceptability and suppression of negative emotion in anxiety and mood disorders. *Emotion, 6,* 587–595. https://doi.org/10.1037/1528-3542.6.4.587

Carrizales, D., Feuerborn, L., Gueldner, B. A., & Tran, O. (2016). *Merrell's Strong Teens: A social and emotional learning curriculum for students in grades 9–12* (2nd ed.). Baltimore, MD: Brooks.

Carver, C. S., & Scheier, M. F. (2014). Dispositional optimism. *Trends in Cognitive Sciences, 18,* 293–299. https://doi.org/10.1016/j.tics.2014.02.003

Carver, C. S., Scheier, M. F., & Segerstrom, S. C. (2010). Optimism. *Clinical Psychology Review, 30,* 879–889.

Chang, E. C. (2009). An examination of optimism, pessimism, and performance perfectionism as predictors of positive psychological functioning in middle-aged adults: Does holding high standards of performance matter beyond generalized outcome expectancies? *Cognitive Therapy and Research, 33,* 334–344.

Chang, E. C., Yu, E. A., & Hirsch, J. K. (2013). On the confluence of optimism and hope on depressive symptoms in primary care patients: Does doubling up on *bonum futurun* proffer any added benefits? *The Journal of Positive Psychology, 8,* 404–411. https://doi.org/10.1080/17439760.2013.818163

De France, K., & Hollenstein, T. (2017). Assessing emotion regulation repertoires: The Regulation of Emotion Systems Survey. *Personality and Individual Differences, 119,* 204–215. https://doi.org/10.1016/j.paid.2017.07.018

Diener, E., & Chan, M. (2011). Happy people live longer: Subjective well-being contributes to health and longevity. *Applied Psychology: Health and Well-Being, 3,* 1–43.

Green, M., DeCourville, N., & Sadava, S. (2012). Positive affect, negative affect, stress, and social support as mediators of the forgiveness–health relationship. *Journal of Social Psychology, 152,* 288–307. https://doi.org/10.1080/00224545.2011.603767

Greenberg, L. S. (2002). *Emotion-focused therapy: Coaching clients to work through their feelings* (2nd ed.). Washington, DC: American Psychological Association.

Gross, J. J. (2001). Emotion regulation in adulthood: Timing is everything. *Current Directions in Psychological Science, 10,* 214–219.

Gross, J. J. (2015). The extended process model of emotion regulation: Elaborations, applications, and future directions. *Psychological Inquiry, 26,* 130–137. https://doi.org/10.1080/1047840X.2015.989751

Gross, J. J., & John, O. P. (2003). Individual differences in two emotion regulation processes: Implications for affect, relationships, and well-being. *Journal of Personality and Social Psychology, 85,* 348–362. https://doi.org/10.1037/00223514.85.2.348

Hettler, B. (1976). *Six dimensions of wellness.* Stevens Point: University of Wisconsin, National Wellness Institute.

Kashdan, T. B., & Breen, W. E. (2008). Social anxiety and positive emotions: A prospective examination of a self-regulatory model with tendencies to suppress or express emotions as a moderating variable. *Behavior Therapy, 39,* 1–12. https://doi.org/10.1016/j.beth.2007.02.003

Kashdan, T. B., Zvolensky, M. J., & McLeish, A. C. (2008). Anxiety sensitivity and affect regulatory strategies: Individual and interactive risk factors for anxiety-related symptoms. *Journal of Anxiety Disorders, 22,* 429–440. https://doi.org/10.1016/j.janxdis.2007.03.011

Lambert, M. J., & Barley, D. E. (2002). Research summary on the therapeutic relationship and psychotherapy outcome. In J. C. Norcross (Ed.), *Psychotherapy relationships that work* (pp. 17–32). New York, NY: Oxford University Press.

Lyubomirsky, S., King, L., & Diener, E. (2005). The benefits of frequent positive affect: Does happiness lead to success? *Psychological Bulletin, 131,* 803–855. https://doi.org/10.1037/0033-2909.131.6.803

Mayer, J. D., & Salovey, P. (1997). What is emotional intelligence? In P. Salovey & D. Sluyter (Eds.), *Emotional development and emotional intelligence: Educational implications* (pp. 3–31). New York, NY: Basic Books.

Mayer, J. D., Salovey, P., & Caruso, D. R. (2004). Emotional intelligence: Theory, findings, and implications. *Psychological Inquiry, 60*, 197–215.

Meevissen, Y. M., Peters, M. L., & Alberts, H. J. (2011) Become more optimistic by imagining a best possible self: Effects of a two week intervention. *Journal of Behavior Therapy and Experimental Psychiatry, 42*, 371–378.

Myers, J. E., & Sweeney, T. J. (Eds.). (2005). *Counseling for wellness: Theory, research, and practice.* Alexandria, VA: American Counseling Association.

O'Sullivan, G. (2011). The relationship between hope, stress, self-efficacy, and life satisfaction among undergraduates. *Social Indicators Research, 101*, 155–172.

Richman, L. S., Kubzansky, L., Maselko, J., Kawachi, I., Choo, P., & Bauer, M. (2005). Positive emotion and health: Going beyond the negative. *Health Psychology, 24*, 422–429. https://doi.org/10.1037/0278-6133.24.4.422

Schutte, N. S., Malouff, J. M., Thorsteinsson, E. B., Bhullar, N., & Rooke, S. E. (2007). A meta-analytic investigation of the relationship between emotional intelligence and health. *Personality and Individual Differences, 42*, 921–933. https://doi.org/10.1016/j.paid.2006.09.003

Seligman, M. (2011). *Flourish: A visionary new understanding of happiness and well-being.* New York, NY: Simon & Schuster.

Smith, T. W., Glazer, K., Ruiz, J. M., & Gallo, L. C. (2004). Hostility, anger, aggressiveness, and coronary heart disease: An interpersonal perspective on personality, emotion, and health. *Journal of Personality, 72*, 1217–1270. https://doi.org/10.1111/j.1467-6494.2004.00296.x

Tuck, N. L., Adams, K. S., & Consedine, N. S. (2017). Does the ability to express different emotions predict different indices of physical health? A skill-based study of physical symptoms and heart rate variability. *British Journal of Health Psychology, 22*, 502–523. https://doi.org/10.1111/bjhp.12242

Valle, M. F., Huebner, E. S., & Suldo, S. M. (2006). An analysis of hope as a psychological strength. *Journal of School Psychology, 44*, 393–406.

Worthington, E. L., Jr. (2003). *Forgiving and reconciling: Bridges to wholeness and hope.* Downer's Grove, IL: InterVarsity Press.

Worthington, E. L., Jr. (2006). *Forgiveness and reconciliation: Theory and practice.* New York, NY: Brunner-Routledge.

Young, M. E. (2017). *Learning the art of helping: Building blocks and techniques* (6th ed.). Upper Saddle River, NJ: Prentice Hall.

Zeidner, M., Matthews, G., & Roberts, R. D. (2009). *What we know about emotional intelligence: How it affects learning, work, relationships, and our mental health.* Cambridge, MA: MIT Press.

Zeidner, M., Matthews, G., & Roberts, R. D. (2012). The emotional intelligence, health, and well-being nexus: What have we learned and what have we missed? *Applied Psychology: Health and Well-Being, 4,* 1–30. https://doi.org/10.1111/j.1758-0854.2011.01062.x

Zeidner, M., Roberts, R. D., & Matthews, G. (2002). Can emotional intelligence be schooled? A critical review. *Educational Psychologist, 37,* 215–231.

Chapter 8

Connection

I define connection as the energy that exists between people when they feel seen, heard, and valued; when they can give and receive without judgment; and when they derive sustenance and strength from the relationship.

—Brené Brown

• • •

Social connection is central to human existence. Some of the most powerful words that I (Phil) heard from mentors in counselor education relate to this aspect of wellness. I recall a mentor stating that the best way to learn about ourselves is through connection with others. Another mentor commented to clients in recovery that "connection is the opposite of addiction." In other words, the road to recovery is through connection, and the pathway to addiction is paved by isolation. In my work counseling people diagnosed with dementia and their families, I quickly learned that receiving a diagnosis such as Alzheimer's disease sends shockwaves through that person's and their caregiver's social system. However, when that social system can find ways to support each other, well-being can remain throughout the journey with the disease for both the individual diagnosed and their loved ones.

Social support can literally save your life! Shor, Roelfs, and Yogev (2013) analyzed 50 studies totaling more than 100,000 participants and reported that "the risk of death for people with lower social support levels was 11% higher than the risk among those with higher levels of social participation" (p. 633). Social support can enhance one's outlook during trying times (e.g., Boyraz, Horne, & Sayger, 2012) and help one handle difficult emotions. As valuable as it is to receive social support from others, researchers have validated that supporting others also improves mental and physical health (Brown, Nesse, Vinokur, & Smith, 2003; Doré, Morris, Burr, Picard, & Ochsner, 2017). U.S. citizens spend more than 40 hours per week working (Bureau of Labor Statistics, 2017). Thus, social support from employers and colleagues can significantly affect one's well-being.

We define *connection wellness* as follows: the experience of interacting with and forming relationships with others through the use of interpersonal skills and resources resulting in increased well-being. For many, connection wellness would be rated as the domain that is most important to them. If this is the case for you, what would be your rationale for this wellness area being primary for you? Think about several of the clients with whom you have worked. How has a lack of connection or positive connection been related to their presenting concern or to their progress in counseling? In this chapter, we first explore why it is that *connection*—in other words, social or interpersonal wellness—is so important to overall well-being. We then identify and describe empirically supported domains that constitute connection wellness and how they are relevant to wellness counseling with clients. Assessing connection and developing interventions to address this wellness domain are discussed.

Social Support

There are multiple forms of social support. It is important to first discuss components that constitute social support as we delve into the impacts that it can have. Social support can generally be differentiated between emotional and instrumental (also called task or tangible) support (Thoits, 2011; R. J. Turner & Brown, 2010). Emotional support involves simply feeling supported. This can be experienced in several ways that have been operationalized in social support measures. For example, on the Interpersonal Support Evaluation List (Short Version) measure, emotional support was divided into an Appraisal scale and a Belonging scale (Cohen, Mermelstein, Kamarck, & Hoberman, 1985). *Appraisal social support* is defined as "the perceived availability of someone to talk to about one's problems," whereas *belonging social support* is defined as "the perceived availability of people one can do things with" (Cohen & Hoberman,

1983, p. 104). Some research has indicated that an individual's perception of social support is more valuable in positive mental and physical health outcomes than actual social support (R. J. Turner & Brown, 2010). This finding is important for those using wellness counseling, given that a client may report having a lot of friends or family, but this client may rate their social support as low. Conversely, the client's social support network may be small, but the client may experience a high level of social support. Instrumental support can manifest through a person receiving information or concrete support, such as a friend babysitting one's child so that one can work.

Often, social support systems can include friends, family, partners, colleagues, and beyond (Nurullah, 2012). Thoits (2011) noted that primary social support people have a closer relationship to the support recipient than secondary groups whose "interactions are more formal" (p. 146). For people with mental health or addiction concerns, social support directed at the presenting concern may be more valuable than general social support. Several addiction researchers have demonstrated that social support aimed at nonuse is highly implicated in non-substance-using outcomes (e.g., Beattie & Longabaugh, 1999; Lawhon, Humfleet, Hall, Reus, & Muñoz, 2009; Wasserman, Stewart, & Delucchi, 2001). The value of specific social support is also evident in the success of systemic interventions for family members of people diagnosed with severe and persistent mental health disorders. Family psychoeducation, which in part informs family members on helpful ways to support their loved one, has resulted in decreased symptomology in adults and children with mental health diagnoses (e.g., schizophrenia and mood disorders) and decreased stress for significant others, according to some studies (e.g., Lucksted, McFarlane, Downing, & Dixon, 2012).

Supporting Others

Social support is a two-way street. Anecdotally, we may view providing social support to others as simply part of the "golden rule." We may neglect to recognize that in helping our friends and family, we in turn help ourselves. The research bears this finding out in remarkable fashion. First, one should note that the provision of support to one's social network can be in the form of all of the aforementioned types of receiving social support (Brown et al., 2003). Let's begin by discussing the health implications of supporting others. When pitting the provision of social support against receiving social support in a sample of older adults, giving to others was associated with lower mortality risk, whereas receiving social support was not (Brown et al., 2003). This outcome was found for both instrumental and emotional support. Looking at specific indicators of health, the more we help others, the healthier our levels of blood pressure (Piferi & Lawler, 2006). The association between giving and blood pressure is contingent on improving one's self-efficacy, which reduces stress and therein lessens blood pressure. Thus, providing assistance (emotional or practical) to those we care about makes us more stress resistant (Inagaki & Eisenberger, 2016).

There may be additional variables at work that help explain the healing power of helping someone. We have all heard the wisdom that we learn from teaching others. Researchers used a creative study design that showed that emotion regulation skills offered to others as a form of social support yielded a rise in the use of that skill by the provider of that support (Doré et al., 2017). So remember, giving back might be the catalyst for change for some of your clients.

Social Isolation

To fully understand social support, it is important to examine the "other side of the coin," which is social isolation. It can also be helpful when learning about social support, to consider the experience of an absence of social support. Social isolation can be a perceived or actual experience for our clients. Because high perceived social support is often related to increased wellness, many clients who seek counseling may feel or be socially isolated. Social isolation can be classified as "socially avoidant," "actively isolated," and "socially disinterested" (Niño, Cai, & Ignatow, 2016, p. 96). The interrelationship between social isolation and well-being was shown in a study of 2,923 middle and older adults in which increases in social isolation corresponded with decreases in physical health. Similar findings emerged when exploring the relationship of social isolation and mental health (Miyawaki, 2015). Social isolation can affect our child and adolescent clients as well. Matthews et al. (2015) identified several possible issues that may arise in youth development and precipitate social isolation, including rejection, self-imposed avoidance of interactions, mental health concerns that predated the social isolation, and the snowball effect of social skill challenges from earlier social isolation that become exacerbated as the individual matriculates into adolescence.

Mental health concerns seem to co-occur with social isolation for both youths (Matthews et al., 2015) and adults (Linz & Sturm, 2013).

In a study that assessed children at 5 and 12 years old, participants whose parents were classified in the low-socioeconomic-status group and endorsed several criteria of antisocial personality disorder had elevated levels of social isolation. Social isolation for children with behavior issues (including attention-deficit/hyperactivity disorder) increased between 5 and 12 years old (Matthews et al., 2015). For adults with severe mental illness (SMI), stigma and alienation may contribute to social isolation (Linz & Sturm, 2013). Stigma entails "the process of labeling," whereas "alienation differs from the experience of stigma in that the individual with SMI may be affected by stigma, but is foremost affected by their psychiatric symptoms" (Linz & Sturm, 2013, p. 248).

Clients from cultural backgrounds other than the United States may experience increased social isolation. A study of Latinx immigrants in North Carolina revealed that approximately 20% of the individuals experienced a high level of social isolation (Mora et al., 2014). Social isolation increased as the number of people living with the participant decreased. People who had less education, lived in the United States for a shorter period of time, and lacked confidence with the English language were more socially isolated. Furthermore, Latinx immigrants who were more socially isolated endorsed lower levels of physical and mental health. Conversely, social support may safeguard against acculturation stress. In the following sections, we elaborate on the benefits of social support for people who have experienced trauma and individuals with SMI.

Benefits of Connection Wellness

Trauma

A person's family and friends can be harmful to trauma recovery if they interact with him or her in a manner that minimizes or instills guilt for what happened (James & Gilliland, 2017). Social support members of the traumatized person can be affected because of the symptoms of trauma, thoughts, feelings, and behaviors exhibited by their loved one—many of which may differ greatly from how the person typically presents. The Trauma Informed Care movement signals the need for providers to be prepared to provide appropriate and effective services given a reasonable likelihood that any given client has experienced trauma (Substance Abuse and Mental Health Services Administration, 2014). Connection wellness is a substantial healing factor in addressing the effects of trauma.

Cognitive symptoms of trauma experienced by people with post-traumatic stress disorder merit being addressed by counselors as they perpetuate the disorder. Researchers uncovered that in a sample of 378 individuals involved in either an interpersonally violent relationship or a car crash, self-reported support of family and friends was correlated with reduced posttraumatic thoughts (Woodward et al., 2015). In a study assessing the history of several types of childhood abuse and neglect in adults, social support influenced reductions in trauma symptoms, provided that the symptomology did not exceed medium levels (Evans, Steel, & DiLillo, 2013). Findings varied in that family versus friend support differed in effect depending on gender and type of abuse. Social support is among the factors associated with posttraumatic growth.

SMI

Clients with SMI live with mental health diagnoses with acute and chronic symptoms that affect multiple activities of daily living, including employment, education, self-care, and social functioning. A focus group study with 52 people with SMI was conducted that asked participants about helpful and nonhelpful social support (Chronister, Chou, Kwan, Lawton, & Silver, 2015). Four of the six domains that emerged were related to instrumental support such as "support accessing and receiving services" and "activities of daily living" support. However, at least one of the domains centered on emotional support, including support people exhibiting an "enduring attitude of respect, worth, and value." A second qualitative study capturing the voice of people with SMI on family support resulted in emotional support, rather than instrumental support, being most frequently noted as beneficial (Aldersey & Whitley, 2015). Emotional support was in the form of encouragement, availability, and position of non-judgment regarding the loved one's mental illness. Instrumental support entailed aid with finances, transportation, and activities of daily living. Obstacles posed by family to positive coping from SMI involved the opposite of the aforementioned benefits; for instance, feeling invalidated and stress and strain in the family.

Yanos and Rosario (2014) conducted 20 interviews per participant with 27 participants with SMI to pinpoint the coping skills that they use. Connecting with their social support (speaking to family members, peers, or friends) was the skill incorporated most often (24% of interview days) and by the greatest number of participants (81%).

Quantitative research has been informative on social support for people with SMI. Davis and Brekke's (2014) path model revealed that increases in social support are related to increases in cognitive coping. Social support also had a favorable indirect effect on functioning occupationally, interpersonally, and in activities of daily living. However, this effect disappeared by the posttest that occurred 6 months later.

To understand the mechanism through which social support has such positive benefits on health and well-being, we can look to a clear connection with *mind wellness* through neuroscience. You may have heard about the neurotransmitter oxytocin, as it has been dubbed "the cuddle hormone" or "the love hormone" in pop culture. Oxytocin is what is released when you hug a loved one, nurse a baby, or experience times of intimacy and trust. Oxytocin, however, is actually also a stress hormone because it is released during the stress response. Health psychologist Kelly McGonigal (2016) has written about the power of this knowledge—that our bodies' stress response is nudging us to seek support from others in times of crisis. This idea of interpersonal neurobiology can be empowering when you frame social support as literally changing our brain to help us in times of need by reducing pain, stress, and anxiety and by interacting with dopamine to help us feel good.

Navigating Obstacles to Connection Wellness

One of the factors that may detract from your client's connection wellness is social or interpersonal conflict. In fact, your client's presenting concern may be directly related to conflict with an intimate partner, family member(s), or friends. Interpersonal conflict affects several other wellness areas. For example, social conflict was a trigger to relapse into self-injurious behaviors in a sample of people who had engaged in these behaviors previously (B. J. Turner, Cobb, Gratz, & Chapman, 2016). Additionally, Marlatt's (1985) model of relapse includes interpersonal conflict as a precipitating factor in substance use relapse. Researchers examined, in part, the social conflict–wellness relationship and found that conflict resulted in decreased wellness (life satisfaction and self-esteem; Wickham, Williamson, Beard, Kobayashi, & Hirst, 2016).

Enmeshed and enabling relationships can cause enormous stress for individuals. Enmeshed relationships are present when the boundaries between family members or friends become blurred, often in the form/direction of "overinvolvement" (Hook, 2012). The conflict can also be one of "underinvolvement" that occurs when significant others are disconnected or have problematic interactions. For instance, Edwards (1997) described that problems manifest in families when children cross the parent–caregiver boundary and end up serving a parental role in the family at a young age. Enabling behaviors may detract from your client's pursuits of well-being or can mask the client's wellness struggles. Enabling is an overstepping of boundaries that precludes a person from awareness and actions to address a life problem or from experiencing the natural consequences of failure to take ownership/responsibility for that problem (Miller, Meyers, & Hiller-Sturmhöfel, 1999).

A concrete example of this behavior is a coworker and friend who covers up for the friend's lack of skill on the job by doing tasks for him or her rather than allowing the friend to find ways to learn the job skills or even teaching the friend the skills. When it comes to the topic of "unhealthy relationships," make sure that your client defines healthy relationships for him- or herself rather than you (the counselor) imposing your value and vision of health relationships onto the client. The client has their own unique worldview and what upsets and fulfills the client relationally may contrast with your experience or that of other clients.

Conceptualizing relationships from a wellness perspective allows clients to examine their relationships in an objective and intentional manner, thereby increasing clarity about the client's interpersonal life and reducing the occurrence of resistance dynamics during counseling. For example, if a client feels judged by the counselor that one of their relationships is "unhealthy," they may not fully explore that relationship. Wellness approaches facilitate the client's own self-assessment of their relationships. Reflective wellness-based warning signs that clients can use to evaluate their relationships include the following:

1. *Mind*—The relationship results in negative thoughts about yourself. The person regularly makes negative comments about you. The person consistently disregards, ignores, criticizes your thoughts and opinions, or tells you what to think or believe. Your mind wellness is noticeably hindered by this person.

2. *Body*—The person is physically or sexually abusive (i.e., grabs you, hits you, leaves bruises on you, causes you injury, forces you to be intimate against your will). The person regularly tells you things about your body or physical appearance that result in you feeling bad about your body or yourself. The person lives a lifestyle that consistently discourages you from seeking and achieving body wellness goals that are important to you. Your body wellness is noticeably hindered by this person.

3. *Spirit*—The person does not support you in your religious or spiritual beliefs, disparages your beliefs and practices, or blocks you from fully engaging in your religious or spiritual beliefs. The person criticizes things that bring you meaning and purpose in life. The life path of this person appears destructive and has begun to affect your life path. Your spirit wellness is noticeably hindered by this person.

4. *Emotion*—The person is emotionally abusive (e.g., puts you down, yells at you, threatens you). The person consistently fails to be emotionally supportive. The person denies, ignores, or invalidates your feelings. The emotional tone of your relationship detracts from your wellness. Your emotions regularly change in a negative way when you are with this person. Thinking about or spending time with this person elicits more negative emotions in you than positive ones. Your emotion wellness is noticeably hindered by this person.

5. *Connection*—The person's style of communicating with you results in consistent conflict or tension. This person minimizes or is jealous over important connections in your life and attempts to isolate you from critical sources of your social support system (e.g., family and friends). Time spent with this person is often a negative experience. Your connection wellness is noticeably hindered by this person.

An important caveat is when working with kids and young adults who are in the midst of forming their schema for what a healthy relationship should be. This period is a crucial time to include psychoeducation and empowerment-based counseling that helps foster a culture of healthy relationships for young people. As we know from research into adverse childhood experiences, children who witness domestic violence or are subject to physical or sexual abuse themselves are at an increased risk of mental health and substance use issues as adults (Merrick et al., 2017). Therefore, it is critical when working with young people to broach the subject of healthy relationships, teen dating violence, active consent, and the effects of (and ways to dismantle) rape culture from a trauma-informed lens.

Social Skills

Providing and receiving social support is a difficult task if one is missing the skills that are critical in cultivating and maintaining relationships. Clients, for many different reasons, may have problems actualizing certain social skills. Problems can occur because of lack of modeling of effective skills by caregivers, failure to navigate certain developmental tasks (Matthews et al., 2015), mental health problems, neurodevelopmental disorders, personality traits, and so forth. After reflection, there are a multitude of social skills needed to function in society and facilitate successful relationships that we likely take for granted. We list and describe some of the most important social skills for youths and adults.

Foundational social skills for children and adolescents include reciprocity, self-disclosure, "following rules of play," "listening to others," "entering a group," "expressing feelings," and "asking for what one wants/needs" (Bloomquist, 2013, p. 113). Bloomquist (2013) listed "stopping, thinking, and planning to resolve a conflict or disagreement" as one of the more complex social skills (p. 113). Research supports the relevance of social skills on connection wellness. Segrin, McNelis, and Swiatkowski (2016) described the following outcomes in their study on social skills in a sample of 211 college students: "[P]eople with poor social skills may be vulnerable to the development of psychological distress because they have less access to the protective effects of social support" (p. 130). Hence, before leaping into helping clients increase their social support and improve relationships, counselors need to first understand the social skills of their client.

Social Media

The use of social media is becoming ubiquitous, especially among younger generations. Whether it's Facebook, Instagram, Snapchat, or WhatsApp, sometimes the challenge to connection wellness is actually a connection overload. Although there certainly are benefits to being able to connect with others in a moment's notice at the tip of your fingers, social media can give a false sense how connected and happy others seem and leave you actually feeling more isolated. Research bears out this idea of social media leading to a phenomenon of "being alone together."

Related to the media literacy skills we discussed in Chapter 4, working on healthy social media habits can be important for enhancing real work social relationships and overall wellness. Opening social media and receiving instant feedback causes the brain to release dopamine, just like other addictive quick fixes. So similar to sugar or drugs, over time we need more to keep feeling good, and what was once an effective coping strategy can become a harmful habit that negatively affects wellness. Ways to limit social media use and exploring what needs are getting met from "likes" and finding ways to meet those needs with real-world interactions are useful topics to explore with clients.

Cultural Considerations in Connection Wellness

The experience of social support and social support needs are influenced by the personal culture of the client. For clients who espouse collectivistic values, their social support may manifest differently than people who hold values of individualism. For instance, a client from a collectivist context may prefer not to request aid from a significant other to avoid inconveniencing the person (Kim, Sherman, & Taylor, 2008). The counselor–client relationship is a form of connection wellness; hence, a counselor who holds cultural traditions that favor requesting help from family and friends while overlooking the client's culture may (a) experience countertransference feelings of frustration toward the client out of a desire for him or her to be more vulnerable in session and (b) implement interventions that are not culturally informed; for instance, encouraging the client to ask loved ones for help more often (Kim et al., 2008).

As we leap into the assessment of connection wellness and related interventions, we wanted to offer a few ideas for connection wellness boosters—that is, simple interventions that can be enacted by the client in a short period of time that bolster wellness in the social domain:

1. *Five-minute phone call*—In today's world, we often text and message friends in social media but do not take the time to connect with them directly. A brief phone call to the friend or family member who grounds or makes you smile can have an instant positive impact on your wellness. Set aside 5 minutes and call this person.

2. *Do one small nice thing for someone*—The idea of "paying it forward" is a cliché, but this is because it works. Take an extra moment to ask someone about their day, help someone with a brief task, and so forth.

3. *Share a laugh*—A genuine laugh can shift one's mindset quickly. It can be doubly powerful when shared with another. Share a funny story or humorous moment from your day with someone.

4. *Connection without distraction*—Spend a few minutes talking face to face with a person in your life who is emotionally supportive with no distractions from television, computer, or phone. If it is your romantic partner, consider cuddling or kissing.

5. *Schedule a social outing*—Having a social experience to look forward to can provide a boost to one's well-being. This activity could be as simple as setting aside 1 hour for dinner or coffee with a friend.

Assessment and Intervention

One helpful starting point when working in the connection domain is to use a formal assessment of connection wellness. There are numerous social assessments that can inform both client and counselor on the client's social skills, types of social support that exist or are lacking in the client's life, the presence of social conflict, and so forth. A listing of connection wellness assessments is beyond the scope of this book. However, we wanted to underscore that formal measures can be an asset in clarifying the client's interpersonal strengths and areas for growth. We now elaborate on components of informal assessments of connection wellness.

The counselor must obtain a clear understanding of the relationship between connection wellness and the client's presenting concerns. For example, if the primary issue that brought the client to counseling is depression, ascertaining links between lack of connection wellness and depression is key. You should also ensure that you are aware of how the client defines connection wellness. These processes often occur during the overall wellness assessment in the first and second sessions (see Chapter 9). To take this step further, engage in an analysis of the client's social supports, conflicts, and obstacles.

Refer back to the scaling question or assessment of connection wellness. When asked to rate their level of connection wellness on a 10-point scale ranging from 1 (*minimal perceived social support*) to 10 (*maximum perceived social support*), most clients will not rate a 1 here. Starting the conversation from a strength-based, solution-focused perspective, inquire about why the client rated what they did rather than a lower number. Then dig deeply into ways in which the client does feel supported. Follow-up questions can explore how (if at all) this social support has buffered the client from further issues directly or indirectly related to the presenting concern.

Now it is time to get more specific. Start with the question, "Who is in your social circle?" The client can even draw an inner circle and outer circle to depict primary and secondary social supports. Use of genograms may be beneficial in the client seeing a visual depiction of stronger and weaker familial relationships. To increase specificity, the counselor can ask the client to discuss each member of their inner circle and the ways in which they feel supported by each person. Be sure to provide psychoeducation to the client about different forms of social support (e.g., instrumental, emotional). This analysis of emotional support contains therapeutic value because the client may realize that they have more social support than initially realized. If "aha" moments occur, make sure to take the time to process the meaning of this new insight with the client. Alternatively, the counselor can ask the client to "name one person in your life who you feel supported by. In what ways do they support you?" You can repeat this process for several support people.

To address the other side of the coin, you can return to the sliding scale and inquire why the client rated what they did rather than give a higher score. The purpose of this question is to elicit information about the client's struggles related to social well-being. To funnel the process, the counselor can ask, "What is the biggest factor or problem resulting in your connection wellness being lower than you would like?" This question may reveal specific and major social conflict or isolation issues that are central to lack of connection wellness that can be addressed in counseling. Here are some additional questions the counselor can ask to raise the client's awareness about obstacles to connection wellness:

1. "Who in your inner or outer circle do you want to feel more supported by or have an improved relationship with?"
2. "With whom in your inner circle do you have the most conflict/strain with? How has this affected you?"
3. "What specifically occurred that led the conflict to reach its peak?"

As you and the client delve into these topics, dialogue about how problems with connection wellness have affected the client's presenting concerns. Denisha Champion (assistant director for programming and prevention, Wake Forest University Counseling Center), who uses this approach with college students, emphasized that the counselor can also assess for "abusive, neglectful, or potentially harmful social dynamics" while discussing the shadow side of the client's inner and outer circles (personal communication, January 4, 2018).

Unhelpful relationships can often be the culprit in client's presenting concerns and struggles with connection wellness. During the inner–outer circle discussion, the counselor can have the client place a star next to relationships that make him or her a better person, an

"X" next to any relationships that cause the client problems in their well-being, or a "?" if the client is unsure. Again, clients may not recognize or be able to objectively identify destructive relationships, so the exploration of potential concerning relationships is a start. A decisional balance can be used to explore the costs and benefits of relationships that might be questionably healthy to the client (Miller & Rollnick, 2002). Also, the counselor can explore whether others in the client's life have expressed concerns about the client's relationship with that person (or those persons). Finally, obstacles to the person achieving the level of connection wellness that the client desires should be fully examined. Shyness, lack of assertiveness or self-esteem, and difficulty with social skills can all block clients from getting what they want socially. Ask clients, "What has gotten in the way of you improving relationships or getting the social life or social support that you want?"

Difficulty asking for help is a common theme that many of us have experienced personally or heard from clients during counseling. It is thus important to explore whether problems asking for help has gotten in the way of the client getting the support that they desire. This topic should only be explored if it aligns with the client's beliefs and goals. Get specific by asking, "What type of social support do you want more of?" Talk with the client about examples of what has gotten in the way of asking for help. Who does your client want more support from, and what support is the client looking for?

Instrumental support is, at times, overlooked by the counselor or client. Thus, there is immense therapeutic potential in dialoguing with clients about instrumental support needs. Many formal social support assessments contain instrumental support subscales or items. Using these measures or items can be helpful in beginning the conversation on this topic. Remember, instrumental support is task-based support provided by others, such as assistance with medical care of self or others, help maintaining one's home, employment seeking, transportation, social services, and so forth. I (Phil) learned the importance of instrumental support when counseling caregivers of people with dementia. Caregivers frequently sought counseling in a state of being overwhelmed. A large portion of the crisis was related to lack of instrumental social support or challenges in mobilizing that support. For instance, clients often needed help in caring for their loved one while they worked or tended to their own self-care needs. Connecting caregivers with adult day centers or in-home nursing was a useful solution for many of my clients. Creative problem solving led to additional options, including increasing family involvement in care of their loved one with dementia and using resources through the client's church. As you and the client assess for instrumental support needs, pinpoint and prioritize what the most pressing ones are.

Whether you and the client are processing emotional or instrumental support, recognize that a discussion of barriers to obtaining this support is necessary. Using solution-focused questions about failed solutions (O'Connell, 2012; O'Hanlon & Weiner-Davis, 2003; e.g., "What attempts did you make in the past to get this instrumental support that did not work? What are some reasons these efforts were not successful?") reduces the risk that you and the client will treatment plan with strategies that have not worked. Solution-focused questions about what has worked in the past to acquire social support can call forward some insights and actions that were effective for the client previously.

One of the most therapeutic actions that a client can take that potentially fosters multiple wellness domains, including connection, is to give to others. Whether that giving involves sharing one's time through voluntarism or providing social support to a friend or family member, taking these steps can boost positive emotion, self-esteem, enhance relationships, meaning and purpose, and so forth. This intervention is not appropriate for clients who are enmeshed or who give overly to others to the neglect of themselves. For clients not engaging in what is sometimes labeled codependent behaviors, giving in relationship or to others gets one outside of oneself, potentially reducing depression and improving other areas of mental health.

As the counselor, you want to get to know ways that the client is supportive of those in their inner and outer circles. In what ways does the client seek to improve as a support person to others? Two extremes to listen for are under- and oversupporting. Clients who undersupport in their relationships may find that strain occurs because of lack of mutuality. Clients who oversupport may be in enmeshed or codependent relationships in which they always put others first to the neglect of themselves. The cumulative stress can factor into the client's presenting concern. However, beware that clients may not be accurate in reporting on this situation. One way to somewhat circumvent this occurrence is to figuratively bring the support person into the counseling office by asking the following questions: "If person X was in the room with us right now, what would they say about you as a friend or family member? What would they say about how you could be a better friend or family member? What would they say about you putting others before yourself?"

Many clients can benefit from discussing and practicing assertiveness as well as communication and social skills. For instance, social support is a key component of the stabilization phase for clients in recovery from complex trauma (James & Gilliland, 2017; H. Lambert, personal communication, November 19, 2012). Teaching the client basic reflective listening skills can improve their ability to communicate.

Remember the solution-focused and strength-based aspects of wellness counseling. We do not want to reinvent the wheel when it comes to wellness, and that includes connection. Make sure to help clients identify specific social skills that are an asset in relating to others. Inquire about positive things about the client that benefit others who are in their social support network. Discuss any giving the client has done that they feel good about that involves the provision of instrumental or emotional support to primary or secondary support people or voluntarism. Finally, identify the relationships that are nourishing to the client. Find out what specifically makes these relationships meaningful. What ideas does the client have for transferring these skills and qualities toward the purpose of increasing social support, improving relationships, increasing social skills, or navigating obstacles to social support?

Your own self-awareness as the counselor may be triggered regarding social skills on the basis of how you experience the client in session. Immediacy and feedback skills can be used to gently offer constructive comments to the client about their social behaviors that occur within session or that are discussed in session. This feedback must only be done when appropriate and after rapport is built (Skovholt & Rivers, 2007). Feedback must be based on observable behaviors rather than the abstract. Facilitating opportunities for clients to role play social support skills can be a potent connection intervention (Bloomquist, 2013).

Interconnected Interventions

Because wellness is atheoretical/transtheoretical, several intervention options are available and—because of the uniqueness of each client—are too numerous to discuss here in full. However, several principles of practice that we list here may be helpful in preparing and implementing your connection wellness interventions. At different times in the wellness counseling process, certain domains of wellness will emerge at the forefront of the client's focus. This occurrence may be due to the client setting connection as a goal area or identifying connection as a strength or grounding area. The purpose of this section is to prime you to (a) think about how connection wellness may benefit other aspects of your client's well-being, (b) identify other avenues for enhancing your client's connection wellness, and (c) discover ways that connection satisfactorily pairs with other wellness domains to create a positive effect that exceeds the power of either wellness domain in isolation.

First, the domains of the wellness model provide a useful template for exploring potential interventions. How can you engage other aspects of the client's well-being in the service of a wellness goal area? We provide an example of paired interventions between connection wellness and each remaining wellness domain.

Connection and Body

A client feeling low on connection wellness—specifically, one who is experiencing loneliness or a smaller than desired social support network, might be able to link their love for exercise into an avenue for increasing social support. For instance, the client may elect to join a running club and attend 1 day per week, thereby increasing the likelihood of sparking primary or secondary social support.

Connection and Spirit

Clients who are experiencing spiritual emptiness as well as a lack of social support may find dual benefit from merging the two wellness areas and seeking the support of a religious or spiritual leader, church, or faith community. EcoWellness interventions can combine connection and spirit wellness by going for a hike or walk with a family member or friend (Reese & Myers, 2012).

Connection and Mind

Interventions to build protective skills against mental illness stigma as well as social skills interventions use cognitive pathways. Furthermore, Thoits (2011) noted that self-esteem factors into social support, because if a person does not view him- or herself positively, he or she may not take the time to build healthy relationships. Consider using cognitive interventions that build self-esteem and challenge cognitive barriers to social skills. This process may open the door to enhanced connection wellness.

Connection and Emotion

Emotional intelligence is a necessary ingredient for connection (Goleman, 2005). If a client cannot identify/articulate and regulate their emotions, relationships can quickly become destructive or distanced (Bloomquist, 2013). Build one's emotion regulation skills via "emotional-containment" skills (Murphy & Dillon, 2011). Validate and reinforce your client's healthy expressions of emotion that occur in session.

Conclusion

In completing your reading of this chapter, you have learned that there are many routes and influences that affect connection wellness. Counselors need to assess and understand the ecology of the client. A significant part of that is the client's relationships or lack thereof. Understanding social isolation, the characteristics of healthy and toxic relationships, and the client's interpersonal needs empowers the counselor to facilitate more effective interventions. The counselor's awareness to view the client's connection wellness through a cultural lens is critical. Finally, connection wellness interventions will fall flat if the client has a dearth of social skills. Knowledge on cultivating interpersonal skills and building on the client's existing abilities are important for the wellness counselor.

Reflection Prompts

1. How do you believe technology (e.g., smartphones, social networking) has affected social relationships? What are some positive effects? What are some negative effects? What are some implications for mental health and the counseling profession?
2. What are some of the benefits and burdens of your social relationships? How happy are you with your level of support? How well do you balance your social wellness with other aspects of your life?
3. What are some characteristics of healthy/helpful relationships that you have? What are some characteristics of unhealthy/harmful relationships?
4. What do you think about our claim that "for many, connection wellness would be rated as the domain that is most important to them"? Do you agree or disagree? Please explain your response.
5. We defined *connection wellness* as "the experience of interacting with and forming relationships with others through the use of interpersonal skills and resources resulting in increased well-being." What would you add to or change about this definition?
6. Recall one instance in which you received meaningful social support. Recall an instance in which you provided meaningful social support to another. How were these experiences similar or different? In what ways did these experiences enrich your connection wellness and any other domains of your well-being?
7. In what ways can you begin incorporating healthy forms of giving-related connection wellness interventions with your clients?

Learning Activities

Inner Circle–Outer Circle[1]

Mark closest relationships in the inner circle, next closest relationships in the next circle, and so forth. Put "I" next to the person's name who provides instrumental support (helps with tasks), "E" next to the name if they provide emotional support, or both "I" and "E." Draw a "star" if the relationship increases wellness, an "X" if it decreases wellness, or a "?" if you are unsure.

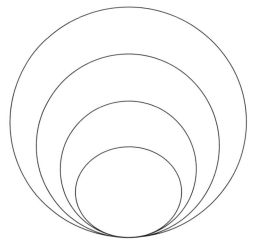

Wellness Booster Activity

Select one (or more) of the wellness boosters from this chapter to implement. Make a note of how you were feeling both before and after enacting the wellness booster.

- What (if any) impact did the wellness booster have on your connection wellness, other domains of wellness, and overall well-being?

Resources

National Alliance on Mental Illness—"Find Support"

https://www.nami.org/Find-Support

The multiple links on this webpage contain mental health information, ways to identify mental health services, and suggestions for helping people with mental health struggles.

---

[1]Adapted with permission from Denisha Champion, PhD, LPC, Assistant Director for Programming and Prevention, Wake Forest University Counseling Center.

Substance Abuse and Mental Health Services Administration Self-Help Groups Treatment Locator
https://findtreatment.samhsa.gov/locator/link-focSelfGP
Social support can come in the form of counseling or self-help groups. This webpage allows people to find self-help groups near them.

Volunteer Match
https://www.volunteermatch.org/
This website links prospective volunteers to volunteer placements.

References

Aldersey, H. M., & Whitley, R. (2015). Family influence in recovery from severe mental illness. *Community Mental Health Journal, 51,* 467–476.

Beattie, M. C., & Longabaugh, R. (1999). General and alcohol-specific social support following treatment. *Addictive Behaviors, 24,* 593–606.

Bloomquist, M. L. (2013). *Skills training for struggling kids: Promoting your child's behavioral, emotional, academic, and social development.* New York, NY: Guilford Press.

Boyraz, G., Horne, S. G., & Sayger, T. V. (2012). Finding meaning in loss: The mediating role of social support between personality and two construals of meaning. *Death Studies, 36,* 519–540.

Brown, S. L., Nesse, R. M., Vinokur, A. D., & Smith, D. M. (2003). Providing social support may be more beneficial than receiving it: Results from a prospective study of mortality. *Psychological Science, 14,* 320–327.

Bureau of Labor Statistics. (2017, June 27). *American Time Use Survey: 2016 results.* Retrieved from https://www.bls.gov/news.release/archives/atus_06272017.pdf

Chronister, J., Chou, C. C., Kwan, K. L. K., Lawton, M., & Silver, K. (2015). The meaning of social support for persons with serious mental illness. *Rehabilitation Psychology, 60,* 232–245.

Cohen, S., & Hoberman, H. M. (1983). Positive events and social supports as buffers of life change stress. *Journal of Applied Social Psychology, 13,* 99–125.

Cohen, S., Mermelstein, R., Kamarck, T., & Hoberman, H. M. (1985). Measuring the functional components of social support. In I. G. Sarason (Ed.), *Social support: Theory, research and applications* (pp. 73–94). Dordrecht, the Netherlands: Springer.

Davis, L., & Brekke, J. (2014). Social support and functional outcome in severe mental illness: The mediating role of proactive coping. *Psychiatry Research, 215,* 39–45.

Doré, B. P., Morris, R. R., Burr, D. A., Picard, R. W., & Ochsner, K. N. (2017). Helping others regulate emotion predicts increased regulation of one's own emotions and decreased symptoms of depression. *Personality and Social Psychology Bulletin, 43,* 729–739.

Edwards, J. T. (1997). *Working with families: Guidelines and techniques* (4th ed.). Durham, NC: Foundation Place.

Evans, S. E., Steel, A. L., & DiLillo, D. (2013). Child maltreatment severity and adult trauma symptoms: Does perceived social support play a buffering role? *Child Abuse & Neglect, 37,* 934–943.

Goleman, D. (2005). *Emotional intelligence: Why it can matter more than IQ.* New York, NY: Bantam Books.

Hook, M. K. (2012). Alcohol addiction and families. In D. Capuzzi & M. D. Stauffer (Eds.), *Foundations of addiction counseling* (2nd ed., pp. 278–300). Upper Saddle River, NJ: Pearson.

Inagaki, T. K., & Eisenberger, N. I. (2016). Giving support to others reduces sympathetic nervous system-related responses to stress. *Psychophysiology, 53,* 427–435.

James, R. K., & Gilliland, B. E. (2017). *Crisis intervention strategies* (8th ed.). Belmont, CA: Brooks/Cole.

Kim, H. S., Sherman, D. K., & Taylor, S. E. (2008). Culture and social support. *American Psychologist, 63,* 518–526.

Lawhon, D., Humfleet, G. L., Hall, S. M., Reus, V. I., & Muñoz, R. F. (2009). Longitudinal analysis of abstinence-specific social support and smoking cessation. *Health Psychology, 28,* 465–472.

Linz, S. J., & Sturm, B. A. (2013). The phenomenon of social isolation in the severely mentally ill. *Perspectives in Psychiatric Care, 49,* 243–254.

Lucksted, A., McFarlane, W., Downing, D., & Dixon, L. (2012). Recent developments in family psychoeducation as an evidence-based practice. *Journal of Marital and Family Therapy, 38,* 101–121.

Marlatt, G. A. (1985). Relapse prevention: Theoretical rationale and overview of the model. In G. A. Marlatt & J. R. Gordon (Eds.), *Relapse prevention: Maintenance strategies in the treatment of addictive behaviors* (pp. 3–70). New York, NY: Guilford Press.

Matthews, T., Danese, A., Wertz, J., Ambler, A., Kelly, M., Diver, A., . . . Arseneault, L. (2015). Social isolation and mental health at primary and secondary school entry: A longitudinal cohort study. *Journal of the American Academy of Child & Adolescent Psychiatry, 54,* 225–232.

McGonigal, K. (2016). *The upside of stress: Why stress is good for you, and how to get good at it.* New York, NY: Penguin Random House.

Merrick, M. T., Ports, K. A., Ford, D. C., Afifi, T. O., Gershoff, E. T., & Grogan-Kaylor, A. (2017). Unpacking the impact of adverse childhood experiences on adult mental health. *Child Abuse & Neglect, 69,* 10–19.

Miller, W. R., Meyers, R. J., & Hiller-Sturmhöfel, S. (1999). The community reinforcement approach. *Alcohol Research and Health, 23,* 116–121.

Miller, W. R., & Rollnick, S. (2002). *Motivational interviewing: Preparing people for change* (2nd ed.). New York, NY: Guilford Press.

Miyawaki, C. E. (2015). Association of social isolation and health across different racial and ethnic groups of older Americans. *Ageing & Society, 35,* 2201–2228.

Mora, D. C., Grzywacz, J. G., Anderson, A. M., Chen, H., Arcury, T. A., Marín, A. J., & Quandt, S. A. (2014). Social isolation among Latino workers in rural North Carolina: Exposure and health implications. *Journal of Immigrant and Minority Health, 16,* 822–830.

Niño, M. D., Cai, T., & Ignatow, G. (2016). Social isolation, drunkenness, and cigarette use among adolescents. *Addictive Behaviors, 53,* 94–100.

Nurullah, A. S. (2012). Received and provided social support: A review of current evidence and future directions. *American Journal of Health Studies, 27,* 173–188.

O'Connell, B. (2012). *Solution-focused therapy* (3rd ed.). Thousand Oaks, CA: Sage.

O'Hanlon, B., & Weiner-Davis, M. (2003). *In search of solutions: A new direction in psychotherapy* (2nd ed.). New York, NY: Norton.

Piferi, R. L., & Lawler, K. A. (2006). Social support and ambulatory blood pressure: An examination of both receiving and giving. *International Journal of Psychophysiology, 62,* 328–336.

Reese, R. F., & Myers, J. E. (2012). EcoWellness: The missing factor in holistic wellness models. *Journal of Counseling & Development, 90,* 400–406.

Segrin, C., McNelis, M., & Swiatkowski, P. (2016). Social skills, social support, and psychological distress: A test of the Social Skills Deficit Vulnerability Model. *Human Communication Research, 42,* 122–137.

Shor, E., Roelfs, D. J., & Yogev, T. (2013). The strength of family ties: A meta-analysis and meta-regression of self-reported social support and mortality. *Social Networks, 35,* 626–638.

Skovholt, T. M., & Rivers, D. A. (2007). *Helping skills and strategies.* Denver, CO: Love Publishing.

Substance Abuse and Mental Health Services Administration. (2014). *Trauma-informed care in behavioral health services* (Treatment Improvement Protocol [TIP] Series, No. 57, HHS Publication No. [SMA] 13-4801). Rockville, MD: Author.

Thoits, P. A. (2011). Mechanisms linking social ties and support to physical and mental health. *Journal of Health and Social Behavior, 52,* 145–161.

Turner, B. J., Cobb, R. J., Gratz, K. L., & Chapman, A. L. (2016). The role of interpersonal conflict and perceived social support in nonsuicidal self-injury in daily life. *Journal of Abnormal Psychology, 125,* 588–598.

Turner, R. J., & Brown, R. L. (2010). Social support and mental health. In T. L. Scheid & T. N. Brown (Eds.), *A handbook for the study of mental health: Social contexts, theories, and systems* (2nd ed., pp. 200–212). Cambridge, England: Cambridge University Press.

Wasserman, D. A., Stewart, A. L., & Delucchi, K. L. (2001). Social support and abstinence from opiates and cocaine during opioid maintenance treatment. *Drug & Alcohol Dependence, 65,* 65–75.

Wickham, R. E., Williamson, R. E., Beard, C. L., Kobayashi, C. L., & Hirst, T. W. (2016). Authenticity attenuates the negative effects of interpersonal conflict on daily well-being. *Journal of Research in Personality, 60,* 56–62.

Woodward, M. J., Eddinger, J., Henschel, A. V., Dodson, T. S., Tran, H. N., & Beck, J. G. (2015). Social support, posttraumatic cognitions, and PTSD: The influence of family, friends, and a close other in an interpersonal and non-interpersonal trauma group. *Journal of Anxiety Disorders, 35,* 60–67.

Yanos, P. T., & Rosario, A. (2014). Preventive coping among people with severe mental illness in daily life: Strategies used and associations with mood. *International Journal of Social Psychiatry, 60,* 489–491.

Part III
Wellness Counseling
in Action

Chapter 9

Assessment and Case Conceptualization

The greatest compliment that was ever paid me was
when one asked me what I thought,
and attended to my answer.

—Henry David Thoreau

• • •

Assessing wellness is a tricky and important endeavor. Wellness assessment starts as soon as we meet the client. The purpose of assessment in general is to understand the presenting concerns of the client and the factors precipitating it. The assessment also should provide a deeper knowledge of the client's strengths because these assets can be applied to alleviate the presenting problem(s). Hays (2017) provided the following definition of assessment: "an umbrella term for the evaluation methods counselors use to better understand characteristics of people, places, and things" (p. 4). Wellness assessment can be defined as a method for increasing understanding of client component-specific and holistic wellness as well as their effect on the client's presenting concern. Conversely, the assessment informs counselor and client about the influence of the presenting problem on the client's well-being. The wellness assessment involves identification of wellness strengths possessed by the client. An important part of wellness assessment is empowering the client to explore his or her own results to inform goals that are client driven.

A comprehensive wellness assessment leads to an effective client conceptualization. *Client conceptualization* is the incorporation of theory and client information to formulate connections that explicate the client's presenting concerns and possibilities for positive change related to these concerns. Wellness-based client conceptualization fosters an understanding of the client's presenting problems and goals. We include the words "presenting goals" because clients may want to explore strengthening different domains of their well-being or bolstering their wellness for prevention purposes. In wellness counseling, we focus on presenting goals through applying a wellness lens. Wellness models help transform assessment information into maps of contributing dynamics among wellness areas underlying the concerns that led the client to seek or be referred to counseling. Wellness models can be used alone in conceptualizing the client or in conjunction with other theories that aid in understanding the client.

The topics in this chapter range from initial steps of the wellness assessment (e.g., collaborating with the client to establish an agreed on definition of wellness) to transforming the assessment into a client conceptualization. The use of formal and informal wellness assessment is described, as is an approach for wellness-based conceptualization. Wellness assessment for clients in crisis and multicultural considerations are also discussed.

Co-Creating Definitions of Holistic and Domain-Specific Wellness With Your Client

The wellness assessment begins with the informed consent process. The wellness counselor should emphasize his or her use of a wellness perspective on the informed consent form. In reviewing the informed consent with your client, this is an excellent opportunity to explain what wellness counseling entails. Here is a sample blurb that you can include in your informed consent:

> My approach to counseling is grounded in holistic wellness. This means that I inquire about different aspects that make up your life and that you believe contribute to making you well or less well. These sometimes include mental wellness, body wellness, spirit wellness, emotional wellness, and connection wellness. My view is that imbalance or deficits in one of more these areas may be related to your presenting concern. I also believe that by identifying and mobilizing your wellness strengths, we will be well equipped to address the concerns that led you to seek counseling. Within this wellness framework, I use additional counseling approaches, including _____. This wellness

approach is also focused on prevention: In other words, sustaining wellness can reduce your risk of future mental and medical problems. Should you have further questions about my wellness counseling approach, do not hesitate to ask.

It is possible that clients may have misconceptions or questions about wellness counseling and assessment; hence, the informed consent process provides a space for further discussion. For instance, prospective clients may want to know what differentiates wellness counseling from fitness coaching or counseling in general. In the next section, the wellness assessment process is described.

During the assessment process, it is important to inquire about different aspects of well-being, whether you use the five domains from this book as a guide or a wellness model of your choice. You will want to learn about the client's history across the various wellness components, examples of times when his or her well-being was highest, and instances when wellness was at its lowest. The counselor should also discuss wellness areas most affected by the presenting concern. To accomplish this, the counselor should start by providing a definition of wellness. We have used Myers, Sweeney, and Witmer's (2000) wellness definition listed in Chapter 1. Read Practitioner Spotlight 9.1, written by Cirecie A. West-Olatunji, because it is a powerfully informative anecdote illustrating the significance of ascertaining the client's definition of wellness.

Cirecie A. West-Olatunji's story reminds the wellness counselor to first ask the following questions:

- What does wellness mean to you?
- How do you define wellness?
- What does being well look like for you?

You should then present a diagram of the five domains of wellness or a wellness model of your choice and information on each wellness domain so that the client and counselor can experience it visually. The Five-Domain Model of Wellness is pictured in Figure 9.1.

When using the Five-Domain Model of Wellness, the subcomponents of each wellness domain can be co-created by the client with help from the counselor. If the client is unsure what could compose certain domains, the counselor provides sample definitions of that wellness area and factors that can be a part of each domain. We have included a definition for each wellness domain in their respective chapters. The counselor can elaborate on the range of definitional possibilities to spark ideas and understanding for the client. For

Practitioner Spotlight 9.1

Reflection

Cirecie A. West-Olatunji

As we think about counseling and wellness, it is important to realize that the concept of wellness can have different meanings and context outside of Eurocentric norms. I know this all too well as a multicultural counseling scholar and from my own lived experiences as an African American female. I, as well as other multicultural scholars, have long asserted the need to expand our conceptualization of wellness to include diverse worldviews and values. This issue became all too apparent during a visit to Turkey several years ago.

In 2013, as president-elect of the American Counseling Association, I was sitting on a panel in Istanbul at the International Association for the Advancement of Counselling conference to discuss the current issues of counseling and professional identity. I had prepared my presentation for the 10 or so minutes to offer perspectives from my association. However, as I sat listening to the other panelists share their views, I had a moment in which I reflected on how distinctly Western our views were. Coupled with that, from where we were seated, we could look through the windows of the auditorium to see the Blue Mosque, the great wall, and the sea. I was struck by the antiquity of it all. The Blue Mosque, built in the early 1600s, was shimmering ethereally—a smoky blue in the afternoon sun; moreover, the Bosphorus Strait that connects the Black Sea and the Sea of Marmara separating Asia and Europe was glistening a cobalt blue. I could even see a bit of the ancient city walls build by Constantine in the 6th century. My first thoughts were of marvel and grace. I felt honored to be in the presence of living history. Then, I felt concern about bringing intellectually adolescent concepts to Istanbul, a city that contains deeper truths than the New World has ever experienced. I thought, "Shouldn't they be the panelists, explaining to us what counseling is and could be?"

So, when it was my turn to speak, I abandoned my prepared 10-minute speech to, instead, address the here and now. I spoke about the need to incorporate language and meanings from other societies that would give broader, deeper, historical conceptualizations to humanism. I suggested that, when thinking about multicultural counseling, counselors from the United States often pride ourselves on our pluralistic society in contrast to many other nations that have less diverse citizenry. Yet, when we consider people of Istanbul, who have for centuries straddled the East and the West, we must acknowledge that they know something about coexistence, collaboration, and cultural competence. It is only in our cultural privilege, our world dominance, that we insist on defining, in this case, wellness and counselor identity. Today, as I did several years ago, I assert that it is time that we open our minds to a true exchange and dialogue about the present and future of counseling globally. Only then can we get to deeper truths and advance the discipline of counseling and wellness to meet the needs of diverse clients.

● ● ●

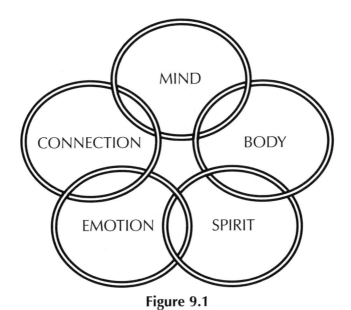

Figure 9.1

Five-Domain Model of Wellness

example, the counselor might state that *spirit wellness* can include a sense of meaning and purpose, one's religious life whether related to faith community experiences or personal prayer, one's sense of connectedness to the universe or environment, personal spiritual activities or experiences, and so forth.

One way to ensure comprehension of the chosen wellness model and that the client's views of wellness are accurately represented is to elicit examples from the client. Hence, if we are talking about *mind wellness*, we can ask the client for an example of an activity or a time when they experienced this domain. Always allot opportunities for the client to ask questions. We recommend that the counselor ask the client whether the wellness domains and factors composing each domain fit for him or her. For wellness models with established definitions, factors, and sub-factors—such as the Indivisible Self model (Myers & Sweeney, 2004)—the counselor should also inquire, "How would you add to or change the definitions, factors, or subfactors?" For the Five-Domain Model of Wellness, the counselor or client should write down the subcomponents for each domain of wellness as perceived by the client.

Critical Concepts in Wellness Psychoeducation During Assessment

The counselor should be clear to explain several important wellness concepts:

1. *Interconnectedness/holism.* This idea posits that each wellness domain does not exist in a vacuum. They each affect and are affected by each other. The implications of this concept are multiple: When one experiences wellness deficits in one or more areas, this shortfall can negatively affect other areas. Ask the client whether they can identify an example of this occurrence in his or her own life. A positive implication is that increases in one or more areas of wellness can perpetuate increases in other areas of wellness.

2. *Small changes can yield large results.* Because of the holistic nature of wellness, one can make a small change in one area of wellness, and that can lead to positive changes not only in that area of wellness but in others.

3. *Strengths are as important as struggles.* Explain to your client that the literature on strengths cannot be overlooked. Similar to reinforcement being more effective than punishment, cultivating strengths and addressing problems by using one's strengths can be helpful.

4. *Life balance discussion.* Find a metaphor to discuss how balance in each wellness domain is needed or else the client may fall out of balance in life. One metaphor used is that of the mobile that you put over a child's crib. After one portion of the mobile dips to one side, the whole balance of the mobile gets thrown off. As Myers and Sweeney (2006) have noted, it is not possible to achieve perfect wellness, yet in seeking to do this, we may live a more balanced life.

Assessing Wellness Strengths and Goals

Now that we have a mutually agreed upon model of wellness, counselor and client must increase the level of clarity about the client's perceived levels of wellness holistically and across domains. Using scaling questions can be beneficial here to assess levels across factors. Ask the client to rate his or her current overall level of wellness and domain-specific wellness on a 1–5 or 1–10 scale (Myers & Sweeney, 2005a). Ask the client to explain his or her ratings. Inquire about the *lowest* that the rating has been in the past (you can specify past year, past 5 years, or lifetime). This question often connects with information about trauma or challenging life events or issues that may still affect the client today. Use discretion with the depth of exploration here. If the client brings up a past trauma, be mindful about allowing the client to take the lead with how far the conversation goes, possibly needing to slow the client's depth of disclosure, or respecting the client's choice to not elaborate on reasons for his or her lowest ratings.

Inquire about the *highest* that the rating has been in the past (you can specify past year, past 5 years, or lifetime). The responses here are worth their weight in gold. Often, clients will report a high level of domain-specific or overall wellness at some point in their life. It is now your job as the counselor to explore this further and build on it. Hence, you will want to use prompts and ask questions such as the following:

- What were you doing differently then that resulted in this wellness area being higher?
- Can you share a story about a wellness "success" from this time and what it means to you (Randolph, Hermann-Turner, & Fullen, 2017)?
- What has changed that your wellness level in this area has since declined?
- What lessons can you carry forward from that time in your life that might help you increase your wellness in this area today?

Another solution-focused technique is to uncover the strengths within reports of lower wellness. For instance, if the client notes that his or her wellness is a 4 out of 10, the counselor could reply, "Tell me about your reasons for rating a 4 and not a 3?" As you begin the goal-setting process, you can query what the client would like to attain for a goal wellness level and his or her ideas for steps toward achieving that level.

You can next explore the impact of the client's levels of well-being across domains on his or her presenting problem or goal (Clarke, Adams, Wilkerson, & Shaw, 2016). You can ask interaction questions such as the following: "How have any struggles with spirit wellness factored into your depression? On the other side, how have your spirit wellness strengths affected your depression?" Be sure to ultimately ask the client how his or her level of holistic wellness is connected to the presenting concern. The purpose of this step is both one of consciousness raising for the client and gathering assessment information for counselor and client. It also reinforces the point that all wellness domains are interwoven. For instance, the client may note that challenges in his or her ability to exercise or eat healthy meals have contributed to increased daily worry and anxiety. A client may disclose that he or she was sexually assaulted 1 year ago and has felt disconnected and disgusted by his or her body since that time. You might ask, "Have your body wellness challenges negatively affected other wellness domains for you?" Perhaps the client has been avoiding looking in the mirror, because whenever they see the reflection, negative automatic thoughts start spiraling, affecting mind wellness.

Perhaps the client's connection wellness is off balance because they have stopped going to yoga class with a friend because of not feeling comfortable in his or her own skin.

Whenever you use interaction questions, you can begin exploring interconnections among the areas of wellness that might yield important information that would not come up if you only asked about wellness domains in isolation. This information aids the counselor's conceptualization of the client—the ability to identify causative factors and their interplay. Remember to also explore the other side of things. Process with the client his or her strengths in each area and how that may moderate the negative impact of the presenting concern. Continuing the example, perhaps the client who feels low body wellness following assault is able to identify a good core network of friends who have supported him or her since the trauma, thus citing connection wellness as a strength.

You could use that strength in one domain to help lift up another. Maybe the client would agree to attend a yoga class with one of his or her close friends. This experience would help him or her learn breath work to use when automatic negative thoughts creep in and offer a new way of connecting back with his or her body through the physical postures of the practice. Exploring domain interactions can help the counselor and client hone the focus of their treatment targets during treating planning, using the strengths the client already has.

The wellness pie activity is a creative way to assess wellness, engage visual processors, and interact with children or adults (Myers, Clarke, Brown, & Champion, 2012). If one were using the five wellness domains, the client draws each component to the size of its proportion in a pie with five slices. Specifically, strong areas of wellness are reflected in a larger slice of pie, and weaker areas are represented by smaller pieces of pie. Observing and thinking about one's high and low areas of wellness by seeing its image on the page may be informative for the client and may precipitate positive change. The wellness pie for the client in our case example is pictured in Figure 9.2. What initial inferences can you make about the client's well-being based on his or her wellness pie?

Wellness Measures

Ideally, your informal wellness assessment can be paired with formal wellness assessments. Wellness assessments fall into two general categories: domain specific and holistic. Domain-specific wellness assessments can be most helpful when examining wellness areas

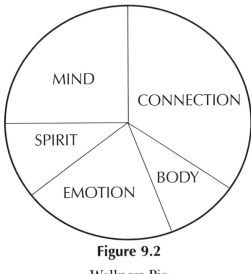

Figure 9.2

Wellness Pie

of struggle for the client or wellness goal areas. They may or may not corroborate the results of your informal wellness domain assessment. These measures will provide a specific and more detailed starting point for your treatment planning and can add context or detail to your understanding of the wellness deficit. Holistic wellness measures can be more difficult to obtain. These measures include some sort of general, overall, or total wellness score (and can also include domain-specific scores).

The Five Factor Wellness Inventory (Myers & Sweeney, 2014) is one of the most comprehensive wellness assessments, and the Perceived Wellness Survey (Adams, Bezner, & Steinhardt, 1997) is also highly used. Other wellness assessments can be found in the positive psychology and quality of life literature. Whenever administering a formal wellness assessment, the principles of effective assessment still apply. Take time to debrief results with the client, and ask what findings the client agrees with and which ones do not fit for him or her (Miller, Forcehimes, & Zweben, 2011; Miller & Rollnick, 2012; Myers & Sweeney, 2005a, 2006). Table 9.1 contains an abbreviated list of wellness assessments.

Balancing Wellness and Clinical Assessments

One beneficial assessment technique described by Clarke et al. (2016) and Myers et al. (2012) is to integrate clinical and wellness measures during the assessment process. After a client has completed

Table 9.1

Wellness Assessments

Assessment Type	Reference
Holistic	
Five Factor Wellness Inventory	Myers & Sweeney (2005b)
Perceived Wellness Survey	Adams et al. (1997)
Quality of Life Enjoyment and Satisfaction Questionnaire–Short Form	Endicott et al. (1993)
Body wellness	
Global Physical Activity Questionnaire	World Health Organization (n.d.)
Godin Leisure-Time Exercise Questionnaire	Godin & Shephard (1997)
Connection wellness	
Social Connectedness Scale	Lee & Robbins (1995)
Multidimensional Scale of Perceived Social Support	Zimet et al. (1988)
Emotional wellness	
Emotion Regulation Questionnaire	Gross & John (2003)
Heartland Forgiveness Scale	Thompson et al. (2005)
Scale of Positive and Negative Experience	Diener et al. (2009)
Subjective Happiness Scale	Lyubomirsky & Lepper (1999)
Mind wellness	
Philadelphia Mindfulness Questionnaire	Cardaciotto et al. (2008)
Self-Regulation Questionnaire	Brown et al. (1999)
Spirit	
Daily Spiritual ExperiencesScale	Underwood & Teresi (2002)
Meaning in Life Questionnaire	Steger et al. (2006)
Spiritual Intelligence Self-Report Inventory	King (2008)

the assessment battery of both clinical (e.g., Beck Depression Inventory—II; Beck, Steer, & Brown, 1996) and wellness (e.g., Five Factor Wellness Inventory; Myers & Sweeney, 2014) assessments, the counselor should ask the client to place a star or other mark next to two or three questions on the clinical assessments that are causing him or her the most problem as it relates to the presenting concern(s). The counselor then processes with the client how the items the client marked are affecting each domain of wellness and the client's overall well-being. Subsequently, the counselor explores with the client ways in which wellness deficits have factored into or exacerbated the client's presenting issue. The risk of this process is that the client becomes discouraged by noticing the multiple areas that are being affected by the presenting concern. The key, if the counselor notices this outcome, is to then shift the client's focus to the *interconnection* notion that addressing small aspects of the presenting concern and wellness can cause benefits to multiple areas of wellness and improve the client's presenting concern. Additionally, the counselor should engage the client in dialogue about strengths identified in the wellness assessment that may be helpful in addressing issues related to the clinical items noted by the client. This dialogue raises the client's awareness about interconnection, the importance of strengths, resources to address the presenting concern, and the impact of the presenting concern.

Multicultural Considerations

It is critical to meet your clients where they are. A significant part of this method is understanding and respecting the personal culture of the client and making considerations for how a wellness counseling approach fits. One of the benefits of a wellness approach is that it may be at a lower risk of being as culturally encapsulated as other approaches. This result is because wellness or wellness domains are concepts that exist in some form in many cultures (Pesek, Helton, & Nair, 2006). Pesek et al. (2006) stated that, "There are several themes regarding cultural traditions on health and wellness that illustrate the understanding that the health and wellness of an individual are reliant on the integrated effects of mind, body, and spirit" (p. 114).

Additionally, the client is empowered to define wellness in ways that fit for him or her. The client is encouraged to remove any domains of wellness that do not fit for him or her and to define the components of the different areas of wellness. However, it is imperative that the counselor obtains the client's definitions of wellness and wellness domains. The idea of interconnectedness may resonate more with certain cultures than others (D'Andrea & Daniels, 2012). Furthermore, given that each client has his or her own unique personal culture, the salience of each domain of wellness will differ from client to client. Clients who hold a collectivist worldview may experience the concept of wellness differently than a client who values individualism.

One critique that we have heard from clinicians is that wellness is not clinically relevant to clients whose basic needs are not being met—for example, clients who are struggling with chronic homelessness and food insecurity or who are living pay check to pay check. Wellness is co-constructed between counselor and client. The true author of the client's wellness is the client. Our five-domain model provides a potentially useful structure for framing wellness discussions with all clients, because it is our belief that working toward wellness should be a right of all people, not just those with privilege.

Indeed, at its core, wellness counseling is about honoring and valuing all individuals by seeing them for who they are and the strengths they have, not simply their deficits. The client who is barely making ends meet may need help conceptualizing how to mobilize the task-based social support (connection wellness) of family members or friends to help with child care so they can work an overtime shift. The refugee client may benefit from connecting with a local community center that offers group fitness to find grounding and connection among his or her mind, body, and new home. Finally, the expectant mom who is experiencing preterm labor complications for no medical reason other than the chronic stress that comes with expecting racism and poverty on a daily basis could find small moments of peace and solace through guided meditation and stress-reduction techniques.

Wellness-Based Client Conceptualization

Client conceptualization is the link between assessment and treatment planning. It involves the counselor looking for patterns, piecing together information, and testing hypotheses to paint a picture of the client's life. That painting should include the colors of the client's strengths as well as his or her struggles. Wellness-based client conceptualization ensures that we paint the picture of the whole client rather than one portion of the painting. A wellness orientation informs the counselor that each client is composed of multiple components of wellness that, when combined, are more than the sum of their parts—similar to a whole painting being more powerful than even a well done corner of a piece of art.

Completing the wellness model with the client will result in the counselor already having much of the painting filled in. Therefore, the first step is examining the wellness-related information we know. The counselor will want to ask him- or herself reflective questions for building a wellness-based case conceptualization, such as the ones below:

1. How are the client's wellness deficits feeding the presenting problem?
2. What specific domains are having the most negative impact on the presenting problem?
3. What aspects of wellness are being most negatively affected by the presenting problem?
4. What are the client's greatest wellness strengths?
5. What wellness victories did the client report that may be helpful in understanding the client and addressing the presenting concern?

6. What wellness information do we need to find out more about?
7. At what levels of importance, confidence, and readiness is the client, to make a change?
8. What barriers to wellness exist?
9. What wellness resources does the client possess?
10. What patterns of wellness problems have occurred in the client's life?
11. How do the client's culture and context interact with his or her wellness and the presenting concern?
12. Does a clinical diagnosis need to be made?

When conducting your wellness-based client conceptualization, you can proceed through each of the aforementioned questions and build your conceptualization of the client. Remember that because wellness is a framework for counseling, other theories can be applied in the assessment process. We like to think of wellness assessment and conceptualization as the starting point. After the dynamics among the wellness areas and the presenting problem/goal are identified, the counselor's preferred theories can be the next lens for funneling to understand the client. Using an integrative perspective, the counselor can use the wellness assessment results to target the best theory for further explaining the client's concerns. For instance, if the client's challenges or goals revolve around family conflict infiltrating several wellness domains, additional conceptualization through a family systems theory might be prudent.

Benefits of Wellness Assessment

It is often overlooked that assessment *is* an intervention. An effective holistic wellness assessment fulfills this notion. A substantial part of wellness assessment is about *enhancing awareness* and *motivation for change*. A wellness assessment may be one of the first times the client has reflected on him- or herself holistically. Assessment can be misunderstood as a tool for the counselor, which is limiting. Through the wellness assessment, the goal is for the client to become more aware of where they have balance in life. Additionally, the client becomes increasingly aware of his or her strengths and resources. This experience can be empowering and eye-opening for the client. The assessment experience can be particularly therapeutic for clients who have low self-esteem, who are focused predominantly on certain areas of their lives to the exclusion of others, and who have been disempowered by people or systems. For instance, the client who is being physically and emotionally abused may gain a lot from giving attention to his or her strengths. This client's awareness of the negative impact of the abuse may be heightened through the wellness assessment process, which eventually may prompt steps for him or her to leave the toxic relationship.

A motivating component of the assessment is the client learning that *small changes can yield large results.* Clients can get stuck in negative behaviors because of the belief that large changes need to be made for positive results to occur. The wellness model shows the beneficial and balancing effects that one change in one subcomponent of wellness can have. The wellness assessment process is highly valuable to the counselor who may be at risk of viewing the client myopically and missing key aspects of the client's well-being. I (Phil) can think of several times when I have neglected to explore the client's spirituality with enough depth, for example.

Wellness facilitates a clear and motivational path for tracking client progress via ongoing assessment. When the counselor uses a wellness model for assessment and conceptualization, counselor and client can observe and experience domain-specific and holistic changes that manifest in the client's life. The client will notice, for example, that the number of strengths on his or her wellness map have increased or that the strengths that were small have become large ones. This process can also happen with the domains and holistic wellness. Clients' motivation tends to increase as they notice improvement in areas of wellness and overall well-being or decreases in the impact of clinical symptoms. When clients become stuck or motivation declines, a wellness model can serve as a "road map" for getting unstuck and for reminding the client of progress and strengths. This information might be one of the few things keeping the client motivated during a dark time.

Applying Wellness Concepts With Clients in Crisis

The notion of wellness counseling and wellness assessment as an approach for working with clients in crisis may seem inappropriate or even unethical to some. We contend that aspects of wellness counseling can be appropriately used to inform your assessment, conceptualization, and coping plan for clients in crisis. From a wellness perspective, a client is experiencing a mental health crisis when a major deficit occurs in one or more of the five wellness domains, overwhelming the client. If overall wellness were represented by a balance beam lying peacefully and perfectly balanced in the middle, crisis is represented by the balance beam tipping completely in one direction because of loss of wellness in multiple areas, leading to a resounding thud of the balance beam striking the ground. The wellness assessment processes and questions are not necessarily appropriate for a client in acute crisis. Using a crisis assessment that has a holistic perspective is appropriate. The Triage Assessment System (Myer, Williams, Ottens, & Schmidt, 1992) is one such example because it is composed of a structure that is similar to the Five-Domain Model of Wellness. However, the assessment prompts are specific to gathering information about the client's crisis state (Myer & Conte, 2006). Wellness counseling interventions can be used to facilitate writing a coping plan for the client in crisis.

During the short-term holistic assessment process with a client in crisis, the counselor will want to identify the client's strengths. Even in a crisis situation, some aspects of wellness remain intact. The counselor must tap into these in a more directive way with the client who may be struggling with executive functioning in the moment. Wellness interventions can be used whether the client is in crisis or ongoing counseling. The wellness model provides a helpful reminder of strengths to identify and incorporate into the crisis coping plan. It can be useful to make sure to consider each wellness domain.

For instance, with a client who is having suicidal thoughts related to depression and the recent breakup of a romantic relationship, the counselor and client may (a) identify soothing self-talk to use as part of the safety plan when the client experiences nonconstructive cognitions (mind wellness), (b) link the client to several friends and family members as well as a crisis hotline to combat feelings of loss and loneliness and increase safety (connection wellness), or (c) build in pleasant body wellness activities to use as distractors, such as taking a bath or going for a walk. If a spiritual wellness practice such as prayer is helpful, that can be added. Some clients may benefit from attending a place of worship, speaking with their spiritual leader, or engaging in a meaningful activity in which they lose themselves (Csikszentmihalyi, 1990) or that connects them to the universe or personal meaning. An emotion wellness part of the crisis plan can entail pinpointing ways to mute painful emotions when needed (Murphy & Dillon, 2011).

Between-sessions conceptualization can be done through the Five-Domain Model of Wellness or another model. It is more appropriate to conduct the type of wellness assessment that is described in this chapter after the client is stabilized. In concluding this chapter, you now have a greater sense of the value and skills needed to be effective in wellness assessment. We encourage you to review the discussion prompts, activities, resources, and handouts on this topic.

Conclusion

Wellness assessment is a multifaceted process. The counselor must be adept at administering wellness measures, integrating clinical assessments and diagnostic information, and identifying client strengths and challenges. These pieces form a holistic perspective of the client, leading client and counselor into the intervention phases. When done successfully, the assessment inspires insight and motivation from the client. Wellness assessments are diverse in their utility, given that they serve a purpose for both clients in crisis and not in crisis.

Reflection Prompts

1. What do you believe are the benefits of wellness assessment? What are the biggest challenges involved in wellness assessment?
2. Find and review one of the wellness or related assessments listed in this book. Complete this wellness assessment. Did the results seem accurate? How could incorporating this assessment with a client be helpful or not helpful? What considerations are needed when administering wellness assessments to clients? How might this assessment be helpful in your work with clients? Review the literature and identify a wellness assessment not listed in this book.
3. Identify your own creative approach for informally assessing wellness in children and adolescents using the guidelines presented in this chapter. What steps would be involved? In what ways would your approach be similar to or different than wellness assessment with adults?
4. In what ways do you currently incorporate formal or informal wellness assessment into your work with clients? In what ways can you begin incorporating wellness assessment into your work with clients?

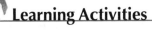

Learning Activities

TV Break Part I

Watch an episode of a television show or a movie clip with a character dealing with a life stressor or mental health issue. Use the Five-Domain Model of Wellness or a model of your choice as your lens for conceptualizing this person or character. How do the wellness areas affect each other? What are the reciprocal relationships among the client's presenting problem and wellness domains? Go through all of the relevant conceptualization questions that were described in the chapter.

TV Break Part II

Practice incorporating another theory within the wellness structure for conceptualizing the "client" from the TV Break Part I activity. Explain your rationale for selecting the theory that you did. Write out or present your full assessment and conceptualization of the client.

Peer Practice

Conduct a wellness assessment on a peer from your counseling class. Consider incorporating both a wellness measure and an informal assessment.

Reverse Case Example

See Handout 2 for instructions.

Wellness Self-Assessment

Complete a formal wellness assessment (e.g., Five Factor Wellness Inventory) and an informal wellness assessment such as the wellness pie activity (use Handout 3) or scaling questions. Reflect on what you learned about your own wellness and about conducting a wellness assessment from this experience. What surprised you about your self-assessment results?

Handout 1
Assessment Questions for the Five-Domain Model of Wellness

1. What does wellness mean to you? How do you define wellness?

2. What are the factors that make you well or less well in mind, body, spirit, emotion, and connection?

3. On the back of this handout, rate your overall level of wellness on a 1–10 scale. Do the same for each of the mind, body, spirit, emotion, and connection domains (with 1 = *lowest possible wellness* and 10 = *highest possible wellness*). As you look at your ratings, what surprises you? What did you learn?

(continued)

Handout 1 *(continued)*

4. Which areas of wellness have increased or decreased over the past year? What are some possible reasons for these changes? What did you do differently that resulted in any wellness increases? *(Note:* Identify a specific wellness success story from the past year.)

5. Looking at your current wellness levels, in what ways has the concern that brought you to counseling affected your mind, body, spirit, emotion, connection, and overall wellness? Which domains of your well-being have been most affected? Please explain.

6. Looking at your current wellness levels, in what ways have any domains in which your wellness is lower had an impact on the concern that brought you to counseling? Identify at least one example.

7. Identify at least one wellness strength and one way in which it might be helpful in addressing the concern that brought you to counseling.

8. By the time our work together is concluded, what is one positive change you would like to make in addressing the concern that brought you to counseling? Identify at least one way in which this positive change would improve your mind, body, spirit, emotion, connection, and overall wellness.

Handout 2
Reverse Case Example

Create a fictitious case example based on the wellness pie below. The case example should include (1) describing the client's background and presenting concern, (2) stating how the presenting concern has affected the wellness domains, (3) identifying how wellness deficits may have worsened the presenting concern, (4) highlighting details about the client's strengths, (5) stating ideas for how the client's strengths could be mobilized to address the presenting concern, and (6) identifying 2–3 measurable wellness counseling goals based on your responses to Prompts 1–5. The purpose of this activity is to hone your skills in wellness assessment and conceptualization.

(continued)

Handout 3 *(continued)*
Wellness Pie

Complete the wellness pie activity using the circle figure below. Draw each of the five wellness domains to the size of its proportion in your life. Specifically, strong areas of wellness are reflected in a larger slice of pie, and weaker areas of wellness are represented by smaller pieces of pie. Reflect on what you learned about your own wellness and about conducting a wellness assessment from this experience. What surprised you about your self-assessment results?

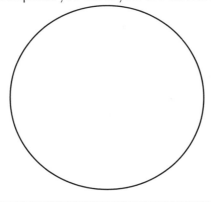

Resources

Center for Disease Control and Prevention—
Workplace Health Promotion

https://www.cdc.gov/workplacehealthpromotion/model/assessment/index.html

Assessments and interventions for fostering organizational wellness are included on this webpage and its various links.

National Wellness Institute Six Dimensions of Wellness

http://www.nationalwellness.org/page/Six_Dimensions

A wellness model that may be useful in work with clients is the Six Dimensions of Wellness. Details about the model are linked to this webpage.

References

Adams, T., Bezner, J., & Steinhardt, M. (1997). The conceptualization and measurement of perceived wellness: Integrating balance across and within dimensions. *American Journal of Health Promotion, 11*, 208–218.

Beck, A. T., Steer, R. A., & Brown, G. K. (1996). *Manual for the Beck Depression Inventory—II*. San Antonio, TX: Psychological Corporation.

Brown, J. M., Miller, W. R., & Lawendowski, L. A. (1999). The self-regulation questionnaire. In L. Vande Creek & T. L. Jackson (Eds.), *Innovations in clinical practice: A source book* (Vol. 17, pp. 281–289). Sarasota, FL: Professional Resource Press.

Cardaciotto, L., Herbert, J. D., Forman, E. M., Moitra, E., & Farrow, V. (2008). The assessment of present-moment awareness and acceptance: The Philadelphia Mindfulness Scale. *Assessment, 15*, 204–223.

Clarke, P. B., Adams, J. A., Wilkerson, J., & Shaw, E. G. (2016). Wellness-based counseling for caregivers of persons with dementia. *Journal of Mental Health Counseling, 38*, 263–277.

Csikszentmihalyi, M. (1990). *Flow: The psychology of optimal experience.* New York, NY: Harper and Row.

D'Andrea, M., & Daniels, J. (2012). Humanism and multiculturalism. In M. B. Scholl, A. S. McGowan, & J. T. Hansen (Eds.), *Humanistic perspectives on contemporary counseling issues* (pp. 45–62). New York, NY: Routledge.

Diener, E., Wirtz, D., Tov, W., Kim-Prieto, C., Choi, D., Oishi, S., & Biswas-Diener, R. (2010). New measures of well-being: Flourishing and positive and negative feelings. *Social Indicators Research, 39*, 247–266.

Endicott, J., Nee, J., Harrison, W., & Blumenthal, R. (1993). Quality of Life Enjoyment and Satisfaction Questionnaire: A new measure. *Psychopharmacology Bulletin, 29*, 321–326.

Godin, G., & Shephard, R. J. (1997). Godin leisure-time exercise questionnaire. *Medicine and Science in Sports and Exercise, 29*(Suppl.), S36–S38.

Gross, J. J., & John, O. P. (2003). Individual differences in two emotion regulation processes: Implications for affect, relationships, and well-being. *Journal of Personality and Social Psychology, 85*, 348–362.

Hays, D. G. (2017). *Assessment in counseling: Procedures and practices* (6th ed.). Alexandria, VA: American Counseling Association.

King, D. B. (2008). *Rethinking claims of spiritual intelligence: A definition, model, and measure* (Unpublished master's thesis). Trent University, Peterborough, Ontario, Canada.

Lee, R. M., & Robbins S. B. (1995). Measuring belongingness: The Social Connectedness and the Social Assurance Scales. *Journal of Counseling Psychology, 42*, 232–241.

Lyubomirsky, S., & Lepper, H. S. (1999). A measure of subjective happiness: Preliminary reliability and construct validation. *Social Indicators Research, 46*, 137–155.

Miller, W. R., Forcehimes, A. A., & Zweben, A. (2011). *Treating addiction: A guide for professionals.* New York, NY: Guilford Press.

Miller, W. R., & Rollnick, S. (2012). *Motivational interviewing: Helping people change* (3rd ed.). New York, NY: Guilford Press.

Murphy, B. C., & Dillon, C. (2011). *Interviewing in action in a multicultural world* (4th ed.). Belmont, CA: Brooks/Cole.

Myer, R. A., & Conte, C. (2006). Assessment for crisis intervention. *Journal of Clinical Psychology, 62,* 959–970.

Myer, R. A., Williams, R. C., Ottens, A. J., & Schmidt, A. E. (1992). Crisis assessment: A three-dimensional model for triage. *Journal of Mental Health Counseling, 14,* 137–148.

Myers, J. E., Clarke, P. B., Brown, J. B., & Champion, D. A. (2012). Wellness: Theory, research, and applications for counselors. In M. B. Scholl, A. S. McGowan, & J. T. Hansen (Eds.), *Humanistic perspectives on contemporary counseling issues* (pp. 17–44). New York, NY: Routledge.

Myers, J. E., & Sweeney, T. J. (2004). The Indivisible Self: An evidence-based model of wellness. *Journal of Individual Psychology, 60,* 234–244.

Myers, J. E., & Sweeney, T. J. (Eds.). (2005a). Assessing wellness: Formal and informal approaches. In *Counseling for wellness: Theory, research, and practice* (pp. 39–42). Alexandria, VA: American Counseling Association.

Myers, J. E., & Sweeney, T. J. (2005b). *The five factor wellness inventory.* Menlo Park, CA: Mind Garden.

Myers, J. E., & Sweeney, T. J. (2006). *The wellness and habit change workbook.* Greensboro, NC: Author.

Myers, J. E., & Sweeney, T. J. (2014). *Five Factor Wellness Inventory (FF-WEL): Adult, teenage, and elementary school versions.* Menlo Park, CA: Mind Garden.

Myers, J. E., Sweeney, T. J., & Witmer, J. M. (2000). The Wheel of Wellness counseling for wellness: A holistic model for treatment planning. *Journal of Counseling & Development, 78,* 251–266.

Pesek, T. J., Helton, L. R., & Nair, M. (2006). Healing across cultures: Learning from traditions. *EcoHealth, 3,* 114–118.

Randolph, A., Hermann-Turner, K., & Fullen, M. (2017, July). *Wellness and resilience.* Session presented at the Association for Adult Development and Aging Annual Conference, New York, NY.

Steger, M. F., Frazier, P., Oishi, S., & Kaler, M. (2006). The Meaning in Life Questionnaire: Assessing the presence of and search for meaning in life. *Journal of Counseling Psychology, 53,* 80–93.

Thompson, L. Y., Snyder, C. R., Hoffman, L., Michael, S. T., Rasmussen, H. N., Billings, L. S., . . . Roberts, D. E. (2005). Dispositional forgiveness of self, others, and situations. *Journal of Personality, 73,* 313–359.

Underwood, L. G., & Teresi, J. A. (2002). The Daily Spiritual Experience Scale: Development, theoretical description, reliability, exploratory factor analysis, and preliminary construct validity using health-related data. *Annals of Behavioral Medicine, 24,* 22–33.

World Health Organization. (n.d.). *Global Physical Activity Questionnaire (GPAQ): Analysis guide.* Retrieved from http://www.who.int/ncds/surveillance/steps/resources/GPAQ_Analysis_Guide.pdf

Zimet, G. D., Dahlem, N. W., Zimet, S. G., & Farley, G. K. (1988). The multidimensional scale of perceived social support. *Journal of Personality Assessment, 52,* 30–41.

Chapter 10

Treatment Planning

If you don't know where you are going,
you'll end up someplace else.

—Yogi Berra

• • •

In this chapter, we include an overview of the three-tiered intervention model (i.e., primary prevention, secondary prevention, tertiary intervention) and how it applies to individuals' wellness. For example, wellness treatment planning at the prevention level frequently involves psychoeducational wellness approaches when compared with tertiary interventions with a client who might be struggling with severe mental health concerns. Tertiary level wellness counseling often merits treatment plans containing behavioral wellness interventions such as psychotropic medication adherence (body wellness) for emotion regulation (emotion wellness). We discuss strategies for collaborating with clients to develop wellness-oriented goals and treatment plans. The chapter also includes a case example of how to develop wellness goals, a treatment plan template, a learning activity, discussion prompts, and resources to use in practice.

The idea of wellness may appear to be a concept that is most applicable to clients who are already functioning at a high level and who may be labeled "growth seekers." Although we believe this can be the case and are advocates for prevention, we also believe an integrative wellness framework is applicable for all clients. We conceptualize treatment from the prevention model (i.e., primary, secondary, tertiary) described by multiple authors (Caplan, 1964; Capuzzi & Gross, 2019; World Health Organization, 2002). Although this model is often used to describe approaches to disease prevention related to physical health, we believe it coincides well with mental health and holistic wellness promotion. *Primary prevention* includes interventions targeted to the general public or the population as a whole. Some examples include school counselors providing psychoeducation to each class in a school on stress management or a college counseling center conducting workshops on college student well-being. *Secondary prevention* is focused on early identification of risk for a problem and intervention to prevent the problem from developing further. As an example, a pediatrician may require mothers to complete depression screenings during their child's well visit. The physician might refer a new mother to counseling and provide her with coping resources after she reports relatively mild feelings of sadness. The counselor may work with the mother to develop a holistic plan to help prevent depression from occurring. *Tertiary prevention* refers to interventions that are implemented after a problem has occurred, with a goal of rehabilitation and to prevent the problem from worsening.

There is some controversy related to the interdisciplinary concept of prevention, particularly about how prevention is differentiated from mental health promotion. The prevention model works well in relation to medical disorders, but it is hard to apply to mental health because of the multifaceted nature of how mental health concerns develop. Some theorists combine prevention for predictable problems with promoting wellness in the same category (Bloom & Gullota, 2003). Other authors believe primary prevention consists of promoting protective factors for groups that are at a greater risk (Mrazek & Haggerty, 1994). We view the process similarly to the World Health Organization, in that we believe prevention and promotion can be simultaneous and complementary activities. This concept is especially true related to mental health because it challenges to identify all the factors an individual is experiencing at a given time that may place him or her at risk.

Although some of the treatment planning processes may be similar at each level of prevention, client goals and intervention strategies may differ significantly in terms of intensity, duration, and monitoring. For example, an individual who receives services at the primary prevention level may attend a workshop and set a single wellness goal specific to healthy eating habits. There may or may not be any follow-up workshops to assess how well the individual followed through with this goal. Conversely, a client at the tertiary level may set several goals on social support, coping, and spirituality to help avoid relapse from an addiction. The counselor and client may check in weekly on goal progress and adjust the interventions accordingly.

Wellness-focused treatment planning is guided by the client's presenting concerns, desired growth areas, and personal goals. Additionally, treatment plans are developed from a holistic and integrated perspective and address all aspects of an individual's functioning. Other terms you might use for this process are wellness plans, intervention plans, or personal growth plans. Some important factors to consider in treatment planning are (a) the client's level of readiness or stage of change; (b) severity of the client's presenting concerns; (c) the client's values and their cultural, religious, and spiritual background; and (d) the available research on effective strategies related to the client's concerns (Barden, Conley, & Young, 2015).

Plans are developed in collaboration with the client and often include consultation with other members of an interdisciplinary team (e.g., primary care physicians, nutritionists, teachers, psychologists). Treatment planning is a continuous process throughout the course of a counseling relationship rather than a one-time activity. Counselors use information from assessments and evaluation to help guide the interventions they implement with clients. Following is a description of the wellness intervention planning process.

Wellness Intervention Planning Process

The following tasks are essential steps in the wellness intervention planning process. Although the tasks are in chronological order, counselors will often have to cycle back through various steps throughout the process:

- Review holistic formal and informal assessment data from the client.
- Discuss the data with the client and process the results.
- Brainstorm specific focus areas.
- Work collaboratively to set mutually agreed upon goals.
- Select appropriate interventions.
- Assess client confidence and commitment to goals.
- Assess goal attainment throughout the relationship.
- Adjust goals as needed.

Most of the practical application in this chapter is related to working with clients at the secondary and tertiary levels, which is primarily facilitated through individual or small group counseling. However, we first review some strategies that can be used at the primary prevention level and can be facilitated through multiple modalities.

Intervention Planning at the Primary Level

As previously mentioned, intervention planning at the primary level may be different than planning at the secondary or tertiary level. Primary prevention is typically done in large groups through workshops, trainings, or web-based formats. As a result, intervention and planning activities at this level typically involve less intimate conversations and goal-setting processes. Sometimes attendees are simply receiving information from a website, and there is no contact. Other times, the workshop is the intervention, and there is no follow-up. Nevertheless, when possible, it is helpful for clients, participants, or consumers to commit to some type of action to get the most out of the information. This process can be as simple as having workshop attendees verbally identify the most important thing they learned and what they will do differently as a result of attending. We prefer to require participants to commit to a goal through a written format. To facilitate goal setting in a psychoeducational format, it can be helpful to include information about how to set a specific, measurable, attainable, realistic, and time-related (S.M.A.R.T.) goal (this topic is discussed later in the chapter). In a large group, it may be helpful to have participants discuss goals together and then share some examples with the large group. It is helpful to provide participants with a goal-setting worksheet, either as a hard copy or through an electronic medium.

Intervention Planning at the Secondary and Tertiary Levels

Transtheoretical Model (TTM)

We believe that the TTM (Prochaska & DiClemente, 1984; Prochaska & Norcross, 2014) provides a helpful framework for counselors when determining the most helpful wellness interventions for clients. The TTM was originally developed to explain behavior changes related to addictions, but it has since been applied to many aspects of behavioral and mental health. The TTM is integrative and draws on aspects of the major counseling theories that are currently available. Two prominent dimensions within the TTM include change processes and stages of change. By matching the change processes (and techniques to facilitate the processes) to the client's stage of change, we can maximize the efficiency of interventions and capitalize on effective strategies of adapting to client readiness.

Change Processes

Change processes consist of how various counseling theories promote change for clients. The processes are strategies people use to modify relationships, thinking, emotions, or behavior in relation to a particular problem. Prochaska and Norcross (2014) identified 10 change processes that are most supported by research:

- Consciousness raising (increasing one's knowledge of self and the problem)
- Catharsis/dramatic relief (experiencing and expressing pent-up feelings about problems and solutions)
- Self-reevaluation (self-assessment about how one thinks and feels about oneself in relation to a problem)
- Environmental reevaluation (modifying one's internal response to external events)
- Self-liberation (awareness of new alternatives and choosing new ways of living)
- Counterconditioning (changing one's behavior in response to stimuli; substituting incompatible behaviors for the problem)
- Stimulus control (changing one's environment; e.g., avoiding environmental triggers)
- Contingency management (reinforcement of behaviors; e.g., rewards for positive behaviors)
- Social liberation (environmental or societal changes that increase options for clients)
- Therapeutic relationship (a strong relationship between the counselor and client)

The change processes are common to many of the counselor theories, with consciousness raising being the most common change process. As you will notice, some of the processes are insight or awareness focused (consciousness raising, catharsis, self-liberation, self-reevaluation), and others are more action oriented (environmental reevaluation, counterconditioning, stimulus control, contingency management). Within the TTM, the processes are emphasized more at various stages of the client's change process. Therapeutic relationship and social liberation are emphasized throughout the course of counseling and are not specific to one stage. In Table 10.1, we include a synthesis of stages, processes, and example interventions.

Stages of Change

The Stages of Change Model (Norcross, Krebs, & Prochaska, 2011) is particularly helpful in assessing the client's readiness to engage in behavioral change within the wellness domains. Authors of the model have pointed out that clients often attend counseling with different perspectives, attitudes, intentions, and behaviors related to their problems and the idea of changing. From a holistic wellness perspective, clients may also be in different stages within the various wellness domains. For example, a client may be willing to address physical wellness but may be unaware that the amount of time they are dedicating to exercise is contributing to a relationship conflict with their partner. Counselors must keep the interconnected and holistic nature of wellness in mind when assessing stage of change for client problems. The model includes five stages: precontemplation, contemplation, preparation, action, and maintenance.

Precontemplation

Clients in the precontemplation stage of change are not aware that a problem exists or may not acknowledge the behaviors that are contributing to a problem. Consequently, these clients are not planning to make any changes in the near future. Clients in this stage are often

Table 10.1

Change Processes and Techniques Emphasized at
Each Stage of Change

Change Process	Stage of Change	Techniques/Interventions
Consciousness raising	Precontemplation to contemplation	Confrontations; reading; awareness exercises
Catharsis/dramatic relief	Precontemplation to contemplation	Role-play; expressive arts
Self-reevaluation	Contemplation	Imagery; value clarification
Environmental reevaluation	Contemplation	Perspective-taking exercises; empathy
Self-liberation	Preparation	Decision-making exercises; commitment-enhancing strategies
Counterconditioning	Action/maintenance	Relaxation; assertiveness training; desensitization
Stimulus control	Action/maintenance	Avoiding high-risk situations; modifying relationships
Contingency management	Action/maintenance	Contingency contracts; self-reward; reinforcement

referred to counseling and may have been coerced by a partner or family member or may be mandated to attend counseling through the legal system. As a result, they may present as disengaged from the change process. A client in this stage may have the mindset that "Everything is fine, I don't need to change anything." For example, a male client who is in counseling for stress also has high cholesterol. The client talks about his busy schedule and reports that he eats a lot of fast food because he is on the go. When conducting a holistic assessment, the client states, "My diet is the least of my worries. I don't have time to cook for myself. That would just add more stress." Clients in this stage tend to need insight-oriented change processes, such as consciousness raising or catharsis, to move to the next stage of change. Working within the body wellness domain, a counselor might encourage the client to read some information on the impact of food on health and mood to help raise his awareness (consciousness raising) about the importance of a healthy diet.

Contemplation

Clients who are in the contemplation stage are aware that a problem exists and are seriously considering making some changes to address the issue. Clients in this stage are typically contemplating how much effort it will take to make a change, but they are hesitant to make a strong commitment to changing. Clients tend to stay in the contemplation stage for a long time. Clients in this stage may acknowledge, "Yeah, I should really do something about this problem." For example, a woman who is invested in her career is starting to realize that her job stress is negatively affecting her family. She comes home irritable and becomes easily frustrated with her kids. She is considering changing something to manage her emotions but is not committed to making any permanent changes. Clients in this stage also benefit from insight and awareness processes, such as consciousness raising, dramatic relief, and self-reevaluation. A counselor working within the heart domain in this stage may use a values checklist (self-reevaluation) to help the client reassess what is most important to her. A counselor could also facilitate a guided imagery to help the client visualize how her family members might feel about her behavior toward them (environmental reevaluation).

Preparation

Clients in the preparation stage are ready to take action in the near future. They may have already started to make small changes or may have gotten things in order to follow through with their primary goals. Clients in this stage need to set specific goals and commit themselves to a firm plan of action. For example, a male client who is committing to improving his physical health has looked into gym memberships and has found a nutritionist to work with to find healthy food options. He now needs to decide what he is going to do for exercise and how he is going to go shopping for the right food to cook. Clients in this stage need to become aware of their choices through the self-liberation change process. A counselor who is helping this client within the body wellness domain in this stage could help the client brainstorm options about what type of physical activity he enjoys doing or is open to trying and then prioritize the list (emphasizing the client's autonomy to choose) and develop an action plan in which he indicates when the activity will take place and who can help him stay accountable (commitment enhancement).

Action

Clients in the action stage have successfully altered their behavior, are overcoming their problems, and report having modified their behavior for 1 day to 6 months. They have the perspective that "I am putting forth a lot of effort in making this change." For example, a female client who has recognized that her stress from school has become overwhelming is actively working on stress-reduction techniques. Clients in this stage tend to benefit most from change processes that are action oriented, such as stimulus control, contingency management, and counterconditioning. A counselor working in the mind wellness domain might teach the client progressive muscle relaxation and encourage the client to attend a mindfulness group (counterconditioning).

Maintenance

Clients who are considered in the maintenance stage have been engaging in new behaviors or have been "problem free" for more than 6 months. These clients are actively working to maintain the positive changes they have made and are avoiding relapse. They may say something such as, "Things are going great, but I want to make sure I continue with this progress." For example, a female client might report that she has really reconnected with her spiritual community, which has helped her reestablish her meaning in life and has also helped her social connection. She has missed the formal service the past couple of weeks because of work responsibilities and wants to make sure she does not fall into a routine of not attending.

Similar to clients in the action stage, clients in the stage benefit most from action-oriented processes, such as counterconditioning, stimulus control, and contingency management. In this example, the counselor working with the client on spirit wellness might help her set healthy boundaries with her employer (assertiveness training), so when she is asked to work on projects, she is able to articulate that she has prior commitments rather than passively agreeing to work (counterconditioning). From a wellness perspective, it is important to attend to this stage with equal consideration as the others. Counselors can help clients identify strengths and capitalize on positive behaviors that may help with success in other areas. The client's spirit wellness is related to other domains (e.g., connection, heart). Maintaining her spirit wellness will also affect these other areas.

We acknowledge that counselors' approach and intervention selection will likely differ on the basis of their theoretical beliefs. The TTM provides an integrative framework that is naturally compatible with a holistic wellness approach. One can address wellness domains from a variety of perspectives, so the emphasis on change processes opens the door for counselors from a variety of approaches to select interventions from multiple sources to best meet clients' wellness needs. Prochaska et al. (2012) found support for the TTM in improving individuals' exercise, stress management, diet, depression risk, physical health, and emotional health. Although there are strengths to using the TTM to facilitate client wellness, there are also special considerations. Clients may not fit cleanly into one stage, particularly when considering multiple wellness domains. Clients often cycle back through the stages after a relapse back to problem behavior, and it is important to normalize this setback to keep clients engaged in the process of change rather than feel discouraged and give up. When conceptualizing clients and selecting interventions, counselors must respect clients' values, worldview, culture, and family influences. There are some instances in which change in a particular area will not be appropriate for a client. For example, just because a client does not practice a particular religion or view spirituality as important does not mean we must raise their consciousness about the importance of spiritual or religious practices. We should assess how important this domain is and help clients work within their own value system. Practitioner Spotlight 10.1 illustrates the application of the TTM.

Practitioner Spotlight 10.1

Ambivalence and Marijuana

Linda Hancock

A female student in her late teens comes to you complaining of "anxiety." She states that she gets nervous in social settings and that it's getting harder to go to class, especially if she needs to do a presentation. As you take her history, you find that her father has lung cancer and alcohol use disorder. Because of this experience, she never drinks alcohol or smokes cigarettes. Her life dream is to become a pharmacist. In struggling with anxiety, she has found that marijuana helps her calm down and focus on homework. She strongly believes that marijuana will soon be legalized in all states and that it is has many medical benefits.

Take a Breath and Ask the "Good Things/Not-So-Good Things" Questions

Health choices related to substances are fraught with ambivalence. Users are often entrenched in their views and have read a lot on the Internet to support those views. As a counselor, it's crucial to be skilled in motivational interviewing. Take a breath and avoid the urge to point out inconsistencies or contrary findings. From a wellness counselor's position, you can certainly see the glaring risk in her family history and you can easily spot the dichotomy between her future goals and her current behavior. However, the power to change lies within the individual. If you voice all the reasons to change, she will have nothing left to say. People mostly believe what comes out of their own mouths. So don't rush in. Strive first to get on the same side of the picture book and understand the client's point of view. Then, get the client to talk through their ambivalence. One of the best ways to understand ambivalence is to ask the "good things/not-so-good things" question. When asking her more about "the good things" marijuana does for her, she says it helps her bond with her boyfriend, focus on her homework, feel good, and fall asleep. When you ask her about the "not-so-good things," she admits that it's getting expensive; her use has increased from occasional to several times a day, and that makes her a little concerned.

Planting Seeds of Nonjudgmental Self-Awareness

Obviously, anxiety management skills are going to be important for this client. So focus on those needs first. However, after starting that process, the marijuana use also needs to be addressed. One way to do this step is to engage her in being an objective "scientific" observer in her own symptoms. Ask her to notice how what she eats and drinks affects her anxiety or panic either immediately or in a delayed fashion. Research shows that the "CATS" (caffeine/cannabis, alcohol, tobacco, sugar/sweeteners) can affect physical sensations and increase anxiety. Some patients even go so far as to check their pulse before and after caffeine or cannabis use. There is a lot of power in nonjudging observation and supportive listening.

• • •

A key aspect of the treatment planning process is collaboration between the counselor and the client (Norcross & Wampold, 2011). Therefore, the counselor and client must work together as a team to implement treatment goals. Following is an introduction to the treatment planning process, starting with brainstorming and then developing goals.

Brainstorming

A unique consideration in treatment planning from a wellness perspective is the preventive and holistic nature of the goal-setting process. Although treatment plans include targeted interventions to address clients' current presenting concerns, wellness planning also includes proactive interventions in multiple wellness domains to promote optimal functioning and to prevent future problems. Treatment planning from a wellness perspective also considers the interconnected nature of the various aspects of wellness. Therefore, plans address each aspect rather than focusing only on areas where the client is experiencing concerns.

Counselors use formal and informal assessment data to help clients target specific focus areas within each domain. Often, goals will be based on areas in which the client would like to improve. However, we believe it can also be helpful to formalize goals based on areas in which the client would like to maintain positive behaviors. For example, a client may identify physical wellness as a particular strength during the holistic assessment process. The counselor can help the client identify what they are doing well in that area and how the behavior can continue. During this process, it is important to maintain a strengths perspective toward clients and avoid overwhelming them. Clients may experience anxiety or stress when looking at the holistic view of their functioning and planning to engage in new behaviors within each domain. They may also experience guilt or shame for not doing more in one or more of the areas. We certainly do not want clients to feel bad about their progress, so it is important to maintain a positive, encouraging approach while considering clients' readiness to make changes in various areas.

The counselor can also brainstorm with the client how to capitalize on the interconnected nature of the wellness domains to help improve in areas where growth is needed. For example, a counselor might say, "Your physical wellness is an area of strength for you, I'm wondering whether there is a way you could connect some of your physical activities to help improve your social wellness." Some ideas that may emerge are joining a running club or a gym that also holds social functions. Counselors can use the wellness mapping exercise discussed in the previous chapter to help make connections among the various wellness domains when developing goals and interventions with clients.

Goal Setting

We believe it is important to emphasize the therapeutic relationship within wellness counseling because it is strongly related to counseling outcomes (Norcross & Wampold, 2011). An important aspect of the therapeutic relationship is mutually agreed upon goals between the counselor and client. The first step in developing goals is to identify the most important focus areas. Using holistic assessments at the start of counseling can help provide insight into potential target areas. At minimum, assessment results provide a starting point for discussion around focus areas. For example, I (Jonathan) supervise counselors-in-training who conduct personal growth and wellness sessions with undergraduate student clients. The counselors use the Quality of Life Enjoyment and Satisfaction Questionnaire—Short Form (Endicott, Nee, Harrison, & Blumenthal, 1993) to assess their client's satisfaction in a variety of areas. The counselors use the assessment results to help start the brainstorming process around potential goals. For example, the counselor may say, "I noticed you rated your satisfaction with social relationships lower than other areas. I'm wondering whether that's an area you would like to explore." The assessment can also be used to identify client strengths that can be formulated into goals so the client can continue to be satisfied in those areas.

S.M.A.R.T. Goals

In our clinical experience, we often find it challenging for clients to identify goals that are specific and measurable. Although each counselor's style will vary, we recommend a balanced approach to goal setting, during which the counselor encourages and challenges the client to pinpoint specific goals without being overly direct or confrontational. A common way to frame a good goal is through the S.M.A.R.T. (specific, measurable, assignable, realistic, and time-related) goal acronym, which was first developed by George T. Doran (1981) for application in management. The acronym has since been applied in various settings and has also evolved to represent different meanings. Following is an outline of how we prefer to apply S.M.A.R.T. goals.

Specific

The goal should be easy to identify with a clear understanding about what is going to happen. The counselor and client should develop a shared understanding about the expectations. Specific goals also mean that the goal is stated in a positive, rather than negative, way. We should be able to know what the client is going to be doing instead of having a negative goal, such as, "I am going to stop eating so bad," or "I'm going to stop being so stressed out."

Measurable

We should be able to determine in a quantifiable way whether the goal has been met or whether the client is making progress toward the goal. Some qualifiers that can help quantify goals are intensity, frequency, and duration. This process can help the client feel a sense of accomplishment, and it can help us determine whether we need to make adjustments to the interventions and when it is appropriate to terminate.

Attainable

Although it is important to set high expectations for what we would like to accomplish, the goals should be reasonable for the client. If the goals are too challenging or are beyond clients' readiness level, they are more likely to feel discouraged or give up if they do not experience any initial progress.

Relevant

Goals should be personally meaningful to the client. At times, it might be easier for the client (as well as the counselor) to have the counselor simply create goals for him or her. However, clients are more likely to be invested in the outcome if they are involved in the goal-setting process. Counselors work with clients to help them assess the importance of their goals. At the same time, counselors can help ensure that the goals are relevant related to clients' areas of focus and overall wellness.

Time Related

Setting timelines for goals can help facilitate urgency and accountability for the client. It can help promote action and creates an opportunity for predetermined checkpoints throughout the counseling process. Even if the client does not accomplish the goals by the set time, it allows the counselor and client to assess progress and readjust the goals as needed.

Solution-focused questioning can be particularly helpful in formulating goals. Questions such as, "When things are going well with your physical wellness, what is going on at that time?" or "Tell me about some times when your social life was going really well. What kind of things were you doing?" can help the client and counselor identify potential goals. When pinpointing specific behavioral objectives, it can help to ask things such as, "What are you going to be doing instead of arguing with your partner?" Other questions, similar to the miracle question, such as, "If you could wake up tomorrow and you were implementing your ideal, balanced wellness plan, what would that look like?" can help to enhance growth in all the wellness domains.

Selecting Interventions

There are multiple factors to consider when selecting the most appropriate interventions to implement to help clients reach their goals and maintain a high level of wellness.

Evidence-Based Interventions

Counselors must be knowledgeable about evidence-supported interventions and have the appropriate skills to implement them. Counselors need to stay current with the research and professional literature on best practices. Some of these practices are summarized in the domain chapters of this book. Some other opportunities to stay current include peer-reviewed journal articles, professional development (e.g., conferences), or professional organization websites.

Client Readiness

As discussed earlier in the chapter, clients may vary in their readiness to address their immediate concerns or make behavioral changes in areas to promote optimal wellness. Counselors must consider clients' level of readiness and stage of change when developing treatment goals and interventions. Readiness may also include consideration of clients' previous trauma. Some interventions (e.g., exposure) may trigger clients, leading to further trauma. Counselors must be able to assess for this history as much as possible and to be sensitive to it. Typically, clients who are at a lower level of readiness benefit from insight and awareness interventions, whereas clients at a higher level of readiness benefit from behavioral and action interventions (Prochaska & Norcross, 2014).

Client Culture, Religion, Values, and Family System

Counselors must consider clients' unique circumstances and characteristics when helping them set goals and implementing interventions. In addition to readiness and specific concerns, counselors need to consider clients' cultural, religious, and spiritual background; unique worldview and values; and their family dynamics. Although wellness goals are specific to the individual, we cannot ignore the influences that affect our clients' functioning. Additionally, it is not advisable for clients to pursue goals in a vacuum. Their behavioral changes influence others in their lives, and clients' ability to engage in behaviors is affected by others. Counselors can obtain much of this information during the assessment process; however, it is important to ensure that goals fit with clients' values. Counselors can work with clients to reassess how well the goals fit with religious or spiritual beliefs or how behavioral changes may affect others in a client's family or the family dynamics.

Scope of Practice and Collaboration

When addressing a client's holistic functioning, it is important to develop goals and implement interventions that are within the scope of the counselor's competency. For example, many goals may be associated with physical health. It is appropriate for a counselor to help clients set behavioral goals related to modifying physical activity or eating habits. However, if a client plans to make major changes to exercise, diet, or supplements, a nutritionist or physician should be involved in planning. Additionally, it is imperative that any interventions related to medication management also be implemented in collaboration with a psychiatrist or primary care physician. Counselors are encouraged to become familiar with the research and best practice on complementary and alternative medicines (CAMs) that can be used in conjunction with traditional interventions. If counselors plan to use CAMs in their practice, they must seek out the appropriate trainings, credentials, or certifications to ethically implement the practices. Alternatively, counselors should consult with practitioners who are using CAMs, specifically if their clients prefer to participate in them as part of counseling.

After you have developed a treatment plan, review the goals with the client. It is helpful to assess the goals for confidence and importance—in other words, determine how important the goal is to the client and how confident they are that it can be reached. During this stage in the process, it can be helpful to use strategies from the motivational interviewing approach (Miller & Rollnick, 2013). Some examples include asking clients to rate how important the goal is and how confident they are in their ability to meet the goal on a 0–10 scale. Goals can be adjusted as needed to fit best with the client's needs and aspirations. In Table 10.2, we provide an example of potential interventions based on the client's wellness concern and stage of change.

Now that we have covered the general process of wellness treatment planning, we have included a case example of how it applies in practice. We know there are many factors to consider beyond the information provided, but this example is a good start. As you read the case, think about the client's readiness, concerns, strengths, and areas of focus for a treatment plan. What else would you want to know about the client? What are some potential interventions that come to mind for you? We include an example plan after the case example.

Case Example

A client, M.G., is a 22-year-old woman who is currently enrolled at a local university. She is a full-time student and also works part time.

Table 10.2

Example Interventions

Client Concern or Growth Area	Wellness Domain	Stage of Change	Change Process to Emphasize	Potential Interventions
High levels of stress	Mind	Precontemplation	Consciousness raising	Education about the stress response and how it affects health; full physical from a physician
Career change	Spirit	Contemplation	Self-reevaluation	Career values sorter to identify priorities Career construction interview
Improving social life	Connection	Preparation	Self-liberation	Brainstorm socialization options; develop a plan for one social event for the client to attend
Maintaining an exercise routine	Body	Action	Contingency management	Help the client identify a self-reward for following through on an exercise routine for a week
Anger management	Heart	Maintenance	Stimulus control; counter-conditioning	A feeling log to help the client identify and avoid situations that trigger anger; feedback practice exercise to help the client express feelings appropriately

She has come to counseling on her own and talks about having some work- and school-related concerns. She talks about having a lot on her plate between her classes and trying to maintain her work schedule. She is supporting herself financially through school, so she must maintain employment. Through some formal assessments and informal interviewing, the counselor learns that M.G. is aware that she is feeling anxious and stressed related to her work and school. She seems to lack confidence in herself and is apprehensive about soliciting feedback from supervisors or professors. She is motivated to do well in school and at work. She appears committed to attending counseling and working on her concerns with the counselor. When the counselor inquires about previous things she has tried to relieve stress, she mentioned that she tried a couple of mindfulness workshops last year at her university and she really enjoyed them. Although she lives far away from her family, M.G. identifies her social and spiritual connections with her church as strengths that help her cope with stress. The counselor works with M.G. to brainstorm, set goals, and develop an intervention plan. Figure 10.1. is an example treatment plan that could be developed with this client.

Conclusion

Counselors who approach treatment planning from a wellness perspective consider the clients' holistic functioning, including areas for growth and strengths. An effective plan includes S.M.A.R.T. goals that address areas where the client would like to improve as well as strategies to help the client maintain positive behaviors. Interventions align with clients' readiness, values, and culture. Essentially, a wellness treatment plan is focused on intervention and wellness promotion for clients.

Reflection Prompts

1. Think about your current or intended work setting. How could you incorporate primary prevention activities within your practice?
2. Think about a time you set a goal for yourself, perhaps a New Year's resolution or a general personal goal. What was challenging about setting the goal? What was challenging about following through with the goal?
3. Think about a time when you have successfully set and accomplished a goal. What was helpful during the goal-setting and implementation process? How will you consider these experiences when working with your clients?

Original _____
Revised _____

Clinical Services: Counseling Plan

Date: __6/4/2018__ Client: ____M.G._____ Client Date of Birth: _10/13/1996_

Reason for Counseling/Presenting Concern: <u>General feelings of anxiety; difficulty concentrating;</u>
__problem with school and work_____

Diagnosis (if applicable): _____

Services Needed   **Anticipated Number of Sessions**

Intervention	1–2	3–7	8–10	11–20	21–40	41+
❑ Assessment						
■ Individual			✓			
❑ Couple						
❑ Parent Consultation						
❑ Filial Therapy						
❑ Family						
❑ Group						
❑ Other						

Client Concerns/Issues/ Wellness Domain	Goals/Objectives	Interventions

Feelings of anxiety related to school and work
(Heart, Mind)
	To decrease anxiety and increase feelings of confidence related to school and work
	    Contribute at least 1 comment in each class every week for the rest of the semester
	    Ask for clarification or feedback from supervisors at least once per week at work
		Individual counseling
		
		Thought log
		
		Loving-kindness meditation and gratitude journal to increase positive self-affirmations

Managing stressful situations and ability to concentrate
(Mind, Heart, Body)
	To increase positive emotions and focus
	    Engage in at least 15 minutes of relaxation each day or as stressful feelings arise
	    Spend at least 30 consecutive minutes, 3 times per week, focused on school- or work-related planning
		Individual counseling
		
		Strengths/exceptions
		
		Mindfulness meditation to increase concentration and relaxation

Connection with her individual spirituality and spiritual community (Spirit, Connection)	To increase involvement in spiritual activities Attend at least 1 volunteer function with the church small group per month	Individual counseling Spiritual journal to explore meaning and purpose

Referrals/Recomendations for Outside Services: _____
_____

I have discussed the intervention plan above with my counselor, understand the recommended strategies, and agree to participate as an active member in my intervention plan _____ or my child's intervention plan ____.

_____
    Client Signature   *Date*
_____
Client Parent or Guardian Signature *Date*
_____   _____
    Counselor Signature   *Date*   *Supervisor Signature*   *Date*

Figure 10.1

Sample Counseling Plan

4. Discuss how your culture, religion, or spirituality and family dynamic influence the individual goals you might set for yourself. How would you consider these areas when developing personal goals?
5. What would be most challenging for you when developing an intervention plan for a client?
6. How do you believe treatment planning from a wellness perspective is unique from treatment planning for other approaches?
7. Regarding the Practitioner Spotlight, what techniques related to the Transtheoretical Model (TTM)/stages of change did the counselor use? In what additional ways can the TTM/stages of change be helpful in treatment planning and working with this client?

Learning Activities

1. Work individually or with a partner to develop a wellness goal. Brainstorm several possibilities and commit to one area of focus. After developing a goal, evaluate how well it fits the S.M.A.R.T. (specific, measurable, attainable, realistic, and time-related) criteria and adjust the goal as needed.
2. Work with a partner and develop an individualized treatment plan using the template provided in this chapter. Use the information in this chapter and previous chapters to select the most appropriate interventions.

Sample Intervention Plan for Wellness Workshops

Topic

- What did you learn about yourself during the workshop?
- Develop a S.M.A.R.T. (specific, measurable, attainable, realistic, and time-related) goal for yourself related to the topic covered today.

Goal

- What will you be doing differently as a result of pursuing the goal?
- How will you know that you've been successful in reaching your goal?
- Who can help you be accountable for reaching your goal?
- What are some potential barriers to reaching your goal and how can you overcome them?

Personal growth plans should include a focus area/wellness domain, goal and objectives, and interventions. It should be agreed on and signed by the client, counselor, and supervisor.

Resources

Habits Lab at the University of Maryland Baltimore County
https://habitslab.umbc.edu

Substance Abuse and Mental Health Services Administration Guide to Evidence-Based Practices
https://www.samhsa.gov/ebp-web-guide

References

Barden, S. M., Conley, A. H., & Young, M. E. (2015). Integrating health and wellness in mental health counseling: Clinical, educational, and policy implications. *Journal of Mental Health Counseling, 37,* 152–163.

Bloom, M., & Gullotta, T. P. (2003). Evolving definitions of primary prevention. In T. P. Gullotta & M. Bloom (Eds.), *Encyclopedia of primary prevention and health promotion* (pp. 9–15). New York, NY: Kluwer Academic.

Caplan, G. (1964). *Principles of preventive psychiatry.* New York, NY: Basic Books.

Capuzzi, D., & Gross, D. R. (2019). *Youth at risk: A prevention resource for counselors, teachers, and parents* (7th ed.). Alexandria, VA: American Counseling Association.

Doran, G. T. (1981, November). There's a S.M.A.R.T. way to write management's goals and objectives. *Management Review, 70*(11), 35–36.

Endicott, J., Nee, J., Harrison, W., & Blumenthal, R. (1993). Quality of Life Enjoyment and Satisfaction Questionnaire: A new measure. *Psychopharmacology Bulletin, 29,* 321–326.

Miller, W. R., & Rollnick, S. (2013). *Motivational interviewing: Helping people change* (3rd ed.). New York, NY: Guilford Press.

Mrazek, P. J., & Haggerty, R. J. (Eds.). (1994). *Reducing risks for mental disorders: Frontiers for preventive intervention research.* Washington, DC: National Academy Press.

Norcross, J. C., Krebs, P. M., & Prochaska, J. O. (2011). Stages of change. In J. C. Norcross (Ed.), *Psychotherapy relationships that work* (2nd ed., pp. 279–300). New York, NY: Oxford University Press.

Norcross, J. C., & Wampold, B. E. (2011). Evidence-based therapy relationships: Research conclusions and clinical practices. *Psychotherapy, 48,* 98–102. https://doi.org/10.1037/a0022161

Prochaska, J. O., & DiClemente, C. C. (1984). *The transtheoretical approach: Crossing the traditional boundaries of therapy.* Homewood, IL: Dow Jones-Irwin.

Prochaska, J. O., Evers, K. E., Castle, P. H., Johnson, J. L., Prochaska, J. M., Rula, E. Y., . . . Pope, J. E. (2012). Enhancing multiple domains of well-being by decreasing multiple health risk behaviors: A randomized clinical trial. *Population Health Management, 15,* 276–286.

Prochaska, J. O., & Norcross, J. C. (Eds.). (2014). *Systems of psychotherapy: A transtheoretical analysis* (8th ed.). Stamford, CT: Cenage Learning.

World Health Organization. (2002). *Prevention and promotion in mental health.* Geneva, Switzerland: Author.

Chapter 11

Interventions

Change does not roll in on the wheels of inevitability,
but comes through continuous struggle.
—Martin Luther King Jr.

• • •

Counselors can promote clients' holistic wellness through a variety of theoretical approaches. There are several principles and approaches that are exceptionally effective for counselors when selecting appropriate interventions, helping clients identify growth areas, enhancing client commitment, and identifying client strengths. In this chapter, we review several intervention frameworks to foster client wellness.

We have heard a question repeatedly from counseling students, professional counselors, counselor educators, and friends or family: "What is wellness counseling?" What they really want to know is, "What does wellness counseling look like, and how will I know whether I am conducting wellness counseling?" These are highly valid questions. Next, we offer principles of wellness counseling that can serve as guidelines to self-assess whether you are indeed using a wellness counseling approach. Supervisors can similarly process these principles with supervisees for the same purpose. You can view these principles as questions to ask yourself when session planning, reflecting on your work with clients, and in supervision or consultation to uphold and maintain consistency with your wellness approach.

Principles of Wellness Counseling

Wellness counseling entails attending to the following principles, when appropriate, with the client:

1. Conduct baseline and ongoing assessments of the client through a holistic lens that encompasses the components of the wellness model used by the counselor.
2. Incorporate informal and formal holistic wellness assessments into the counseling process to inform treatment planning and intervention.
3. Administer domain-specific assessments that are integrated within the context of the whole client (the client's overall wellness).
4. Implement domain-specific and holistic wellness interventions to address the client's presenting concerns.
5. Mobilize the client's wellness strengths to address the client's presenting concern or goal and the client's overall well-being.
6. Recognize that wellness can be a *determinant* of mental and physical health rather than solely an *outcome* of mental and physical health.
7. Apply knowledge about the interplay and relationships among the wellness domains so that these interconnections can be maximized to the benefit of the client.
8. Integrate strength-based interventions in conjunction with wellness counseling interventions to draw on the client's internal and external resources.
9. Match the wellness intervention with the client's stage of change.
10. Include developmental, cultural, and environmental considerations in one's wellness counseling approaches.

In this chapter, we focus mostly on the intervention-related principles. We discuss solution-focused approaches and a variety of other strategies to promote client wellness.

Solution-Focused Counseling

Solution-focused counseling is a natural fit for incorporation into wellness counseling. Similar to how wellness counselors using the Transtheoretical Model (Prochaska & DiClemente, 1984; Prochaska & Norcross, 2014) hone their "antennae" or listening ears to identify the client's stage of change, wellness counselors involving solution-focused methodologies hone their antennae for strengths and solutions. This method is what wellness counseling is all about—being able to identify client resources (internal and external) but, more importantly, increasing the clients' ability to do this independently and to get those resources to work for them in their own lives. Part of the idea in solution-focused counseling is that we can be more efficient in counseling if we work with what is already working rather than to presume that the counselor or client has to create new solutions or help the client develop new strengths (O'Hanlon & Weiner-Davis, 2003). There are three key solution-focused techniques used in wellness counseling: (a) the Exception Question, (b) Failed Solutions, and (c) the Noticing Task.

The *Exception Question* entails asking the client about times when their presenting problem is less problematic or nonexistent. The assumption is that a solution lies within the moments when the person is doing something differently, resulting in the issue decreasing in severity (O'Connell, 2012; O'Hanlon & Weiner-Davis, 2003). These moments frequently go unrecognized by clients because they are mired in the problem itself. Thus, the therapeutic value of the Exception Question is in consciousness raising about these exceptions. This approach adapts well to wellness counseling by asking clients to identify and discuss times in their life when their holistic or domain-specific well-being was higher.

Follow-up prompts are necessary to delve deeper here. The counselor will want to explore what specifically the client was doing differently that contributed to higher well-being. Clients may refer to external circumstances as the reason for increased wellness; nonetheless, the counselor must be on guard to keep the focus on things within the control of the client. For instance, if the client states that they worked fewer hours at their old job and hence was more well, it is the counselor's job to redirect the client back to "and what were *you* doing differently during that time?" The next step of the Exception Question process is linking those successes to changes (even small ones) that can be carried forward into the present time. Insights from exceptions can thus be useful.

The other side of the coin is examining *Failed Solutions*—attempts at wellness that were unsuccessful (O'Connell, 2012; O'Hanlon & Weiner-Davis, 2003). The Failed Solutions are equally informative to exceptions because they help the client avoid repeating past ineffective strategies. A similar question sequence can be applied here with the counselor asking about wellness behaviors that were nonproductive. Last, well-being can be bolstered through attending to examples in our daily lives when we live out that wellness. The *Noticing Task* is a homework assignment for clients in which the counselor asks the clients to notice any evidence they can find each day of wellness, wellness behaviors, and progress in well-being (O'Connell, 2012; O'Hanlon & Weiner-Davis, 2003). It can be even more effective to ask the client to write the signs/indicators down in a journal and bring this to session. The directive of looking for evidence of one's wellness can lead the client to engage in more pro-wellness behaviors—a worthwhile self-fulfilling prophecy. It also allows for the identification of additional strengths and solutions.

We now shift to examining the Covert Antecedents Model (Marlatt, 1985) and our adaptation and application of this model to wellness counseling. Our adapted model depicts the connections among wellness, stressors, and mental health symptomology. Processing this model with clients can be a helpful intervention and induction into wellness counseling.

The Covert Antecedents Model of Relapse: A Foundation for Wellness Intervention

The Covert Antecedents Model was developed by Marlatt (1985) in the context of interventions for clients with substance use issues. He essentially proposed that when one neglects one's wellness (i.e., "lifestyle imbalance"), this neglect leads to a longing for instant pleasure and the experience of cravings for a substance, followed by the person ending up in a context that could trigger relapse. We espouse that this model can pertain to relapse with any mental disorder or relapse into stress, being overwhelmed, and decreased well-being.

Think of how when your own life is out of balance, you want to feel good. When we fail to attend to our own well-being, our vices, addictions, and mental health vulnerabilities are at risk of showing themselves (at minimum) and enveloping our lives (at worst). Pictured in Figure 11.1 is our adaptation of Marlatt's (1985) model, which can be used in wellness counseling at the primary, secondary, and tertiary levels.

The starting point of our version of the Covert Antecedents Model is with wellness. This is notable because it corresponds with Wellness Counseling Principle 6, in which wellness affects mental and physical health (and vice versa) rather than wellness being the last step in the equation. When overall wellness is low or when one or more domains are particularly low, a chain of processes can be set off, including an increase in mental disorder symptoms and unhelpful

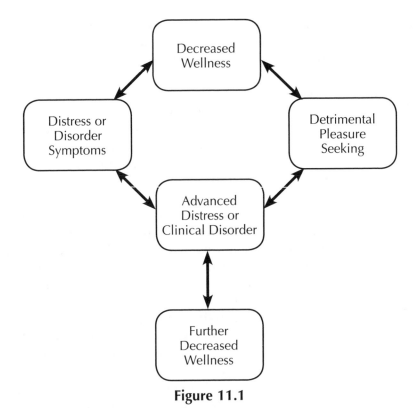

Figure 11.1

Adaptation of the Covert Antecedents Model

Note. From "Relapse Prevention: Theoretical Rationale and Overview of the Model" by G. A. Marlatt, 1985. In G. A. Marlatt & J. R. Gordon (Eds.), *Relapse Prevention: Maintenance Strategies in the Treatment of Addictive Behaviors*, p. 48. Copyright 1985 by Guilford Press. Adapted with permission; permission conveyed through Copyright Clearance Center.

pleasure seeking (within one or more of the five wellness domains). All of these variables can impinge on the other, which is why double-sided arrows connect these factors. Collectively, the windstorm of low wellness, increased symptoms, and unhelpful pleasure seeking can result in a full relapse into a mental disorder or a state of distress. This relapse cycles back into the person's well-being, causing further harm to their domain-specific and holistic wellness.

An example would be a 14-year-old client whose family was facing financial hardship resulting in significantly decreased body wellness. Lower body wellness was influenced by lack of sleep because of inadequate heat in the home during wintertime and improper nutrition. Although the client did not show it, she was distraught (emotion wellness) at overhearing her parents' intense arguments that have escalated over the previous months. This tension led the client to begin experiencing increased feelings of anger and symptoms of depression. The client sought pleasure through the sense of belonging involved in destroying a part of school property with two peers after school, resulting in her facing punishment from the school. Being on punishment at school and at home exacerbated the client's symptoms of anger and depression (relapse into mental disorder), resulting in the client resuming engagement in self-injurious behaviors that she had not done for several months (seeking relief and relapse into distress). The combination of the aforementioned experiences cycled back to negatively affect the client's overall well-being.

Remember to provide psychoeducation on this model to your clients. First, explain the model and what the different terms mean. Then, enhance the clarity of the model by asking the client to apply it to their own life. Specifically, ask the client to think about a time when their wellness was low (holistically or domain specific), and then elicit the client's personal examples of the various components of the model from their own lived experience.

A significant goal is for clients to develop ways to interrupt the negative chain of events before it picks up momentum and ends in relapse or becoming entrenched in active distress or mental disorder (Marlatt, 1985). When incorporating this model in counseling, invest time with the client in identifying patterns of "unhelpful pleasure seeking." Assist clients by offering a general definition that unhelpful pleasure seeking can involve engaging in anything related to mind, body, spirit, emotion, and connection that (a) is inherently deleterious; (b) is not engaged with in moderation, causing risk to well-being and mental health; and (c) has been historically harmful to them.

As instances of unhelpful pleasure seeking come into focus, they can be addressed. Each aspect identified can also be documented by the client as a warning sign that the client is headed toward a backslide into further mental health concerns. Conversely, wellness counselors can use interventions in which clients identify indicators that they are making progress toward well-being. Hence, the flip side of unhelpful pleasure seeking is helping clients become aware of healthy and helpful pleasures. The sections in this chapter on wellness boosters and balancers, as well as the domain-specific chapters, illuminate examples of positive, wellness-enhancing pleasures.

The adapted Covert Antecedents Model also serves as a vehicle for motivating clients to bolster their wellness. Examination of the model makes the lesson clear that neglecting wellness can come at a great cost. Moreover, the model shows the pathways by which low wellness can affect people. Approaches for cultivating wellness are described in this chapter and throughout this book. Counselor and client now have several avenues for intervention.

Wellness Self-Assessment Intervention

We often hear the self-care metaphor highlighting that people treat their cars better than themselves. We take our cars to get serviced and washed, change the oil, put air in the tires, and so forth, yet, many of us are a lot less attentive to caring for ourselves. I (Phil) have incorporated components of the wellness self-assessment intervention when presenting to caregivers of people with dementia and in co-occurring disorders groups. Self-assessment of wellness encourages clients to tune in to themselves and can be done through visualization, in written form, or through verbal discussion. In session, the counselor and client co-construct a metaphor comparing one's wellness to things such as a gas tank, a battery, a fuse connected to a bomb, or a cup of liquid as used in Impact Therapy interventions (Jacobs, 1994). A higher scale, fuller tank, higher battery charge, or longer fuse represents high wellness, and the other end of the spectrum is likened to low well-being.

The counselor educates clients that, throughout the day, they should develop a habit of self-check-ins by picturing one's wellness level at any given moment. This self-assessment information is extremely valuable in that after clients identify their current level of wellness, they (a) have more self-compassion for any current stress that they might be experiencing because of the recognition that wellness is lower and (b) can elect to enact part of the wellness plan in the moment or when the opportunity presents itself to increase their wellness. In the next section, we talk about wellness boosters and wellness balancers that can be fast-acting methods for improving well-being when a plethora of time is not available.

Help the client identify times to use the wellness self-assessment. As you have probably heard before, instruct the clients to use this technique when they are not overstressed so that they become practiced in it and able to incorporate it during more frenzied times. This exercise can be an effective way to start wellness counseling sessions. It allows for an examination of progress or setback. The activity serves as a practice opportunity for using wellness self-assessment and sends a meta-message to the client about the importance of attending to self. The client's response to the check-in can be useful for deep discussions on the client's wellness challenges and victories.

One key recommendation to offer to clients is to identify critical cues for when to use this self-assessment. Discuss signs of unwellness with the client across the five wellness domains that can serve as prompts to do the wellness self-check-in. Cues of unwellness can include physical fatigue, negative thoughts or feelings, stress, or interpersonal conflict. This technique is inspired by Benson and Stuart's (1992) "Stop, Breathe, Reflect, Choose" intervention. Taking 20 seconds to engage in this exercise is therapeutic in and of itself by forcing clients to step away and gain perspective on their current experience. This activity was powerful for caregivers of persons with dementia because, when wellness is decreased, caregivers reported to me (Phil) anecdotally that they became more negatively reactive toward their loved one with dementia—similar to having a "shorter fuse." Taking a brief timeout to draw the wellness cup or to visualize whether the cup was moderately full, empty, or full brought calm so that the caregiver could be more in control and positively responsive to their loved one.

Wellness Boosters

Wellness counselors are wise to include short-term wellness interventions into counseling with their clients. Short-term wellness interventions focus more on supporting clients in the short term, although they are skills that can be used over time. Wellness boosters in particular are skills that can be enacted quickly by the client during times of struggle, yielding increases in well-being and coping. Stress and struggle with wellness are linked to the emergence or exacerbation of symptoms for nearly any mental disorder. As part of wellness counseling, counselors would serve clients well to co-construct a range of wellness boosters that can be used during times of stress or to reduce the impact and severity of mental disorder symptoms. When wellness boosters have favorable outcomes, clients feel empowered, thus clearing the way for them to use their coping skills. Wellness boosters are a significant alternative to the unhealthy pleasures of the adapted Covert Antecedents Model.

Wellness boosters must be readily accessible, meaning that (a) the client does not necessarily have to rely on others to perform the wellness booster, (b) the client can engage in the wellness booster most anywhere and within a short amount of time, and (c) the wellness booster can bring benefit with even brief invoking of the skill. The domain-specific chapters of the book include boosters unique to that chapter's wellness area.

Wellness Balancers

Wellness diagrams are not realistic depictions of wellness because each area of wellness will not be perfectly equal. The notion of wellness balancers takes this concept a step further. All wellness areas are not created equally for any given individual—meaning that each person may have wellness areas that are prioritized over others. These wellness areas hold such power and importance for the individual that a person can have deficits in other aspects of wellness that do not perpetuate a downward wellness spiral as long as their priority wellness areas are fulfilled. These priority aspects "tip the scales" in favor of wellness even when other areas have been neglected.

The point then, from the strengths-based perspective of wellness counseling, is to honor the client's wellness preferences. These preferences are the "north stars" that keep the client on course during rough waters when the client is lost and unwellness pervades. The counselor's work is to find out what these wellness balancers are early on when working with clients. Here are the criteria for wellness balancers: (a) They have been a "go-to" healthy experience that the client has used in the past, (b) they have a sizeable positive impact on the other wellness areas, (c) they can help ground the client during times of distress, and (d) they help the client sustain a functional level of overall wellness even in the midst of low domain-specific well-being.

As a wellness-balancer example, I (Phil) strongly value and have a high need for body wellness via exercise, specifically running. Running facilitates wellness across the domains for me because it makes me feel connected spiritually, is a form of moving meditation (especially when running outside), quiets my mental noise, improves my mood, makes me more pleasant in social interactions, and improves my body image. You can see here that running, as a key component of my body wellness, lies at the center of wellness. I run to prevent myself from falling into full distress or crisis during troubled times, and this activity ensures that my holistic wellness remains afloat when aspects, such as my mind wellness, have declined.

Daily Wellness Practices (DWPs)

Wellness boosters and balancers support the wellness plan on a short-term and "as-needed" basis. However, the wellness plan also needs to be supported by ongoing, long-term interventions. DWPs are wellness behaviors that are built into the client's daily or weekly routine. DWPs can include wellness boosters and balancers, but the differentiating factor is that DWPs are a daily practice that maintain the client's domain-specific and holistic well-being. They are important because they can buffer clients from relapse (prevention), help the client develop positive habits, and facilitate coping with mental disorder and distress symptoms. DWPs therein are composed of wellness-based coping skills and strategies for enhancing well-being.

DWPs should be a part of any wellness-informed treatment plan. Creating a DWP begins with a single question: "What things can you do on a daily or weekly basis that will keep you well and improve your well-being?" For example, a client coming to you related to generalized anxiety disorder symptoms may co-construct DWPs with coping skills for anxiety to be used and improved on a regular basis, such as deep breathing, progressive muscle relaxation, or mindfulness. If the anxiety causes sleep disturbance, a nightly sleep hygiene routine can be incorporated. Three days a week of exercise could be part of the plan as a wellness balancer or booster that also reduces the severity of anxiety symptoms. A DWP handout is included at the end of this chapter.

An additional powerful aspect of DWPs is that they serve as an alert system to the occurrence of the downward spiral conveyed in the adapted Covert Antecedents Model. When a client starts omitting parts of the DWP, that could be a sign that the client is headed toward increased distress or mental disorder relapse. Therefore, wellness counselors should check in each session about adherence to the DWP. Processing any slips can start with an open-ended question—such as asking the client, "What do you make of that?"—to explore the client's perspective. The counselor should listen for barriers that can be addressed to follow through on the DWP. Navigation of any barriers can then be problem solved in session. The counselor should also listen for changes in motivation. For instance, the client may have returned to a state of ambivalence, and the DWP and treatment plan need to be reexamined in conjunction with motivational interviewing strategies.

It is imperative that the counselor assess for any increases in mental disorder or distress symptoms that may relate to nonadherence to the DWP and any declines in domain or holistic well-being. When possible, elicit the client's motivation by discussing connections between adherence to the DWP and increased wellness/decreased symptoms versus increased problems related to nonadherence. Be cautious to frame such discussions in an exploratory manner, meaning that these insights should come from the client and the wellness counselor should remain nonjudgmental.

Working Your Wellness Plan

Wellness in Action

Wellness counseling is conducted most effectively when wellness behaviors, experiences, and processes become a part of the counseling session. Wellness counselors can and should allot space and time for wellness actions to be rehearsed, experienced, and de-briefed during session. Do not wait for clients to practice and engage in wellness on their own outside of the session. Next, we provide a few initial examples (note that the chapters on each of the five domains contain additional domain-specific wellness interventions that can be done during the counseling session):

1. *Mind wellness:* Assist the client to identify unhelpful self-talk that has been contributing to their presenting concern, and then encourage the client to challenge that self-talk and replace it with more constructive thinking. Engaging in mindfulness activities during the session may also increase well-being in this domain.
2. *Body wellness:* Spend time during session practicing deep breathing with a client struggling with stress and anxiety.
3. *Spirit wellness:* Search for volunteer opportunities during session to enhance the client's sense of meaning and purpose. Invite the client to pray or engage in spiritual reflection to cope with an existential or faith-based struggle, if the client wants to do so.
4. *Emotion wellness:* Practice the experience of positive emotions, such as gratitude, or the "containment" of emotions (Murphy & Dillon, 2011).
5. *Connection wellness:* Practice assertiveness skills during session, rehearse drug refusal skills, or role play social skills.

Capitalizing on Success: The Wellness Progress Check-In

When success occurs, it must be celebrated! The research on the power of positive reinforcement suggests that it would be foolish to not ask about and celebrate progress with our clients. Remember each session to conduct a wellness progress check-in—an inquiry about any successes with the wellness plan. Clients will often deny that any progress has occurred, particularly when struggling with low confidence or the cognitive constriction that can come from crisis. Hence, you may have to be persistent. What makes wellness counseling unique is that the counselor should then process how even the "smallest" victory had an impact on other domains of the client's well-being and holistic wellness.

This practice links back to the psychoeducation provided to the client that all wellness areas are interconnected. The consequence is that a small improvement in one component of a wellness domain can result in increases in other wellness domains and overall well-being. Processing these occurrences can be a helpful tool for enhancing both client motivation and insight. For instance, a counselor begins a wellness progress check-in with an adolescent client referred for grief counseling because of the sudden death of his father several months ago. The client reports that, since last session, he participated in his teen grief support group meeting rather than declining to share. He was surprised at the helpful support he received from other group members and how cathartic it felt to share. The counselor asked, "What domains of wellness have been affected by this experience?" The client was able to identify increased emotion wellness because of a growing sense that he could express his feelings to others and be "ok" with it and that others could relate, which decreased feelings of isolation and increased connection wellness.

Conclusion

We have covered a lot of territory in this chapter. You are now more aware of the relevance of the stages of change to wellness counseling. Without meeting clients where they are in the change process, wellness counseling can go astray. The integration of solution-focused techniques was presented. Furthermore, we described holistic short- and long-term interventions. Note that, similar to the Transtheoretical Model, wellness counseling is transtheoretical, meaning that you can use another theory within the framework of wellness counseling. This approach applies for both assessment/case conceptualization and intervention.

Reflection Prompts

1. Think about a behavior you have been thinking about changing (e.g., healthy eating, responsible spending). Discuss where you are on the continuum of the Transtheoretical Model. How well do you think the model describes an individual's change process?
2. Who might you identify as wellness role models in your life? What do you admire about each person? Do you admire different people for different domains?

Learning Activities

Wellness Role Model Intervention

We have talked about wellness models in this book. Here, we discuss ways clients benefit from models of wellness—people who embody holistic or domain-specific wellness in ways that our clients appreciate and aspire to. When you ask yourself or a client, "Who in your life do you view as a pillar of well-being?" Someone almost always comes to mind—a colleague who seems to work diligently and effectively in the workplace but makes time for family and leisure, a sibling who is committed to exercising multiple times per week, or a friend who always makes time for friends or nurturing their faith.

The wellness role model exercise involves identifying one or two people whose wellness the client admires. The client should identify the wellness domains in which each person is successful and then provide examples to illustrate the specific wellness behaviors and processes that bolster the person's wellness. Ensure that clients get as specific as possible so that both you and the client have a clear picture of the wellness-enhancing steps taken by the wellness role model. Then drill down even further. Prompt the client, "What steps does it take (e.g., scheduling time for wellness activities) for the person to make wellness happen for them?" The client may not be sure yet can still speculate. Even if inaccurate, this process can lead to helpful brainstorming of action steps for actualizing wellness. If the client gets stuck at this step, the counselor can assign homework for the client to talk to their wellness role model, asking the person about their wellness successes and action steps for actualizing wellness. In the final stages of the wellness role model activity, the client chooses one aspect of wellness along with a corresponding action steps to integrate into their own life.

> *Note:* The counselor must be careful to explain to the client that the purpose of this activity is to learn from others rather than to compare oneself with others in a way that makes one feel "less than." This exercise may not be appropriate for your client if you determine that they are at risk for falling into this comparison trap to the detriment of their mental health.

Motivation Activity

Take the University of Rhode Island Change Readiness Assessment (URICA): https://habitslab.umbc.edu/urica/. Think of a hypothetical problem and complete the psychotherapy version of the form. Discuss your level of readiness. What are your thoughts about the assessment? How might this assessment help guide your intervention selection with your client?

Daily Wellness Practices

Complete the Daily Wellness Practices handout. Process the activity with a colleague or friend. How helpful is the activity? How might you use it with clients?

(continued)

Handout 1 *(continued)*
Daily Wellness Practices

- List and describe your daily/weekly *mind wellness* practices and the day and time you plan to engage in this practice.

- List and describe your daily/weekly *body wellness* practices and the day and time you plan to engage in this practice.

- List and describe your daily/weekly *spirit wellness* practices and the day and time you plan to engage in this practice.

- List and describe your daily/weekly *emotion wellness* practices and the day and time you plan to engage in this practice.

- List and describe your daily/weekly *connection wellness* practices and the day and time you plan to engage in this practice.

References

Benson, H., & Stuart, E. M. (1992). *The wellness book: The comprehensive guide to maintaining health and treating stress-related illness.* New York, NY: Fireside.

Jacobs, E. (1994). *Impact therapy.* Lutz, FL: Psychological Assessment Resources.

Marlatt, G. A. (1985). Relapse prevention: Theoretical rationale and overview of the model. In G. A. Marlatt & J. R. Gordon (Eds.), *Relapse prevention: Maintenance strategies in the treatment of addictive behaviors* (pp. 3–70). New York, NY: Guilford Press.

Murphy, B. C., & Dillon, C. (2011). *Interviewing in action in a multicultural world* (4th ed.). Belmont, CA: Brooks/Cole.

O'Connell, B. (2012). *Solution-focused therapy* (3rd ed.). Thousand Oaks, CA: Sage.

O'Hanlon, B., & Weiner-Davis, M. (2003). *In search of solutions: A new direction in psychotherapy* (2nd ed.). New York, NY: Norton.

Prochaska, J. O., & DiClemente, C. C. (1984). *The transtheoretical approach: Crossing the traditional boundaries of therapy.* Homewood, IL: Dow Jones-Irwin.

Prochaska, J. O., & Norcross, J. C. (Eds.). (2014). *Systems of psychotherapy: A transtheoretical analysis* (8th ed.). Stamford, CT: Cenage Learning.

Chapter 12

Wellness Counseling for Couples, Families, and Groups

The meeting of two personalities is like the contact of two chemical substances: if there is any reaction, both are transformed.
—Carl Jung

• • •

Up to this point, we have primarily discussed wellness promotion in the context of working with an individual. However, there are several modalities used by counselors to address wellness that require unique considerations and skills. In this chapter, we discuss these considerations and provide practical strategies for promoting wellness when working with couples, families, or groups.

The Importance of Wellness for Couples and Families

Couples

Rarely have we heard the topic of wellness come up when discussing couples, families, and counseling. Many of the clients who seek our counseling services are a partner in a couple, and all are members of a family. Although we believe that wellness counseling for individual clients can be immensely beneficial, we would be remiss to disregard the potential impact of wellness counseling with couples and families. After all, couples mutually affect each other; hence, wellness progress could be sabotaged or misunderstood by the partner not in counseling. The partner not attending counseling will be influenced by the wellness changes of their partner attending counseling. A client struggling with wellness and mental health issues may not sustain increased well-being because of unhelpful dynamics in their family and wellness problems among other family members.

There is empirical support for the impact of marriage on individual wellness. Researchers meta-analyzed 93 studies and found that marriage and wellness are interconnected; increases in one facet correspond with increases in the other (Proulx, Helms, & Buehler, 2007). A multinational meta-analysis with a sample of 72,000 participants indicated that those in healthier marriages are physically healthier than those who are not (Robles, Slatcher, Trombello, & McGinn, 2014). Problems in a marriage or relationship can leak into the family system and vice versa. For instance, deficiencies in marital quality (in conjunction with a weak bond between parent and adolescent) were predictive of worse physical and mental health in adolescents (Hair et al., 2009).

Relationship problems or strengths can derive from the inside out or the outside in. Wellness factors from within the relationship can affect the couple—for example, communication skills (*connection wellness*; Carroll, Hill, Yorgason, Larson, & Sandberg, 2013) or physical intimacy (*body wellness*; Schoenfeld, Loving, Pope, Huston, & Štulhofer, 2017). Regarding outside factors, the "spillover effect" can occur, in which contextual stressors seep into a relationship and cause trouble (Buck & Neff, 2012). Lavner and Clark (2017) stated that "spillover refers to when strains experienced in one domain (e.g., work) are transmitted to another domain (e.g., family) and negatively affect a person's well-being in the other role" (p. 68). Brock and Lawrence (2008) noted that researchers have also identified "life transitions," "economic stress," and "work-related stress" as precipitants of the spillover effect (p. 11).

Attention to wellness can pay dividends when it comes to threats to the well-being of couples. The same negative relational repercussions that result from wellness deficits and stressors can be combatted when wellness strengths are present. Take, for instance, that sharing openly about religious practices and beliefs (*spirit wellness*) between marriage partners correlates with increases in quality of the relationship (David & Stafford, 2015). Relationship education entails providing psychoeducation to couples to enhance their relationship with each other and their families. These interventions tap into *mind wellness* (given the provision of information and skills) and the other components of well-being, yielding positive results (e.g., Williamson, Altman, Hsueh, & Bradbury, 2016).

Families

Wellness offers an important lens through which to understand and intervene at the family level. Numerous studies demonstrate how family variables can both detract from and improve wellness. There is an interconnectedness in families as there is among the domains of wellness. Therefore, studies have shown that tension manifesting in the family relates to depression symptoms in adolescents and, conversely, that the adolescent's depression symptoms foster tension in the family (Kelly et al., 2016). Connection wellness is essential to the parent–child relationship. If parents fail to build a relationship and rapport with their children, the path to wellness for parents and children can be adversely affected (Parcel & Bixby, 2016). All areas of wellness are implicated in couples and family work. If a parent's mind wellness is not fulfilled through their career or other outlets, the parent may then raise their children in a manner that does not fully satiate the child's need for mind wellness (Parcel & Bixby, 2016).

Body wellness has become compromised in the United States to the point that former First Lady Michelle Obama launched a "Let's Move" campaign in an effort to address nationwide weight issues in children (https://letsmove.obamawhitehouse.archives.gov/). According to the National Health and Nutrition Examination Survey that spanned 2011–2014, 17% of children and adolescents met the criteria for obesity (Ogden, Carroll, Fryar, & Flegal, 2015). Barriers to child body wellness and holistic wellness exist, including past or current trauma experienced by the parents or child (Fuemmeler et al., 2017). Food insecurity and access to resources for improving and sustaining body wellness must be navigated. Fuemmeler et al. (2017) reported that "it may be that focused efforts to improve prenatal care and promoting positive parenting during early childhood have a beneficial effect at addressing several problems arising in childhood" (p. 168). Additionally, when individuals have an expansive view of who they deem as family, they are more safeguarded from stress that saps one's well-being (Buchanan & McConnell, 2017).

When counseling couples and families, there are great opportunities for fostering wellness. To take advantage of the encouraging possibilities of keeping wellness at the center of couples and families, we must understand how it fits in with the assessment and intervention process. This information is described in the next sections.

Couples Counseling Assessment

The first step in ensuring that one is integrating wellness counseling with one's couples counseling approach is to include one or more holistic formal or informal assessments in the couples assessment process. There are both individual wellness assessments (see Chapter 9) and wellness-related measures specifically for couples. The wellness-informed couples counselor will provide psychoeducation. Similar to the wellness domains being linked to form the whole of holistic wellness, so is the well-being of the couple. This result occurs because the wellness strengths or deficits of one partner can affect the other and vice versa. The counselor provides information on the spillover effect (described earlier) and crossover effects (e.g., when the stress of one member of the couple infuses into the other member; Neff & Karney, 2007). This stage-setting process by the wellness counselor meets a key therapeutic principle of couples counseling "that it is important to increase the extent to which both partners' view of the relationship is objective, dyadic, and contextualized, rather than one-sided and blaming" (Benson, McGinn, & Christensen, 2012, p. 26).

The couples counselor then reviews each partner's wellness score (whether self-rated through the informal process described in Chapter 9 or rated with a formal assessment tool such as the Five Factor Wellness Inventory; J. E. Myers & Sweeney, 2014). After the counselor briefly processes the wellness strengths and areas of lower wellness with one partner, the counselor can facilitate an enactment in which the listening partner speaks directly to the partner whose wellness assessment was just reviewed to discuss any additional wellness strengths not mentioned or fully discussed by the partner being evaluated. This method serves as both intervention and assessment of communication skills and patterns (Edwards, 1997). The counselor will return to asking the partner whose individual well-being is being examined to discuss how their areas of higher wellness positively affect the relationship, followed by opening the floor to the listening partner to share additional thoughts on the effects of their partner's wellness strengths.

Understanding Couple Wellness

Let's look at how wellness domains intersect with couples-related issues and strengths. The following are questions and reflective prompts to guide your conceptualization of the couple:

1. *Mind wellness.* Does the couple take part in activities that are mentally engaging to them? Are they mindful and attentive to each other's needs and interests? Do they have individual outlets for mental stimulation that cannot be met by the partner? Do the partners experience self-talk that leads them to unhelpful beliefs about or behaviors within the relationship?

2. *Body wellness.* Are there issues with physical intimacy in the relationship? Is the couple on the same page regarding preferences for touch, intimacy, and intercourse (Chapman, 2015)? Do the individuals in the couple take physical care of themselves through nutrition, exercise, hygiene, and so forth? Is there physical or sexual violence in the relationship?

3. *Spirit wellness.* Noted relationship researcher John Gottman (2015) stated, "A relationship is about building a life together, a life that has a sense of shared purpose and meaning. It's not just about being happy" (p. 215). What values are espoused collectively by the couple? What values come into discrepancy and cause conflict?

4. *Emotion wellness.* Do the partners experience difficulty in preventing emotions from becoming toxic during disagreements or in the relationship? Do the partners demonstrate a dearth of positive feelings in the relationship (Gottman, 2015)? What core emotions underlie the surface feelings that manifest overtly in the relationship (Brubacher, 2018)? Is emotional abuse occurring in the relationship?

5. *Connection wellness.* What couples communication skills do the partners possess? What are helpful and unhelpful ways in which the couple encourages and assists each other? Is the couple aware of each other's preferences for support (Chapman, 2015)?

6. *Holistic wellness.* How are individual wellness deficits for each partner affecting the relationship?

7. *Systemic wellness.* What external or internal events have occurred in the relationship or with individual partners that have affected the couple? What domains of relational well-being were affected?

Wellness-Based Goal Setting With Couples

Now that assessment information has been gathered and client conceptualization is in full swing, goal setting can commence. When goal setting with couples, consider providing them with a handout picturing your wellness model of choice. The benefit of using a visual depiction of the wellness domains is that the couple can discuss their areas of higher wellness and areas of lower relational wellness. Similar to the assessment recommendations in Chapter 9, discuss the individual and collective strengths of the couple. Identify ways that the couple can mobilize those strengths to address weaker areas. Then encourage the couple to identify mutual goals. In addition or alternatively, each partner through an enactment can be directed to ask the other partner what domain of relational wellness they would like to see improve. The inquiring partner will then be instructed to ask about specific ways they can play a role in actualizing the couple's goals.

The couple will need some information and practice during this time regarding communication skills. For instance, teach the partners how to paraphrase what they hear each other saying. Goal setting is an excellent opportunity to get a sense of the strengths, weaknesses, and habits in the couple's communication. Wellness-based goal setting with couples also reminds them to each attend to their own individual wellness for the benefit of themselves and their partner (spillover and crossover effects). Each partner should thus identify one or two self-care goals.

Wellness Interventions for Couples

Part of the beauty of wellness counseling is that when developing a wellness plan for the couple, wellness counseling offers the scaffolding for a holistic plan. Leaving no stone unturned, incorporating wellness with couples helps the counselor and clients see the whole picture of the couple, and because of that, the parties involved can co-construct wide ranging and meaningful interventions to improve the couple's well-being. To jump start our journey into wellness interventions, let's read through Practitioner Spotlight 12.1.

Dr. Cashwell's vignette illustrates the difference between a wellness-informed approach to couples counseling and a medical model approach. Dr. Cashwell applied emotionally focused couple and family therapy (Johnson, 2004) toward addressing several aspects of the couple's well-being. The vignette also demonstrates how wellness counseling for couples and families is not intended to replace evidence-based interventions; rather, wellness is a lens to ensure that the counselor and clients are thinking and working holistically. Wellness-specific techniques and interventions can also be incorporated. Let's now examine couples interventions across wellness domains.

Mind Wellness

One example category of mind wellness approaches is mindfulness interventions for couples. *Mindfulness* can be defined as "paying attention in a particular way: on purpose, in the present moment, and non-judgmentally" (Kabat-Zinn, 1994, p. 4). These principles can be applied by asking couples to conduct nonjudgmental self-monitoring and documenting of thoughts, feelings, and behaviors that arise before, during, and after conflict, nonconflict, or positive exchanges (Carson, Carson, Gil, & Baucom, 2004).

Practitioner Spotlight 12.1

Case Study

Craig Cashwell

Mark and Sondra requested couple counseling. Mark was in his late 60s and Sondra in her mid-60s. They had been married for about 12 years, and this was a second marriage for both. Mark had never been to counseling before our first session, and Sondra had been to see a counselor briefly after her divorce. Both were originally from a small rural town where they continued to live.

Both said that they would not divorce under any circumstances, but both were unhappy with how often they fought and the emotional disconnection they felt. As is common in couple counseling, Mark and Sondra initially had different perspectives on the problem. Sondra, a soft-spoken and demure woman, became defensive as she spoke of how mean Mark would be to her at times. Mark said that he did not intend to be mean to Sondra but that he would sometimes get stressed at something else (recent examples were heavy traffic and being underprepared to teach a lesson in his faith community) and that his tone would change. Mark reported that he was not angry at Sondra or in any way directing his anger at Sondra, but rather, he would get angry at something external, and this reaction would trigger an emotional response from Sondra. Tracking the cycle further, it became apparent that when Sondra became upset, Mark began working hard to justify his anger, explaining it to Sondra in logical terms that made Sondra much more upset, at which point she would either pull away from Mark or lash out in anger. These cycles had become more and more frequent over time.

Sondra agreed that the start of the argument was Mark getting angry at something external but quickly added that "He knows I don't like it when he gets angry; if he really loved me, he would stop doing that." Mark responded with, "But I'm not angry at you; you just overreact so much when . . . ," and I quickly intervened to cut off the negative path that the session was taking.

I asked them both to tell me about their first marriages. Both divorces were difficult. Sondra's first husband was emotionally and physically abusive. I introduced and defined the term "gaslighting" and defined the term (manipulation that makes you question your memory, perception, and sanity), and she responded, "That's it. That's exactly what he did!" Mark reported that his first wife had an affair with a close friend. He initially omitted one detail that came to light only after Sondra prompted him—that she justified her affair on the basis of Mark's difficulty getting and maintaining an erection.

Although I began to see both Sondra and Mark through a trauma lens, I wanted to avoid pathologizing what I saw as logical developmental struggles for each of them, so it seemed particularly important to work from a wellness orientation. Because both reported as highly religious, I introduced the idea that whole, healing,

(continued)

and holy were all derived from the same word. Both Sondra and
Mark seemed intrigued by this notion. I then leaned in and slowly
and intensely said, "I think what has happened is that, for each of
you, your wholeness was broken in your first marriages. I think your
work here is about being a healer for the other of what was broken in
the first marriage." My hope was that this frame would externalize the
problem as something to be teamed up against. I went on to state that
I thought what had gotten broken for Sondra in her first marriage was
her sense of safety and a clear sense that she mattered. In contrast,
what had gotten broken for Mark was a sense that he was enough. I
slowed down and spent time on this concept, checking in with each
to see whether my understanding fit with their experience, which it
did. I intentionally chose language that communicated to Sondra that
she mattered and to Mark that he was doing great work in the room,
actively countering their core negative beliefs.

I then tracked the cycle between the two of them, normalizing
the following:

- Mark's irritations and frustrations with everyday events;
- How Mark's change in tone of voice "landed" with Sondra,
  given her history of domestic violence in her first marriage;
- How Sondra's reactions (fight or flight) were perfectly
  understandable and, in fact, predictable responses to fear;
- How Mark's defensiveness and explaining were logical,
  given that his fear of inadequacy was activated; and
- How Sondra's reaction to this was understandable because
  Mark's explanations sounded like excuses to her, which she
  likened to a pattern from her first marriage.

Tracking and normalizing this pattern between the two of them
took multiple sessions of exploring, processing slowly and deeply,
and checking in. Both seemed relieved to have the process normalized and validated, and their distress began to come down. Using
emotionally focused couple and family therapy (Johnson, 2004), we
began to track the cycle in terms of attachment-related emotions
and to create more vulnerable reaches for the other. Building on
their many strengths as individuals and as a couple, they got great
traction and first decreased their distress in the relationship and,
over time, created a stronger and more secure attachment bond.

What I believe makes this a wellness-oriented case study is my
steadfast refusal to pathologize in any way. Had I listened only to
Mark's initial reports about Sondra, I might have considered Sondra to be histrionic. Similarly, Sondra's initial characterizations of
Mark made him sound antisocial. Although there were behaviors
that were not helpful in maintaining their connection, these deeds
were all logical reactions in the context of strong attachment-
related emotions and previous attachment injuries. As I normalized

(continued)

Case Study *(continued)*

and validated their struggle, each person began to feel more safety in the counseling room and could see the problem as something to be tackled together rather than some pathology in their partner.

We terminated our work together by mutual consent after 17 sessions.

• • •

This technique can reduce reactivity through mindfulness and self-monitoring alone and also illuminates triggers to problematic communication. Couples can also participate in *interconnected* interventions that merge mind wellness with other domains such as body wellness. For instance, Carson et al. (2004) discussed using "mindful touch exercises, with each partner paying close attention to the giving and receiving of a gentle back rub, followed by dyadic discussion of the implications of this for sensual intimacy" (p. 479). Couples would need information from the counselor on mindfulness and to practice mindfulness within and outside of session to maximize the benefits of such approaches or to avoid causing further harm to the relationship.

Mind wellness can also entail the couple involving themselves in an activity that is engaging to one or both partners. Gottman's (2015) research supports the importance of "turning toward" the things that are significant to our partners. The couple, for example, can schedule a time to go to paint together, visit a museum, and so forth. With couples in which conflict can easily be triggered, it is advisable to set clear parameters for these shared mind wellness experiences. Identify talk topics to be avoided that the couple knows may lead to an argument.

Body Wellness

Body wellness interventions can range from the couple engaging in physical activity together such as going for a walk or job to attending to physical intimacy in the couple's relationship. Couples counseling provides a unique opportunity for partners to discuss the topic of intimacy. Couples may need to talk in and out of session about what is pleasurable to them (Gottman, 2015). As mentioned previously, "physical touch" might be the "love language" of one partner and not the other, hence bringing this information to light can be eye-opening for the couple (Chapman, 2015).

Spirit Wellness

Regarding spirit wellness, Whitlatch, Judge, Zarit, and Femia (2006) developed a values activity for couples in which one partner is diagnosed with dementia. The goal of the activity is to help the partners better understand what each other values, particularly the person with dementia, so that their care needs and preferences can be maximally understood and respected. Motivational interviewing counselors also incorporate values card sorts to help clients identify what is most important to them and if they are living in a way that contradicts those goals and values (Miller & Rollnick, 2012). Request that clients separately identify and write down their top 5–10 values, with the first value being their highest priority and the last value being significant but less so than the others. You can find lists of values online and print them out for your clients so that they have options to choose from. Facilitate the partners sharing and elaborating on their top five values. Urge clients to be specific in providing examples of what living out that value looks like and means to them. The couple should then process values that are shared from their list.

Couples are also directed to co-create shared values; this list of values would serve as a guidepost for the couple. The counselor should process, "What specific behaviors and decisions will help you make steps forward in your relationship toward living out these shared values?" The couple's individual or shared religious beliefs and faith can become a part of the counseling process. The couple can discuss what about their religious or spiritual selves nurtures them individually and collectively (Clarke, Giordano, Cashwell, & Lewis, 2013). An intervention can also be to assess whether the partners' differences in religio-spiritual beliefs cause tension in the relationship. If so, a powerful intervention might involve applying communication skills to this topic or from an emotion-focused couples therapy perspective, helping clients gain insight into these occurrences and getting attachment needs met (Brubacher, 2018).

Emotion Wellness

What are the emotion wellness triggers for the couple? Providing handouts with examples of emotional triggers and having couples identify and share these samples can be powerful. Interconnected interventions with mind wellness can help with emotion regulation of the partners. For example, teach the couple about the cognitive triangle (see Chapter 4) and the relationship among thoughts, feelings, and behaviors. Give the clients homework to identify and write down the thoughts that trigger reactive or conflict-inducing behaviors. Support the partners in writing down the unhelpful self-talk and pinpointing helpful self-talk to repeat to oneself when nonconstructive thoughts emerge. Help clients identify behaviors that keep them grounded. For example, Gottman (2015) recommended that if the partners become escalated with conflict, they need to be apart for 20 minutes. This recommendation is because attempts at resolving an issue while both partners are activated will likely be nonproductive. Emotion education for the couple may be helpful; assisting the partners in understanding that although they are seeing one emotion from their partner that might seem hurtful to them (anger), their partner's true emotion (loneliness) may be coming from a good place (Brubacher, 2018).

Connection Wellness

Connection wellness is not all just about communication skills. Disagreements and different preferences for the social life of the couple can create conflict. Taking a Myers–Briggs Type Indicator (I. B. Myers, McCaulley, Quenk, & Hammer, 1998) may reveal that one partner is extraverted, whereas the other is more introverted. Discussing these assessment results can spark insight, change, and understanding. The intervention can involve talking about ways that the needs of both partners can be met. Does the couple have social support needs? A couple who is caregiving for a loved one with a medical issue may need task support from family members or health professionals. Lack of assistance can cross over into the well-being of the relationship. The counselor can then help the couple find solutions to getting the support they need, thereby increasing connection wellness.

Understanding Family Wellness

In this section, we use the five domains of wellness to facilitate a deeper comprehension of family well-being. The wellness domains intersect with both family-related issues and strengths. When exploring family concepts, we must be careful not to impose our ideas of family on the client, particularly because notions of family vary for each client. Furthermore, culturally influenced beliefs and practices related to family can hold immense value. The following are questions and reflective prompts to guide your conceptualization of the family.

Mind Wellness

Families who eat together tend to be more well. If this is any indication, families who engage in enjoyable activities usually have higher mind wellness. Families with high wellness in this area have comprehensible rules and boundaries that avoid unnecessary confusion for the child or adolescent (Edwards, 1997). Caregivers facilitate a context of intellectual stimulation in the home.

Body Wellness

What is the physical activity level of the family members individually and collectively? What type of nutrition is consumed and provided by the parents or caregivers? Are there barriers to body wellness such as food insecurity? Is physical or sexual abuse taking place?

Spirit Wellness

Do the parents have a purpose? When the primary caregivers of a family live a listless life, this can affect the family system. Is the family involved in a faith community? Do the children or adolescents report or have a sense of purpose? Do the young people in the family appear lost and struggling with issues such as substance abuse?

Emotion Wellness

What is the emotional tone of the family? You can tell by where and how the family members sit and interact. Where do they fall on the emotional spectrum from overly emotional to muted? How are emotions expressed and handled in this family? Do the parents or children have problems with emotion regulation? Is emotional abuse taking place?

Connection Wellness

What patterns of communication do you observe? What family roles exist? Are some family members aligned, whereas others are left out? Is there enmeshment or disconnection in the family as a whole or between certain members? Do the young people and parents/caregivers have healthy social lives outside of the immediate family? Are there unhelpful social influences involved in the child's or adolescent's life?

Wellness-Based Goal Setting With Families

Families are often in crisis by the time they attend counseling, hence the most pressing issues need to be addressed first, including family violence and obtaining needed treatment for individuals in the family related to domestic violence, substance abuse, or severe mental illness. However, once stabilized and family work is indicated, wellness counseling can have a noticeable impact. Similar to couples counseling, family members should each complete a formal or informal wellness assessment individually. Family members are presented with the idea that if each pursues individual wellness goals, this improvement can benefit the well-being of the entire family.

The family members are to share their wellness strengths and deficits and to share an individual wellness goal. They are to then share how the family can support them in this goal. In a second activity inspired by Edwards (1997), the family should each rate the wellness of the family across the domains and holistically. The counselor will have the family members share their wellness pie or ratings. At times, family members may vary greatly in how they perceive the well-being of the family. Be sure to process what these differences mean to the family members. The family will be assisted in coming to an agreement about no more than two to three family goals, with each member taking responsibility for contributing to family wellness goals. Family members are encouraged to ask each other for help in pursuing the family wellness goals.

Wellness Interventions With Families

Wellness-based family interventions can be a helpful adjunct to many family counseling approaches. The counseling is based around the wellness model chosen by the counselor. A family wellness approach works particularly well in prevention and primary-level family counseling situations in which the severity of crisis is lower. However, it can also be used with families in crisis after they become stabilized. After goals are set, psychoeducation and counseling ensue, targeting counseling goal areas.

Connection Wellness

Connection wellness is frequently one of the first domains covered during family interventions because interactional issues are a common factor resulting in families coming to counseling. If a family cannot communicate at a minimal level, then even balancer activities can have a negative result.

Counseling in this domain focuses on identifying failed solutions of communication patterns—in other words, what components of communication tend to lead to family tension. Additionally, communication exceptions are highlighted in which the family communicates in ways that are more constructive. The wellness counselor should present information on effective communication skills that is sensitive to the client family's culture. The counselor may help the family learn and practice skills such as reflective listening, how to break destructive communication patterns, and walking away from conversations when communication breaks down.

Emotion Wellness

Family emotion wellness psychoeducation can center on learning emotional triggers of different family members and how to respect those. Strategies for providing emotional support for each other is another topic.

Spirit Wellness

Spirit interventions often relate to the caregivers or parents not effectively steering the family ship, thereby preventing the children and adolescents from self-actualizing as well as experiencing collective meaning within the family. Single-parent or couples sessions can empower them to set appropriate boundaries, rules, and a sense of meaning for the parents, individually and as a couple. As the caregiver or couple become more fulfilled, this improvement can benefit the family.

Spirit interventions can also pertain to the family's religious or spiritual beliefs and practices. If religion and spirituality are important to the family and they became disconnected from their faith community, this isolation may be an area for attention. The faith community may add an extra layer of support for the family (Brown, 2008; Ebaugh & Curry, 2000).

Body Wellness

Some families have patterns of being sedentary. Education on healthy food options, exercise options, sleep hygiene and self-care information, supporting healthy body image in children and adolescents, and the benefits of these facets can be discussed. Facilitating discussions among the family as a whole to identify and implement a family wellness enriching activity can be therapeutic.

Mind Wellness

The counselor can ask each family member to list and discuss their hobbies and favorite activities. The children in the family should discuss aloud the activities that they enjoy engaging in the most with their parents and vice versa. The counselor should be aware of families that over- and underschedule activities for their children. Balance is the goal. Thus, an intervention for an underscheduled family can involve helping parents initiate some of the identified activities.

A lack of setting rules, children not understanding rules, and an absence of the enforcement of rules in the home can clutter the minds of children and parents. Wellness interventions can entail assessing existing rules and barriers to follow through with the parents. The counselor then assists the parents in preparing to set and implement their rules. This can include conversations between parents and among parents and older children to determine rules, rewards, and punishments as well as discussions in which parents ensure that the rules of the home are unambiguous to the family (Edwards, 1997).

Family Wellness Balancers and Failed Solutions

Pinpointing family wellness balancers is a good starting point. Engage the family members in a discussion to identify one or more pleasant activities that the family does together and enjoys themselves. The family may groan that such an activity does not exist. This response is where the exception question can be helpful. Ask the family about a recent time in which they were all together and things did not become as tense as they typically do. What were they doing? What did each member do differently that contributed to the family experience being less negative?

An additional alternative is exploring failed solutions. Assist the family in isolating factors of an activity (including the nature of it) and the communication among family members that causes the family gathering to fall apart. Then encourage the family to, piece by piece, construct a family experience that has a chance of going well, including any guidelines that need to be in place for fun and fulfillment to occur.

A wellness model provides a map for the family to identify pleasant activities that support the well-being of different family members. The following list contains some examples of family wellness boosters or balancer activities across domains:

1. *Mind wellness*—Engage in fun activities that stimulate the mind, including attending a play at the community theater, going to a local science center, and playing board games if this is a balancer (avoid if it typically causes conflict).
2. *Body wellness*—Go for family walks or jogs, play a sport together if it is a balancer (avoid sports if they tend to cause conflict), or eat a healthy meal together.
3. *Spirit*—Attend one's religious service or an event held in one's faith community, go for a nature walk together, or volunteer together.
4. *Emotion*—At dinner or during family time, each member expresses gratitude for one thing about each family member; notice and affirm strengths you notice in each family member during family time that elicits pleasant feelings; and engage in family activities that elicit positive emotions.

5. *Connection*—Get together with friends of the family that have a positive influence; practice effective communication skills during and outside of family time.

A Note About Technology

Dr. Ed Jacobs, developer of impact therapy, created an activity in which a beer bottle prop is placed between counselor and client to reflect the barrier that alcohol has posed in the client's life (Jacobs, 1994). Although addiction remains a huge barrier in the lives of many individuals and families, one of the emerging barriers that is, in some ways, comparable is technology. Use of cell phones and the Internet are creating increased problems with couples' and families' ability to connect. How many couples sit in bed at night and become lost in reading Internet articles on their cell phone rather than talking about the day's events? How many couples and families avoid real problems that are going on by zoning out with Instagram or Facebook? Be aware when counseling couples and families to assess for and address the role of technology and how it affects the partners and members.

Strides forward in the area of understanding technology and wellness have been made by people such as Kennedy and Baker (2016), who developed the TechnoWellness Inventory to assist wellness counselors in exploring the role and repercussions (positive and negative) of technology in their clients' lives. The wise wellness counselor will also identify ways to mobilize technology for beneficent purposes in the couple's and family's life. For instance, family or couples exercise challenges using apps or Global Positioning System technology can be an effective interconnected intervention that enhances mind, body, and connection wellness. The counselor must use judgment, because such an activity might cause more tension in some families. Ground rules for making such an activity productive can be co-constructed by the counselor and family.

Wellness in Groups

There are unique advantages and challenges when facilitating wellness groups or infusing wellness concepts into groups that have a specific focus. As we have discussed throughout the book, most aspects of individuals' functioning are interconnected with respect to the wellness domains. By addressing clients' holistic wellness in groups, we can promote healthy coping from multiple angles and perspectives and reinforce clients' strengths in areas where they are functioning at a high level. We believe that groups can be especially effective in addressing wellness-related issues. One aspect that is helpful is the increased accountability within groups. When individuals commit to a goal with others, they are more likely to follow through with it.

The group process itself is a key component for group leaders in promoting members' wellness. Yalom and Leszcz's (2005) therapeutic factors—which are widely known and are considered primary mechanisms by which group counseling is effective—include the following: instillation of hope, universality, imparting information, altruism, corrective recapitulation of the primary family group, development of socializing techniques, imitative behavior, group cohesiveness, catharsis, and existential factors.

Skilled group leaders promote a climate where these factors are present. When the therapeutic factors are present, the group is helpful for clients, regardless of the concern they are experiencing. At the same time, many of the factors may be directly related to aspects of clients' wellness. Connection or social wellness is an obvious area where working with a group could be helpful. Development of socialization techniques and group cohesiveness are specific factors related to connection wellness. Corrective recapitulation of the primary family group, altruism (i.e., helping others in the group), and universality (realizing you are not alone in dealing with problems) are also related to connection and emotion wellness. Instillation of hope (i.e., feeling more hopeful about improvement) and catharsis strongly link to emotion wellness.

Existential factors, such as finding meaning and embracing choice, are linked with spirit wellness. Imitative behavior and imparting information can both be helpful across wellness domains. For example, group members can learn effective strategies for regulating emotions, managing stress, or identifying communication patterns from other group members. Group members can also share helpful practical information, such as who are the good local nutritionists; where some good yoga studios are located; which smartphone apps are most helpful for tracking progress; or which churches are welcoming to lesbian, gay, bisexual, and transgender members. Group leaders who promote wellness can capitalize on the unique dynamics of group counseling and foster the therapeutic factors to facilitate their members' holistic development.

Despite the benefits of wellness promotion in group formats, leaders must be aware of the potential challenges. As with all groups, leaders must screen potential members for appropriateness to be in the group. Group leaders must also attend to members' readiness to address various aspects of wellness and be prepared to have members at different stages. There is a risk that group members may feel self-conscious when other members are making faster progress toward their wellness goals. Group leaders must be sensitive to members' insecurities and foster a climate of support and encouragement rather than one of competition.

Wellness-focused groups are offered from a prevention standpoint or may be implemented with individuals who are already experiencing concerns. Below is a sample of some of the more common wellness-related groups that may be offered in K–12 schools, universities, or community settings:

- Stress management
- Social skills
- Healthy relationships
- Life balance
- Body image
- Career development

- Self-esteem
- Body image
- Self-care
- Mindfulness
- Health

There are multiple approaches to facilitating wellness groups. Following is a general outline for a wellness group to help them deal with stress. Although the example is tailored to students, it could easily be adapted for any population. The group is relatively psychoeducational in nature; however, leaders must attend to the group process and dynamics.

Wellness Group: Session 1

Introduction and Discussion

Objectives
1. To introduce group members and leaders to each other.
2. To help students identify challenges they may face as graduate students in counseling.
3. To help students recognize some of their current wellness practices.

Procedure
1. Group leaders should introduce themselves and talk about the purpose of the group. Also, the logistics of the group should be addressed.
2. Group leaders engage the students in an introductory or "icebreaker" activity of their choice to help the students get to know each other and the leaders.

3. Students break into smaller groups of two or three and develop a list of challenges (e.g., moving, work, relationships) that they expect to face. Then each group reports the list to the larger group.
4. Individually, students will identify one wellness activity in which they currently participate.

Wellness Group: Session 2

Stress and Burnout

Objectives

1. To introduce students to the signs of burnout in counselors and the consequences for clients.
2. To help students to identify when they are burned out.
3. To introduce students to wellness dimensions.

Procedure

1. Individually, students identify two signs (one physical, one mental/emotional) that they are stressed out. Identify what is going on, what are they thinking, and how do they behave.
2. Group leaders describe the characteristics of burnout and stress.
3. The students then formulate a list of potential consequences of burnout for clients. Group leaders lead a discussion, adding any additional information that students may not have identified.
4. As a homework assignment, instruct the students to complete the Five-Factor Wellness Inventory (J. E. Myers & Sweeney, 2005) or another wellness assessment.

Wellness Group: Session 3

Wellness Dimensions

Objectives

1. To introduce students to six areas of wellness.
2. To help students identify their current practices in the different wellness dimensions.
3. To help students identify and prioritize areas of wellness that they need to address to maintain appropriate self-care.

Procedure

1. Check in with students about their results of the wellness assessment. Talk about what their thoughts are (e.g., any surprises, what they expected, what they learned).
2. Distribute the "POSIES" (physical, occupational, spiritual, intellectual, emotional, social) wheel to students. Discuss the various aspects of wellness.

3. Provide students time to fill in each area of the "POSIES" wheel with their current wellness practices in that area. Provide time to discuss the different practices in which they engage. Students will then identify areas where they believe they would like to improve.
4. Go over the guidelines for the wellness plan assignment.

Students will complete and score an assessment of personal wellness; they will then write a two-page "Plan of Action" (including areas for self-care and self-improvement). One to two paragraphs must address how lack of self-care in a student could lead to stress and burnout.

Wellness Group: Session 4

Wellness Grid

Objectives
1. To introduce students to self-care strategies.
2. To help students identify and develop a self-care goal.

Materials: White board; dry erase markers

Procedure: The group leaders will create a grid (see example below) with six dimensions of wellness represented vertically along the left side of the grid. The group members will choose six letters to fill the columns horizontally along the top of the grid. The group leader will give the dry erase marker to one of the group members. The group member will fill in the box with a wellness activity related to the dimension that starts with the letter in the corresponding column. After the group member has filled in one of the boxes, they will pass the marker to another group member. The group will continue this process until the whole grid is filled. Each group member will then choose a wellness activity that they will agree to do in the subsequent week and report back to the group during the following week.

Grid Example:

	R	S	T	L	N	E
Physical	run					
Emotional						
Intellectual				learn some-thing new		
Spiritual						evaluate life goals
Social			talk to friends			
Occupational						

Students will be assigned homework to begin working on a rough draft of their wellness plan.

Wellness Group: Session 5

Wellness Dimension Goals

Objectives
1. Students will evaluate their ability to implement a wellness goal.
2. Students will identify specific, measurable, and attainable wellness goals for each wellness dimension that they will implement throughout their time as a graduate student and as a professional.

Procedure
1. Students will report to the group how successful they were in completing their wellness goal from the previous week. If they were not successful, they can talk about what kept them from completing it and how they might be able to in the future.
2. Students will break into smaller groups of two or three and discuss their rough-draft wellness plans. Students will give each other feedback.
3. Students will individually develop specific, measurable, and attainable wellness goals for each of the dimensions on the "POSIES" wheel. For example, within the physical dimension, one could state, "I will bike ride for 30 minutes, three days per week."
4. Students will share their goals with the rest of the group.

Wellness Group: Session 6

Identifying Barriers and Closure

Objectives
1. To help students identify barriers to implementing their wellness plans.
2. To help students develop a plan to effectively navigate barriers.
3. To provide students with an opportunity to provide each other feedback about their wellness plans.

Procedure
1. Students will break into smaller groups (2–3 students) and identify potential challenges to implementing their wellness plans. Students will then develop strategies to effectively navigate the challenges.
2. Each student will share their wellness plan and strategies when facing challenges with the group by highlighting the main points.

Students will provide each other with feedback about their wellness plans. Students can talk about what they have learned from each other, different wellness strategies that they might try, and hopes for each other.

Conclusion

It is important to address wellness using modalities other than individual counseling. Wellness counseling can be delivered in couples, family, and group formats. These counseling structures offer unique benefits to clients, particularly via working within systems. To conclude, we present Practitioner Spotlight 12.2 from Shannonhouse, Aten, and Davis that exemplifies wellness interventions at an even larger level: the community level.

Reflection Prompts

1. If you were providing psychoeducation on family wellness, what other topics would you consider including in each domain?
2. In your work counseling couples and families, what are the most common wellness struggles that you have noticed that couples and families are facing?
3. What are your reactions to Dr. Cashwell's couples case example? What are the takeaways for you regarding implementing wellness-informed couples counseling?
4. What are some steps you can take to ensure that the culture of the couples and family members you work with is respected as you provide wellness counseling?
5. How has technology been helpful in couples and family relationships? In what ways has it been harmful? How might you handle issues of technology that negatively affect a couple or family while adhering to a wellness counseling framework? In what ways can technology be mobilized in a fruitful way through couples and family interventions?
6. What were some similarities and differences regarding implementing wellness approaches at the community level in the second case study versus the micro level of the counseling office? What ideas do you have for implementing wellness approaches at the systemic level?

Practitioner Spotlight 12.2

A Community-Based Spiritual (Essential Self) Intervention for Those Affected by Disaster

Laura Shannonhouse, Jamie D. Aten, and Don Davis

Globally, approximately 250 million people are affected by some form of disaster every year (International Federation of Red Cross and Red Crescent Societies, 2015). Survivors often turn to their faith to make sense of suffering. Scholars (e.g., Cook, Aten, Moore, Hook, & Davis, 2013) have demonstrated that religion/spirituality constructs are linked to positive and negative psychological outcomes. For example, religious comfort can facilitate positive coping, whereas being angry at, or feeling punished by, God can amplify distress. When survivors are able to integrate their current reality into their belief system, they have been found to experience meaning making and renewed purpose (Haynes et al., 2017). Considering how central religion/spirituality can be to disaster recovery, it is important for counselors to be able to address spiritual distress within the essential-self factor of the Indivisible Self Model of Wellness (J. E. Myers & Sweeney, 2004). This requirement is especially true because wellness scholars (e.g., J. E. Myers, Sweeney, & Witmer, 2000) have proven that positively affecting one area of wellness affects the whole. In a community intervention such as disaster response, we must also consider partnering and working with others in a way that is aligned and respectful of spiritual and cultural values if we are to positively affect holistic wellness.

Many disaster aid volunteers come from, and partner with, local faith-based organizations. Faith-based organizations offer more long-term support when compared with disaster responders deployed during the initial stage of disaster. Partnering with local churches is one means of effectively serving long-term needs. In working with local churches in Baton Rouge (i.e., the Bethany community), we provided trainings in Spiritual First Aid (SFA) to equip local paraprofessionals with skills needed to respond to spiritual distress of survivors.

Those who attended the trainings were highly capable individuals with a desire to be helpful to their community members. To our surprise, attendees were not only from local communities that were not directly affected but also included survivors whose own homes flooded. While "mucking out" each other's houses and rebuilding, there were opportunities for aid workers and neighbors to address spiritual needs. When survivors discussed feeling abandoned by God, those trained in SFA reported being able to listen and respond with humility, as opposed to sharing platitudes and potentially even shaming survivors for being angry with God. Discussing spiritual distress was one of the most immediate ways for them to meaningfully connect with survivors, and it also helped them determine other needs. Many opened their homes to survivors in their faith communities so they had a place to live while their homes were being rebuilt. Sharing food and having a bed to sleep in were common physical needs (physical self) that were addressed by these paraprofessionals.

(continued)

A Community-Based Spiritual Intervention *(continued)*

With spiritual and physical needs being addressed, survivors often coped more constructively (coping self). For instance, survivors who are coping well seek connections with others (social self) in their faith-based community, as opposed to isolating themselves. They turn to sacred writings, hymns, and so forth for answers to faith-based questions, and they consequently find comfort in these beliefs and in community with others. They reengage prior spiritual routines (i.e., prayer practices, attending faith services, and small group). They engage in lament, and they actively grieve the losses they have experienced in fellowship with others. Ultimately, they recognize what they do and do not have control over, and they are able to "give some things over to God" (i.e., the serenity prayer) while focusing energy on things they do have control over.

In a community-based intervention such as SFA, it was essential that we developed an advisory board to learn how the community was doing after we left. This advisory board in Baton Rouge has routinely informed us of progress and needs this past year. Furthermore, it provided a structure for responders to support one another through the disillusionment phase of disaster. In addition, it is important to foster reliance on and interdependence with other community members, as opposed to on us (disaster mental health professionals), because we are there just in the short term. The goal is empowerment and identifying strengths within the community. Last, we have been blessed to witness the social support, and spiritual resources, provided over time by the Bethany community, which undoubtedly has resulted in increased hope and gratitude within its members.

Although we have a lot to learn, the team of researchers who have been organized through the Humanitarian Disaster Institute founded by Jamie Aten routinely collect data by working with disaster-affected populations. The goal is to always develop new resources that foster wellness in communities affected by disaster.

• • •

Learning Activities

Couple and Family Wellness Pie

Use the five-domain model or a wellness model of your choice to explore your own couple or family wellness. On a 1–10 scale, rate your family's collective well-being in each wellness domain and overall. Alternatively, you can self-assess your couples and family wellness through the wellness pie activity in which you draw the domains of wellness as a pie. Draw the areas of strong wellness as larger slices of pie and areas of lower wellness as smaller pieces of pie. Reflect on each rating. Identity components of your couple or family relationship(s) that are positive for each wellness domain

(continued)

Couple and Family Wellness Pie *(continued)*

and any components of each wellness domain in which you could grow as a couple or family. Reflect on what you learned from this experience, particularly regarding how you might incorporate this or a similar exercise with couples and families. What would the impact be when you can have both members of the couple or all members of the family completing this exercise and sharing their findings?

Family Wellness Genogram

Genograms are a wonderful tool of family therapy. They too can be used in family wellness counseling. This activity is intended for your own learning so that you can also use this intervention with individual or family clients, if appropriate. Create a family genogram. A basic Google search on genogram symbols will provide you with information and options for depicting you, your family members, and their relationship to each other. The unique aspect of a family wellness genogram is to uncover generational patterns of wellness in one's family. To do this, you will first write out your genogram, checking with family members to help you complete the genogram. While doing this, ask your family members (immediate and extended) to identify their area of strongest wellness and their area of lowest wellness. You may have to explain and provide some examples of domains that constitute wellness (so study up on your wellness model of choice!). Then document your family members' responses on the genogram by marking two letters next to each family member, with one letter representing the first letter of the domain of highest wellness and the other letter representing the domain of lowest wellness. Then add a "+" or "−" sign next to each letter to indicate the high and low wellness areas. For example, M+ and C− next to a family member denotes *mind wellness* as the strongest domain and *connection wellness* as the lowest domain. When speaking with family members about their well-being, also consider asking each person about one thing that has helped to maintain high wellness in their strongest domain. This step enables you to amass wellness tips that might be useful (similar to the wellness role models intervention in Chapter 11). For family members whom you are unable to contact, simply leave the wellness information blank.

Debriefing Questions for Family Wellness Genogram

The family genogram process can take some time, but it can yield powerful information and insights. Make sure to reflect on the following questions as you are completing, and after you are done working on, your family wellness genogram:

1. What patterns of high wellness do you notice in your family genogram?
2. What patterns of low wellness have emerged (e.g., are there patterns of wellness differences based on gender, geographical location of family members, age, side of the family)?

(continued)

Debriefing Questions *(continued)*

3. What influences in your family have supported your wellness?

4. What influences in your family have detracted from your wellness?

5. What one or two wellness tips from family members were most helpful to you?

6. What are your greatest takeaways in regard to learning about your own and your family's wellness from engaging in this activity?

7. What insights have you gained in regard to using the family wellness genogram as an intervention with clients?

Resources

American Academy of Pediatrics—Resources for Families

https://www.aap.org/en-us/advocacy-and-policy/aap-health-initiatives/NCECHW/Pages/Resources-For-Families.aspx

Wellness information for families across domains such as physical and mental health.

American Psychological Association—Children, Youth, and Families

http://www.apa.org/pi/families/

Topics on this webpage include the mental health and wellness of ethnic minority, refugee, and immigrant children.

American Psychological Association—Family and Relationships

http://www.apa.org/helpcenter/family/index.aspx

Information on divorce, financial wellness, and other topics resides on this website.

Association for Marriage and Family Therapy

https://www.aamft.org/iMIS15/AAMFT/

A plethora of resources exist, such as webinars, readings, credentialing information, job search, and networking opportunities.

Multicultural Family Institute

https://multiculturalfamily.org/

Readings and information about genograms and family counseling reside on this website.

National Parent–Teacher Association—Health

https://www.pta.org/home/family-resources/health

This website will link parents and families to a wealth of wellness resources, such as preparing for college and employment, safety at school and on the Internet, substance use, and ensuring that one's drinking water is appropriate for consumption.

Parent Toolkit
> https://www.parenttoolkit.com/additional-resources/health-and-wellness-resources
>
> This webpage will connect you to several government-supported websites and programs with information for parents on child and adolescent well-being. Topics include dental health, nutrition, exercise, sleep, and others.

References

Benson, L. A., McGinn, M. M., & Christensen, A. (2012). Common principles of couple therapy. *Behavior Therapy, 43,* 25–35.

Brock, R. L., & Lawrence, E. (2008). A longitudinal investigation of stress spillover in marriage: Does spousal support adequacy buffer the effects? *Journal of Family Psychology, 22,* 11–20.

Brown, D. L. (2008). African American resiliency: Examining racial socialization and social support as protective factors. *Journal of Black Psychology, 34,* 32–48.

Brubacher, L. L. (2018). *Stepping into emotionally focused couple therapy: Key ingredients of change.* London, England: Karnac Books.

Buchanan, T. M., & McConnell, A. R. (2017). Family as a source of support under stress: Benefits of greater breadth of family inclusion. *Self and Identity, 16,* 97–122.

Buck, A. A., & Neff, L. A. (2012). Stress spillover in early marriage: The role of self-regulatory depletion. *Journal of Family Psychology, 26,* 698–708.

Carroll, S. J., Hill, E. J., Yorgason, J. B., Larson, J. H., & Sandberg, J. G. (2013). Couple communication as a mediator between work–family conflict and marital satisfaction. *Contemporary Family Therapy, 35,* 530–545.

Carson, J. W., Carson, K. M., Gil, K. M., & Baucom, D. H. (2004). Mindfulness-based relationship enhancement. *Behavior Therapy, 35,* 471–494.

Chapman, G. (2015). *The five love languages: The secret to love that lasts* (5th ed.). Chicago, IL: Northfield.

Clarke, P. B., Giordano, A. L., Cashwell, C. S., & Lewis, T. F. (2013). The straight path to healing: Using motivational interviewing to address spiritual bypass. *Journal of Counseling & Development, 91,* 87–94.

Cook, S. W., Aten, J. D., Moore, M., Hook, J. N., & Davis, D. E. (2013). Resource loss, religiousness, health, and posttraumatic growth following Hurricane Katrina. *Mental Health, Religion & Culture, 16,* 352–366. https://doi.org/10.1080/13674676.2012.667395

David, P., & Stafford, L. (2015). A relational approach to religion and spirituality in marriage: The role of couples' religious communication in marital satisfaction. *Journal of Family Issues, 36,* 232–249.

Ebaugh, H. R., & Curry, M. (2000). Fictive kin as social capital in new immigrant communities. *Sociological Perspectives, 43,* 189–209.

Edwards, J. T. (1997). *Working with families: Guidelines and techniques* (4th ed.). Durham, NC: Foundation Place.

Fuemmeler, B. F., Behrman, P., Taylor, M., Sokol, R., Rothman, E., Jacobson, L. T., . . . Tercyak, K. P. (2017). Child and family health in the era of prevention: New opportunities and challenges. *Journal of Behavioral Medicine, 40,* 159–174.

Gottman, J. M. (2015). *Principia amoris: The new science of love.* New York, NY: Routledge.

Hair, E. C., Moore, K. A., Hadley, A. M., Kaye, K., Day, R. D., & Orthner, D. K. (2009). Parent marital quality and the parent–adolescent relationship: Effects on adolescent and young adult health outcomes. *Marriage & Family Review, 45,* 218–248.

Haynes, W. C., Van Tongeren, D. R., Aten, J., Davis, E. B., Davis, D. E., Hook, J. N., . . . Johnson, T. (2017). The meaning as a buffer hypothesis: Spiritual meaning attenuates the effect of disaster-related resource loss on posttraumatic stress. *Psychology of Religion and Spirituality, 9,* 446–453.

International Federation of Red Cross and Red Crescent Societies. (2015). *World Disasters Report 2015: Focus on local actors, the key to humanitarian effectiveness.* Retrieved from http://ifrc-media.org/interactive/wp-content/uploads/2015/09/1293600-World-Disasters-Report-2015_en.pdf

Jacobs, E. (1994). *Impact therapy.* Lutz, FL: Psychological Assessment Resources.

Johnson, S. M. (2004). *The practice of emotionally focused couple therapy: Creating connection* (2nd ed.). New York, NY: Brunner-Routledge.

Kabat-Zinn, J. (1994). *Wherever you go there you are: Mindfulness meditation in everyday life.* New York, NY: Hyperion Books.

Kelly, A. B., Mason, W. A., Chmelka, M. B., Herrenkohl, T. I., Kim, M. J., Patton, G. C., . . . Catalano, R. F. (2016). Depressed mood during early to middle adolescence: A binational longitudinal study of the unique impact of family conflict. *Journal of Youth and Adolescence, 45,* 1604–1613.

Kennedy, S. D., & Baker, S. B. (2016). Using the TechnoWellness Inventory (TWI) to examine and apply a new wellness construct. *Journal of Counselor Leadership and Advocacy, 3,* 41–51.

Lavner, J. A., & Clark, M. A. (2017). Workload and marital satisfaction over time: Testing lagged spillover and crossover effects during the newlywed years. *Journal of Vocational Behavior, 101,* 67–76.

Miller, W. R., & Rollnick, S. (2012). *Motivational interviewing: Helping people change* (3rd ed.). New York, NY: Guilford Press.

Myers, I. B., McCaulley, M. H., Quenk, N. L., & Hammer, A. L. (1998). *MBTI manual: A guide to the development and use of the Myers–Briggs Type Indicator* (Vol. 3). Palo Alto, CA: Consulting Psychologists Press.

Myers, J. E., & Sweeney, T. J. (2004). The indivisible self: An evidence-based model of wellness. *Journal of Individual Psychology, 60,* 234–244.

Myers, J. E., & Sweeney, T. J. (2005). *The five factor wellness inventory.* Menlo Park, CA: Mind Garden.

Myers, J. E., & Sweeney, T. J. (2014). *Five factor wellness inventory (FFWEL): Adult, teenage, and elementary school versions.* Menlo Park, CA: Mind Garden.

Myers, J. E., Sweeney, T. J., & Witmer, J. M. (2000). The Wheel of Wellness counseling for wellness: A holistic model for treatment planning. *Journal of Counseling & Development, 78,* 251–266.

Neff, L. A., & Karney, B. R. (2007). Stress crossover in newlywed marriage: A longitudinal and dyadic perspective. *Journal of Marriage and Family, 69,* 594–607.

Ogden, C. L., Carroll, M. D., Fryar, C. D., & Flegal, K. M. (2015). *Prevalence of obesity among adults and youth: United States, 2011–2014.* Washington, DC: U.S. Department of Health and Human Services, Centers for Disease Control and Prevention, National Center for Health Statistics.

Parcel, T. L., & Bixby, M. S. (2016). The ties that bind: Social capital, families, and children's well-being. *Child Development Perspectives, 10,* 87–92.

Proulx, C. M., Helms, H. M., & Buehler, C. (2007). Marital quality and personal well-being: A meta-analysis. *Journal of Marriage and Family, 69,* 576–593.

Robles, T. F., Slatcher, R. B., Trombello, J. M., & McGinn, M. M. (2014). Marital quality and health: A meta-analytic review. *Psychological Bulletin, 140,* 140–187.

Schoenfeld, E. A., Loving, T. J., Pope, M. T., Huston, T. L., & Štulhofer, A. (2017). Does sex really matter? Examining the connections between spouses' nonsexual behaviors, sexual frequency, sexual satisfaction, and marital satisfaction. *Archives of Sexual Behavior, 46,* 489–501.

Whitlatch, C. J., Judge, K., Zarit, S. H., & Femia, E. (2006). Dyadic intervention for family caregivers and care receivers in early-stage dementia. *The Gerontologist, 46,* 688–694.

Williamson, H. C., Altman, N., Hsueh, J., & Bradbury, T. N. (2016). Effects of relationship education on couple communication and satisfaction: A randomized controlled trial with low-income couples. *Journal of Consulting and Clinical Psychology, 84,* 156–166.

Yalom, I. D., & Leszcz, M. (2005). *The theory and practice of group psychotherapy* (5th ed.). New York, NY: Basic Books.

Part IV
Wellness Counseling Across the Life Span

Chapter 13

Wellness Counseling With Children, Adolescents, and Emerging Adults

The potential possibilities of any child are the most intriguing and stimulating in all creation.

—Ray L. Wilbur

• • •

Wellness counseling implementation varies depending on the counselors' setting. In this chapter, we discuss practical application and logistical organization of wellness counseling in primary care, K–12 education settings, and postsecondary institutions. Specifically, we discuss how to align wellness with the mission and vision of the educational setting, and we describe strategies for incorporating wellness interventions within comprehensive school counseling programs and general counseling services in postsecondary institutions.

Introduction to Child and Adolescent Wellness

Childhood is a critical period in development, with strong links to individuals' long-term holistic wellness. When children are exposed to high levels of stress or other adverse childhood experiences, it greatly increases their risk for social, emotional, behavioral, and health problems as adults (Edwards, Holden, Felitti, & Anda, 2003). However, it is encouraging that intervention programs can help alleviate the effects of childhood stressors. Preventive social, behavioral, and emotional activities—as well as early screening, identification, and intervention—are critical in promoting children's holistic wellness.

The Substance Abuse and Mental Health Services Administration (see Oppenheim et al., 2016) identified five primary approaches to promoting childhood wellness:

- Developmental and behavioral screening in a range of child-serving settings,
- Mental health consultation in early care and education,
- Enhanced home visiting with a focus on social and emotional development,
- Family strengthening and parent support, and
- Integration of behavioral health into primary care.

Counselors can play a critical role in each of these approaches, ranging from being the direct service provider to being a consultant to another service professional. In practice, we know it can be challenging to have children focus on wellness promotion, because parents are more likely to bring their children to counseling after a problem has started. However, two common places where counselors are able to work with children through a prevention perspective are primary care and educational settings.

It is impossible to separate the individual from the environment when thinking about wellness for children and adolescents. Bronfenbrenner's (1979) ecological model, seen in Figure 13.1, is helpful in conceptualizing how to address wellness from a social and environmental perspective. The model includes four contextual environments that influence individuals' perspective on wellness as well as their ability to access wellness resources. Closest to the individual, the *microsystem* includes influences that are prominent in an individual's daily life, such as family, friends, and school. Next, the

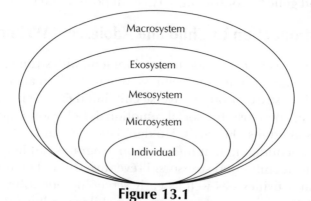

Figure 13.1

Bronfenbrenner's Ecological Systems Model

mesosystem consists of the interaction between members of the micro-system (e.g., the parents' interactions with the school). Continuing to broaden out, the *exosystem* includes environments that indirectly affect children, such as the neighborhood, community, social servic-es, family socioeconomic status, and local school board. Finally, the *macrosystem* includes the individuals' cultural values as well as laws, policies, and programs that are dictated by larger institutions such as the government or education system as a whole. There have been various iterations of this model over time; however, for simplicity and applicability for counselors, we believe that the original model is suitable. It is important for counselors to consider factors in each environmental context in addition to individual factors when pro-moting wellness among children and adolescents.

If you remember back to Chapter 3, we talked about social deter-minants of health and their impact on individual health and wellness. You can see these environmental factors in each level of an ecological model. Children are heavily influenced by their education experi-ences at the microsystem level (participation in an early childhood program or exposure to language and literacy skills). These things are also reinforced (or not) by their family system. Moving out a level creates a mesosystem (the interaction between microsystems), which is largely affected by the broader systems. Therefore, the exosystem influences—such as a family's employment, food, and housing stability—all affect the availability of their caregivers to interact with their teachers and school environments. For example, a caregiver who is working in an hourly paying job to make ends meet is much less likely to be able to take an hour off of work to attend a Parent–Teacher Association meeting or connect with the school counselor.

Last, the macrosystem affects access to exosystem environments through laws and policies. Because of things such as school zoning, tax incentives, policing procedures, and gentrification, those living in poverty often have less access to healthy foods, quality housing, and health care; are more likely to be incarcerated (or have an incarcerated caregiver) and stay incarcerated for longer sentences (than those with a higher socioeconomic status); and face commu-nity challenges such as discrimination and violence. Therefore, if you are a community counselor or school counselor working with individual students, it is impossible to focus on their health and well-ness without taking into account the impact of social determinants of health throughout their ecosystem. Therefore, it is important for the wellness counselor working with children and adolescents to advocate for community-level change in regard to laws, policy, and access. In addition, it is imperative to keep these challenges in mind when planning programs and other ways to involve caregivers—for example, varying the schedule of when things are offered, sending information home in native languages, working to understand specific needs such as food insecurity over the weekend, and so forth.

Wellness in Primary Care

The integration of behavioral health services in primary care settings is an emerging and exciting paradigm for promoting wellness among children and adolescents. In this model, the physician includes a mental health professional as part of the treatment team to address social, emotional, and behavioral concerns. This integration is an important step because parents are more likely to seek help from a pediatrician when their child is experiencing emotional or behavioral concerns. However, pediatricians have reported a lack of time, training, and ability to screen as a barrier to addressing mental health concerns (Gadomski et al., 2014). Integrating behavioral health with primary care helps increase social and emotional supports for children and families and alleviates some of the burden on physicians to address the issue. In 2008, the Substance Abuse and Mental Health Services Administration supported a national initiative for 55 sites to implement a program called Linking Actions for Unmet Needs in Children's Health to help improve children's behavioral health. Oppenheim et al. (2016) reviewed the programs and found the following common components implemented at the sites:

- Embedded mental health consultants,
- Inclusion of a family partner/navigator,
- Cross-training,
- Behavioral health screening,
- Wellness promotion and prevention as part of the well-child visit,
- Warm handoff,
- Assessment and brief intervention,
- Parenting groups and health promotion activities,
- Shared recordkeeping, and
- Care coordination.

Many of the skills required to provide these services are developed in counselor training programs. As behavioral health and wellness promotion becomes more integrated into primary care settings, counselors should become familiar with the culture of primary care and how they can best contribute to a multidisciplinary team to support children and adolescents in their holistic health and development. At minimum, counselors in the community should develop strong working relationships with their local primary care providers to build referral sources and to provide resources related to social and emotional concerns.

Wellness in K–12 Schools

Because of the rising rates of mental health concerns among adolescents, the Centers for Disease Control and Prevention (2011) recommended preventive services to reduce risk and promote wellness. School counselors in K–12 school settings are in an ideal position to promote wellness for students within the educational environment. Children and adolescents often first receive mental services through the school, and the school counselor is frequently the first mental health professional to have contact with students. A holistic wellness approach is consistent with the scope and focus of comprehensive school counseling programs (Gysbers & Henderson, 2012). School counselors are expected to implement preventive interventions to promote all students' academic, career, social, and emotional development (American School Counselor Association [ASCA], 2014). These areas of development are parallel to the wellness domains discussed throughout this book and are consistent with a primary prevention framework.

Mindsets and Behaviors

The ASCA (2014) has provided school counselors with standards that include specific mindset and behavioral competencies related to social skills, learning, and self-management that students should acquire as a result of a school counseling program. The standards also include mindsets such as "Belief in development of whole self, including a healthy balance of mental, social/emotional, and physical well-being" (Mindset Standard 1, p. 2). The standards are clearly consistent with a holistic wellness perspective. Following is a discussion of the various modalities that school counselors use to promote students' wellness. Table 13.1 includes a list of resources related to incorporating wellness into school counseling.

Classroom Lessons

School counselors spend a significant amount of their time conducting psychoeducational lessons in classrooms or other large-group

Table 13.1

Resources for Incorporating Wellness in School Counseling

Topic Area	Resource	Wellness Domain(s)	Format/Modality
Social and emotional learning	Carrizales-Engelmann et al. (2016)	Mind, emotion, connection	Large group
Student success skills	Brigman et al. (2010)	Mind, emotion, connection, body	Large and small groups
Spirituality and school counseling	Sink & Devlin (2011)	Spirit	All
Spirituality and school counseling	Sink (2004)	Spirit	All
Student delinquency	Smith-Adcock et al. (2008)	Mind, emotion, connection, body, spirit	Small group
Mindfulness in school counseling	Tadlock-Marlo (2011)	Mind, body, emotion	All
Mindfulness with students in alternative schools	Wisner & Norton (2013)	Mind, body, emotion	Small group
Body image	Akos & Levitt (2002)	Mind, body, emotion	All
Hope and optimism; physical exercise	Miller et al. (2008)	Mind, heart, body	Large and small groups

settings. The content of guidance lessons may be guided by state, district, or school initiatives as well as specific school needs. The format of classroom lessons may vary, but a typical lesson could last between 30 minutes and 1 hour and may include 20–25 students. Counselors ideally select from preexisting, research-supported curriculums. Several curriculums, such as Student Success Skills (Brigman, Campbell, & Webb, 2010) and Strong Teens (Carrizales-Engelmann, Feuerborn, Gueldner, & Tran, 2016), address multiple aspects of students' holistic development. However, curriculums may not exist for all topics, and counselors may need to develop their own lessons. If counselors create their own lessons, we recommend reviewing the literature on effective interventions related to the topic and collecting pre- and posttest student data to demonstrate practice-based evidence. School counselors can also collaborate with health teachers, physical education teachers, and core subject area teachers to develop lessons that are connected to course content. The content is typically preventive (e.g., stress management, healthy relationships).

Although targeting specific topics is important, we believe wellness concepts should also be included within topic specific lessons. Villalba (2007) gave the example of integrating various wellness domains into a substance abuse prevention lesson. Counselors could incorporate impact on personal relationships (social self) or how engaging in physical activity and healthy eating (physical self) can help generate positive feelings about self. Comprehensive programs should also include education related to holistic wellness. Villalba suggested a six-lesson curriculum focused on healthy eating and physical activity (physical self), self-worth and coping skills (coping self), and relationships with friends and loved ones (social self). Students may not be currently experiencing concerns; however, the skills required to prevent negative experiences and mental health concerns can be fostered through psychoeducation.

Small Groups

School counselors offer small groups to students who are experiencing concerns related to their academic or social/emotional development. The structure and format of groups vary on the basis of the age of the students and the school schedule. However, most groups consist of about 6–8 members and last 30 minutes to 1 hour. Small groups are typically tailored to specific themes such as grief and loss, self-esteem, anger management, or divorce. Similar to large-group lessons, school counselors may use structured curriculums or create their own outline for the group. Wellness concepts can be integrated into virtually any group.

For example, Villalba (2007) recommended using the Indivisible Self model of wellness (Myers & Sweeney, 2005) to incorporate wellness into small groups and large groups for elementary school students. Villalba suggested intentionally focusing on concrete aspects of wellness. He gave the example of a divorce group and suggested covering areas such as support systems (social self), how to handle feelings (coping self), and maintaining healthy eating and physical activity (physical self). Each area certainly contributes to a child's ability to cope with a divorce and the changes involved in the family transition. Following is Practitioner Spotlight 13.1, from a professional school counselor who discusses how he addresses wellness with groups of students in a school setting.

Individual Counseling

Students meet with school counselors individually to develop academic goals and to make future plans. Students also are also referred to their school counselors for issues such as academic concerns, career development, or crisis situations. Although each situation involves different contexts, a student's ability to make plans, navigate challenges, and continue to thrive in the face of future adversity is affected by their ability to maintain a healthy balance within the

Practitioner Spotlight 13.1

Wellness in Schools

Matt Shenker

Heading into my final semester of graduate school, and thus beginning my school counseling internship placement, I had a breadth of experience with mindfulness. I had been regularly practicing mindful meditation, I had incorporated mindfulness into individual counseling sessions, I had led a psychoeducational mindfulness-based stress management group with middle school students, and I had even taught several classroom lessons at the high school and middle school levels to introduce mindfulness to students. In fact, as a self-proclaimed acceptance and commitment therapy counselor, I considered my counseling approach to be mindfulness-based. Still, despite having experience with implementing mindfulness into my counseling work and having experience with elementary-age children, I was not particularly confident in my ability to implement mindfulness in a school-counseling program that served prekindergarten to fifth grade.

In my second week at my internship placement, I was beginning to lead classroom lessons in kindergarten through second-grade classrooms. I had decided that I would start introducing some mindfulness concepts and practices with the students this week and that we would learn more as the weeks went on. In the first kindergarten classroom lesson I was leading, we were exploring personal space and the skills that go into students' respecting their own and one another's personal space. For the last 10 minutes or so, we explored and defined the terms "past," "present," and "future." Then, I led all of the students through a mindful listening practice. As we all sat up proudly, with a tall back and two feet flat on the floor, we closed our eyes and began listening to the many sounds around us. I opened my eyes to look around the room, and there was a 5-year-old boy sitting 5 feet away from me, staring angrily at the bell in my hand, and holding his middle finger up toward it. As soon as I looked over at him, he quickly put his hand down and got an embarrassed look on his face. My first reaction was to wonder what could have made that boy so upset that he felt he needed to angrily give me the finger. My second reaction was a flooding of judgments about my abilities as a counselor. ("What a great opportunity for me to practice mindfulness!"—This thought was admittedly not my reaction to those judgments in the moment.) As I talked to that boy after that lesson, he explained that the bell had scared him. The next time I did that lesson, I took more time to explain how the bell would be used in our listening practice, and I rang the bell in varying volumes for the students before we began.

(continued)

Wellness in Schools *(continued)*

As my internship experience went on, I led a mindfulness-based stress management group with 6-year-olds, I continued to incorporate mindfulness into my work with individuals, and I implemented a mindfulness practice into every classroom lesson I led at each grade level. Now I work as an elementary school counselor and have used mindfulness with students as young as 3 years old. Although the ways that I introduce mindfulness to a 4-year-old certainly look different than the ways that I have introduced mindfulness to 24-year-olds, I would not say that the approach is terribly different. I need to be incredibly intentional with how I use language (simplicity, defining basic terms, providing visuals along with explanations), and certain exercises need to be shortened. Keeping those things in mind, it has been astounding to see the ways that students incorporate mindfulness concepts and practices that they learn with their school counselor into their life toolbox.

• • •

wellness domains. Students' academic and career concerns (mind wellness) are interconnected with family and school support (connection wellness) and their personal goals, beliefs, and values (spirit wellness). Crisis situations often emerge from concerns related to emotions (emotion wellness), which may also be related to academic concerns (mind wellness), relationships with friends (connection wellness), or issues related to body image or health (body wellness). As you can imagine, the connections among the domains that influence a particular concern are endless.

Although school counselors are often expected to address students' academic and career concerns, it is important to assess students' holistic wellness and to develop goals and interventions that address the interconnected nature of wellness domains to effectively improve the students' functioning in a particular area. As an example, I (Jonathan) once worked with an incoming high school freshman who had transferred to a high school in Florida from California. His mother was concerned about him because he had always been an active child with a lot of friends. Now, he was spending a lot of time at home, and he was also struggling academically. The mother reported that he seemed unmotivated. After brainstorming different ideas, the student, mother, and I thought it would be a good idea for him to start an extracurricular activity, so he joined the track team. The student eventually made some friends on the team, and he gradually became more engaged in school. We were able to address connection, body, and mind while also addressing his academic concerns. We encourage counselors working in K–12 settings to use the assessment and intervention planning strategies discussed in previous chapters and to modify them as needed to be appropriate for the educational environment.

Recommendations

Earlier in this chapter, we discussed how environmental factors affect child and adolescent wellness. Certainly, the school can have a direct effect on the students' microsystem by implementing a comprehensive school counseling program that includes a strong component of wellness promotion. Students are more likely to embrace wellness concepts when they are exposed to a school culture that adopts and promotes holistic wellness. In addition to providing direct services, there are additional strategies that counselors in schools can implement to promote wellness by addressing other areas of students' environment. Following are some recommendations to promote a wellness culture based on our professional experiences and the recent literature.

Collaborate With Other Service Providers in the School

To promote a culture of wellness within the school, it is important to have strong interdisciplinary collaboration. School counselors should work with the other student service providers in the school— such as nurses, psychologists, mental health counselors, and social workers—to coordinate wellness promotion activities and interventions within the school. Additionally, health and physical education teachers can be important partners in wellness initiatives. Members of each discipline possess unique expertise and skills to contribute to a unified wellness promotion program. Students will receive the most benefits if the service providers convey a clear and consistent message about the importance of holistic wellness. Collaborative teams can use the *Core Competencies for Interprofessional Collaborative Practice* (Interprofessional Education Collaborative Expert Panel, 2011) as a resource to determine role expectations, communication, and goals.

Create a School Wellness Committee

School counselors are expected to create advisory councils to obtain input and feedback about their comprehensive school counseling programs (ASCA, 2014). Similarly, we recommend that school counselors develop a committee to explore wellness within the school. Committee members could include administrators, teachers, students, parents and caregivers, counselors, and other student services providers. A committee could meet annually to discuss wellness needs of the school, brainstorm and prioritize intervention implementation, set goals for the school, and evaluate progress.

Collaborate With Community Organizations and Service Providers

School counselors should not work in a silo, in which the school operates separately from the community. Schools can benefit from engaging in positive working relationships with community organizations and service providers in the field. School counselors can connect with various organizations to exchange ideas, host invited presentations about various topics related to wellness, and collaborate on wellness promotion activities and events. Service providers from the community who conduct counseling sessions with students in the school should also be familiar with wellness initiatives and may also be involved in the planning and implementation of primary prevention strategies related to wellness promotion.

Advocate for School Wellness Policies

As part of the school leadership team, school counselors contribute a unique expertise related to students' mental health and wellness. They can raise awareness about the interconnected nature of the wellness domains, why it is important to address all aspects of students' development, and how holistic wellness relates to students' academic achievement. School counselors should be proactive in sharing their knowledge and perspective in areas related to wellness. For example, school counselors can advocate for wellness awareness initiatives for the whole school, integrating social and emotional learning within the classroom, maintaining physical education programs, and providing healthy food options during breakfast and lunch. Other examples would be to offer a mental health class or heavily integrate mental health into the general health curriculum.

Provide Resources on the School Website

School counselors can facilitate wellness promotion by developing and disseminating helpful wellness resources for students, families, and school staff. Although the most efficient way to do so is typically a school website, counselors could also distribute resources through a school newsletter or on an in-school news and announcements network. Websites can include wellness tips on stress-management strategies, coping skills, healthy relationships, physical wellness, or healthy eating. Websites could also include links to free online resources, community engagement opportunities, and information about the services offered at the school.

Offer Services to Families

In addition to dissemination resources, school counselors can offer services to parents, guardians, and family members. At minimum, school counselors can provide consultation to parents related to wellness promotion. Ideally, school counselors coordinate a variety of trainings and workshops to promote various aspects of wellness. The services can be coordinated with local community organizations, local practitioners, or local university programs.

Postsecondary

There is a current focus in higher education on postsecondary student retention and graduation rates. At the same time, students are struggling with independence from their parents and learning how to balance work, school, social life, career development, and financial responsibility. College counseling centers are reporting a rise in mental health concerns among their students, and many students are facing a broad range of serious issues ranging from food insecurity to being sexually assaulted. With all of these challenges, a focus on building resilience, teaching healthy coping strategies, fostering community connectedness, and implementing other wellness initiatives is imperative.

Postsecondary institutions implement a variety of preventive programs and services to promote holistic wellness for their students, which, of course, includes a counseling center. Counseling centers offer individual counseling services to students that are often limited to 6–10 sessions. Counselors may also offer group counseling services to students. In addition to offering reactive services, counseling centers also tend to offer wellness-focused groups and workshops that are preventive and growth enhancing for students. For example, the University of Central Florida Counseling and Psychological Services agency offers group services related to understanding self and others, social confidence, health, body wellness, strengthening relationships, and mindfulness. Similarly, the University Counseling Center at Wake Forest University offers workshops to small and large groups on topics such as college adjustment, body image, stress management, cultural awareness, and relationships.

University 101

Many universities offer a course for first-year students to help them adjust to college life in their first semester. Topics in a first-year seminar course often include practical information about the services provided by the university, how to use your student identification card, or how to use the student union. However, these courses now tend to cover students' holistic development. The University 101 programs at the University of South Carolina include specific goals and objectives that are related to students' holistic development. The goals include focus areas such as students' personal well-being, development, social responsibility, academic success, and connection to the university. The instructors have autonomy in how the objectives are met; however, some recommended topics include values clarification, stress management, goal setting, and academic strategies.

Campus Wellness Initiatives

Some colleges and universities have campus wellness offices that may be independent or connected to the counseling center. Such offices offer preventive services and workshops for students as well as faculty and staff members. The University of South Carolina Student Health Services Department includes a Healthy Campus Initiatives section that offers a variety of free or low-cost health services to students (https://www.sa.sc.edu/shs/cw/students/). The department approaches students' health holistically and addresses physical, social, emotional, spiritual, intellectual, occupational, and financial wellness. Health educators and peer leaders provide wellness coaching and conduct presentations and workshops. Some of the workshops offered include general wellness, nutrition, sexual health, and relationship communication. The more individualized services include preventive health screenings, stress and time management, physical activity and exercise, tobacco cessation, nutrition, and sexual health.

The Wellness Resource Center at Virginia Commonwealth University also offers common prevention and health services related to smoking cessation, alcohol and drug use, disordered eating and nutrition, stress management, mindfulness, sexual health, and interpersonal violence advocacy. In response to the trends and needs of students, they also have a robust collegiate recovery program, Rams in Recovery (https://thewell.vcu.edu/recovery-support/), that is aimed at fostering wellness. Members of the campus recovery community ride a bicycle-powered cart that serves local artisan coffee (body wellness) that is pour-over style (which takes about 6–7 minutes), and the cups are not "to-go" and thus stay with the cart. This delay gives students and community members an opportunity to spend 15–20 minutes in dialogue (connection wellness) with the student recovery member to normalize, reduce stigma, and encourage involvement in recovery.

Conclusion

Children, adolescents, and emerging adults all face unique challenges during their developmental stages of life. However, these populations are frequently in contact with various systems that have opportunities to promote wellness for these individuals. There is a strong societal emphasis on treating or educating the "whole child." Counselors are one of the primary professionals who have training in promoting holistic wellness and should be at the forefront of leading initiatives that are preventive and reactive in promoting wellness.

Reflection Prompts

1. How comfortable are you discussing mental health concerns with your primary care physician? Have you ever discussed mental health concerns with your doctor? How did the conversation go?
2. What do you view as the most important wellness areas to address with children, adolescents, and young adults today? Reflect on your experiences in various settings as a child and young adult. What types of wellness services were provided? How helpful were they?
3. If you currently work in one of the settings discussed in this chapter, how well is your organization promoting wellness for the populations discussed in this chapter?

Learning Activities

1. Conduct an Internet search for some local K–12 schools. Review several school counseling department websites. Identify wellness-related initiatives within the school, including services offered by the school counselor.
2. Conduct an Internet search, and review some websites for postsecondary institutions. Review the various offices that address wellness initiatives. Review the counseling center website, and identify the groups and workshops that are offered related to wellness.
3. Interview a school counselor or college counselor about how they view wellness promotion in relation to the professional role. What themes emerge from the interview?
4. Review some websites for primary care provider practices. What mental health services are offered? Do they have a protocol for addressing mental health concerns?
5. Work in a group to develop an outline of wellness activities that you could include when developing a K–12 or postsecondary counseling program.

Resources

American College Counseling Association
http://www.collegecounseling.org

American School Counselor Association
http://www.schoolcounselor.org

Association for University and College Counseling Center Directors
http://www.aucccd.org/index.php?page

Substance Abuse and Mental Health Services Administration
https://www.samhsa.gov/treatment

References

Akos, P., & Levitt, D. H. (2002). Promoting healthy body image in middle school. *Professional School Counseling, 6,* 138–144.

American School Counselor Association. (2014). *ASCA mindsets and behaviors for student success: K–12 college- and career-readiness standards for every student.* Retrieved from https://www.schoolcounselor.org/asca/media/asca/home/MindsetsBehaviors.pdf

Brigman, G., Campbell, C., & Webb, L. (2010). *Student Success Skills: Group counseling manual.* Boca Raton, FL: Atlantic Education Consultants.

Bronfenbrenner, U. (1979). *The ecology of human development: Experiments by nature and design.* Cambridge, MA: Harvard University Press.

Carrizales-Engelmann, D., Feuerborn, L., Gueldner, B. A., & Tran, O. (2016). *Merrell's Strong Teens: A social and emotional learning curriculum for students in grades 9–12* (2nd ed.). Baltimore, MD: Brookes.

Centers for Disease Control and Prevention. (2011). *Public health action plan to integrate mental health promotion and mental illness prevention with chronic disease prevention, 2011–2015.* Atlanta, GA: U.S. Department of Health and Human Services.

Edwards, V. J., Holden, G. W., Felitti, V. J., & Anda, R. F. (2003). Relationship between multiple forms of childhood maltreatment and adult mental health in community respondents: Results from the Adverse Childhood Experiences Study. *American Journal of Psychiatry, 160,* 1453–1460.

Gadomski, A. M., Wissow, L. S., Palinkas, L., Hoagwood, K. E., Daly, J. M., & Kaye, D. L. (2014). Encouraging and sustaining integration of child mental health into primary care: Interviews with primary care providers participating in Project TEACH (CAPES and CAP PC) in NY. *General Hospital Psychiatry, 36,* 555–562. https://doi.org/10.1016/j.genhosppsych.2014.05.013

Gysbers, N. C., & Henderson, P. (2012). *Developing & managing your school guidance & counseling program* (5th ed.). Alexandria, VA: American Counseling Association.

Interprofessional Education Collaborative Expert Panel. (2011). *Core competencies for interprofessional collaborative practice: Report of an expert panel.* Washington, DC: Interprofessional Education Collaborative.

Miller, D. N., Gilman, R., & Martens, M. P. (2008). Wellness promotion in the schools: Enhancing students' mental and physical health. *Psychology in the Schools, 45,* 5–15. https://doi.org/10.1002/pits.20274

Myers, J. E., & Sweeney, T. J. (2005). The indivisible self: An evidence-based model of wellness. *Journal of Individual Psychology, 61,* 269–279.

Oppenheim, J., Stewart, W., Zoubak, E., Donato, I., Huang, L., & Hudock, W. (2016). Launching forward: The integration of behavioral health in primary care as a key strategy for promoting young child wellness. *American Journal of Orthopsychiatry, 86,* 124–131. https://doi.org/10.1037/ort0000149

Sink, C. A. (2004). Spirituality and comprehensive school counseling programs. *Professional School Counseling, 7,* 309–317.

Sink, C. A., & Devlin, J. M. (2011). Student spirituality and school counseling: Issues, opportunities, and challenges. *Counseling and Values, 55,* 130–148. https://doi.org/10.1002/j.2161-007X.2011.tb00027.x

Smith-Adcock, S., Webster, S. M., Leonard, L. G., & Walker, J. L. (2008). Benefits of a holistic group counseling model to promote wellness for girls at risk for delinquency: An exploratory study. *Journal of Humanistic Counseling, Education and Development, 47,* 111–126.

Tadlock-Marlo, R. L. (2011). Making minds matter: Infusing mindfulness into school counseling. *Journal of Creativity in Mental Health, 6,* 220–233. https://doi.org/10.1080/15401383.2011.605079

Villalba, J. A. (2007). Incorporating wellness into group work in elementary schools. *The Journal for Specialists in Group Work, 32,* 31–40. https://doi.org/10.1080/01933920600977556

Wisner, B. L., & Norton, C. L. (2013). Capitalizing on behavioral and emotional strengths of alternative high school students through group counseling to promote mindfulness skills. *The Journal for Specialists in Group Work, 38,* 207–224. https://doi.org/10.1080/01933922.2013.803504

Chapter 14

Wellness Counseling With Early, Midlife, and Older Adults

A big part of growing up is bringing all of yourself into a space,
not just the parts of yourself that relate to the people in the room.
                                        —Lin-Manuel Miranda

• • •

The path to wellness is not a linear or static one. As counselors, we cannot forget that the experience of well-being changes throughout the life span. Moreover, "being well" is affected by the environmental factors embedded in the tasks and challenges that we face at different ages and stages of life. When providing wellness counseling, the counselor must include developmental considerations into the counseling milieu. The developmental stage for all of you reading this book falls within this chapter: adulthood. Wellness during emerging adulthood may differ from well-being at midlife and older adulthood. Additionally, making transitions from one stage to the next brings a range of challenges and opportunities. If we have unfinished business from a previous part of life—whether childhood, adolescence, or midlife—wellness counselors can help the client pursue resolution, thereby paving the way for higher levels of wellness attainment.

Similar to the interconnectedness of the wellness components, wellness and development cannot be separated. For example, a wellness counseling prevention approach will not be effective if presented in the same way to adolescents as it would be to older adults. Certain experiences are more salient in the life of an adolescent on a wellness topic that does not resonate for the middle-aged or older adult.

Take a moment and reflect on your current age and stage of development:

1. What was the transition like from your previous stage in life (e.g., emerging adulthood into midlife)?
2. What have been the hardest parts or greatest challenges of making this transition?
3. What have been the hardest parts about this age and stage of life? On the other side, what have been the greatest joys?
4. How was your wellness affected by these life transitions?
5. How were your levels of wellness (across the different domains) similar or different between your previous developmental stage and your current one?
6. What would explain these similarities and differences in wellness?

Mentors have advised us that you should never ask others questions you are unwilling to answer yourself. We have gained much insight into wellness and development from examining our own journey in emerging adulthood and upcoming transitions to midlife.

In this chapter, we present key developmental steps that occur for some individuals in adulthood. Considerations for the impact on wellness are discussed. Research on life transitions and wellness during different parts of adulthood is covered. Interventions that are unique to the developmental stages of adulthood are presented. It is important to explore these facets not only in cultivating our abilities to integrate developmental considerations into wellness counseling but also because it builds self-awareness. We may fall victim to assuming (consciously or subconsciously) that our clients' wellness and developmental crises will mirror our own, or we may unknowingly steer the client toward a solution that worked for us but that may or may not be appropriate for the client's own life.

Developmental Considerations for Emerging Adults

When working with adult clients, it is important to consider and integrate several factors with the wellness perspective. Most clients when you probably see are in some level of crisis. Many people do not want to initially attend counseling if they do not have to. Hence, when providing wellness counseling, typically some precipitating issue that has significantly affected well-being has led the client to counseling. It is the counselor's job to help the client understand the dynamics at play that are feeding the issue and come up with a holistic plan to address it.

As you begin the client conceptualization process and understanding the conflagration of factors leading to your adult client seeking or being referred for counseling, ask yourself the following questions: (1) What is the "unfinished business" from previous developmental tasks? (2) What current developmental tasks and transitions is the client working through across the five wellness domains? (3) In what ways is the client struggling and excelling? (4) How do the developmental considerations in Questions 1–3 intersect with the client's presenting concern?

For individuals 18–30 years of age (Arnett, 2004) or older, people can be conceptualized as emerging adults. Given the importance of "unfinished business," one must remember that "identity versus role confusion" is the Eriksonian stage leading up to the "intimacy versus isolation" of emerging adulthood (Erikson, 1963). Challenges can arise for adolescents in identity diffusion (Marcia, 2010). Adolescents with identity diffusion have minimally investigated who they are. Researchers have discerned multiple problematic routes at this stage, including the young person lacking the self-efficacy for self-discovery, whereas others have been more apathetic about intentional seeking of next steps in life (Schwartz, Zamboanga, Luyckx, Meca, & Ritchie, 2013). What are some reasons why the developmental process might unfold in these ways for some adolescents? What are some ways that the adolescent's wellness might be affected? How could this experience affect the adolescent's well-being in emerging adulthood, young adulthood, or later life? These are the types of developmental questions that will begin to inform your wellness-based conceptualization of the client.

Using the five wellness domains as a map can be helpful here. For instance, an emerging adult who falls into the identity diffuse category and is entering the world of work or college may struggle to find a social network that truly meets their needs (connection wellness). They may be unaware of how to manage the different aspects of well-being, including finding a work–life or school–work–life balance. Spirit wellness may be low at this point because the individual is in the midst of a spiritual struggle, feeling a dearth of meaning and purpose. The individual may then be more susceptible to engaging in problematic substance use (body wellness). To be clear, many of these concerns reflect wellness and are part of the normal developmental path. However, the adolescent with identity diffusion may become more entrenched in these problems or manifest them in a more severe manner. It is important to remember the culture and context (Schwartz et al., 2013).

The Context of Emerging Adulthood

Emerging and young adulthood is a time of great change. Think about the changes in just the microsystems and mesosystems in the ecology of emerging adults. They may be moving away from their parents to start new employment or college, or they may be finishing college and moving to a different location. Their peer group and social system will thus likely change. They will become a part of new institutions and communities (Myers & Sweeney, 2004). This process is just the beginning. Multiple identities exist within any one person, and they intersect with their well-being. These identities include but are not limited to race and ethnicity, religion and spirituality, sexual orientation, and others. Regarding the Indivisible Self model (Myers & Sweeney, 2004), the researchers found that gender identity and cultural identity are among the third-order factors that compose the Essential Self.

When exploring the Essential Self, an individual will search for answers to questions such as the following: What does it mean to me to be an African American female? How do I reconcile identifying as gay with my understanding of the religious beliefs taught to me that may depreciate who I am? These tensions affect wellness. This effect is magnified by being in the stage of intimacy versus isolation, in which the person is finding him- or herself while also learning about him- or herself in relationship with another person.

The Indivisible Self model is particularly useful in broaching such conversations with clients because identity and spirituality are pictured on the model, enabling processing during informal assessment. The Five Factor Wellness Inventory (Myers & Sweeney, 2014) also contains items inquiring about these factors and can be used as a springboard for discussion. A critical part of identity discussion is connecting the client's experience to its impact across the wellness domains. Ask the client about how their experiences have increased their holistic and domain-specific well-being and how it has suppressed wellness. What other changes to the emerging adult's ecosystem come to mind? If you are an emerging adult yourself or are past this developmental phase, how did the context of your life change? How did this affect your well-being? The good news is that some level of diffusion can occur over time through emerging adulthood, a term that is inclusive of exploration (Arnett, 2000, 2004).

What Is Emerging Adulthood?

Arnett (2004) distilled emerging adulthood into the following (p. 8):

- It is the age of identity explorations, of trying out various possibilities, especially in love and work.

- It is the age of instability.
- It is the most self-focused age of life.
- It is the age of feeling in-between, in transition, neither adolescent, nor adult.
- It is the age of possibilities, when hopes flourish, when people have an unparalleled opportunity to transform their lives.

A shadow side exists to these aspects of emerging adulthood that can contribute to decreased wellness and mental health issues in your clients. Although the opportunity for surveying life facilitates finding oneself, an abundance of options can be paralyzing. People with a mental health diagnosis may experience difficulty navigating identity and relational processes (intimacy vs. isolation; Tanner, 2015). Individuals who lose foster care supports when reaching adulthood may have less access to the instrumental and emotional support to identify or maximize the next steps in life (Greeson & Thompson, 2015). A diffusion of identity due to the absence of support could understandably have this result.

Marcia (2010) stated that "the risk is that in sharing oneself deeply with another, one can lose oneself unless one's new identity is sufficiently strongly flexible to permit it to be temporarily lost in merger and then recovered" (p. 22). Hence, connection wellness in the form of a romantic relationship can be detrimental to wellness and self-discovery if one is not grounded in who one is. The benefit of "instability," according to Arnett (2004), is the ability to learn from the rapid changes in one's life to funnel oneself down into a clearer identity. Again though, the emerging adult client who enters your office for counseling may be ineffective in learning from the instability (mind wellness) or flooded with emotions about situations that have arisen (emotion wellness), making sense-making difficult. Confusion across the wellness components from "feeling in-between" will exacerbate mental illness symptoms.

Emerging adulthood is not the "age of possibilities" for everyone, as Arnett (2004) pointed out. Life situations such as caring for a family member with a serious medical or mental health problem may preclude possibilities. Socioeconomic status has an impact on career and lifestyle options. The idea of emerging adulthood is widely known in today's American culture to the point at which it is nearly assumed that all people have the chances and perspective identified by Arnett. The desire for possibilities while living in a real or perceived absence of them could detract from one's well-being. It should also be highlighted that Arnett's five aspects of emerging adulthood are not desirable for all. In collectivist cultures, an extended period of self-focused life might not be desired by the young person (Anderson, 2016; Schwartz et al., 2013). The preference might be to remain at home or return home sooner to work with or care for family.

The Transition Framework

There is one additional lens to be introduced now that can be useful in understanding wellness in adults at any stage in life. It is important to know not only the potential developmental markers and experiences of emerging adulthood but what your clients' perceptions of these occurrences and nonoccurrences are. One of the most striking things that I (Phil) learned in my master's in counseling program 16 years ago was during a class in which we each completed Holmes and Rahe's (1967) Life Stress Inventory. I had not fully considered that a positive life event, such as a wedding, graduation, or birth of a child, could introduce stress into one's life. This is one of the most helpful insights that I incorporate on a regular basis when things are going seemingly well in my (and my clients') life, yet anxiety is occurring.

Goodman, Schlossberg, and Anderson (2006) developed a Transition Framework based on the idea that transitions are a part of one's matriculation through life. Transitions can be experienced as positive or negative depending on several variables, including the nature and perception of the transition. Goodman et al.'s (2006) recognition that "nonevents" can be as powerful as "events" is of particular utility. Projected and desired developmental milestones for the individual that do not happen, such as going to college or obtaining employment, can affect the individual (Goodman et al., 2006). Goodman et al. also cited support that transitions do have a bearing on well-being.

Wellness Interventions for Emerging Adults

Emerging adults referred to or who voluntarily seek counseling with you may feel alone, embarrassed, and broken in their struggle for identity, intimacy, and life goals. Reflective listening and validation from the counselor can be helpful. The validation can come through identifying the number of "role changes" (Goodman et al., 2006) that the client is experiencing. Clients may have an "aha" moment that more of their internal and external life is in transition than they realized, resulting in more empathy for self. One must be careful though not to minimize the client, which is where psychoeducation can be helpful in normalizing. Provide the client with information about transitions that people wrestle with at this time in life. Take a strengths approach and focus on the insights that the client has obtained through this period in life. Administer a transitions scale. Use the assessment as an opportunity for intervention in normalizing how what others may see as exciting transitions can be overwhelming.

Reserve time to process the client's thoughts and feelings about life events that they was hoping for that did not manifest and events that were discouraging. Use psychoeducation to normalize that emotion wellness issues of grief and loss are typical (Goodman et al., 2006) and can affect multiple wellness areas. You might then invest in both helping the client express those feelings and assisting clients in managing those emotions when flooded by them. Use motivational interviewing and solution-focused type wellness interventions to find out what skills across the wellness domain helped the client successfully navigate transitions in the past (Miller & Rollnick, 2013).

If a client appears to have unresolved developmental tasks from earlier in life, identify along with the client chances for working through these tasks (D. A. Johnson, personal communication, October 2, 2017). For instance, if the client's parents were absent during the client's teenage years, the client may not have formed a mental rubric for decision making, thereby short circuiting his or her ability to choose different life paths. A client whose attention-deficit/hyperactivity disorder resulted in his or her having academic problems in youth may have foreclosed on certain career or life paths because of lack of confidence. The youth who was unsure of how to manage emotions and, hence, had strained relationships with peers may have personal barriers to intimacy or friendships following high school.

Clients may lose or lack confidence or motivation in negotiating their identity. Use of the Transtheoretical Model (Prochaska & DiClemente, 1984; Prochaska & Norcross, 2014) can aid understanding of the client's interest in self-exploration. This method enables the counselor to meet the client where they are and then use matched interventions to potentially increase the client's stage of change. For example, the client with attention-deficit/hyperactivity disorder may be in contemplation about exploring a new career path even though they are clearly unhappy in their current one. After the counselor assesses that the client is in contemplation, the counselor can use interventions, such as the decisional balance or values card sort, to develop dissonance and help the client decide whether next steps or changes are warranted in their life (Miller & Rollnick, 2013). In conducting a decisional balance (using some of the language from Dr. Linda Hancock's case example from Chapter 10), the client lists

(a) the "good things" about making a specific change, (b) the "not-so-good things" about making the change, (c) the "good things" about *not* making the specific change, and (d) the "not-so-good things" about *not* making the change (Miller & Rollnick, 2013). New and existing understandings resulting from the activity are discussed. Counselors should also ask the client to identify and dialogue about items from among the four lists that hold more importance than the others. If the primary barrier to positive change is confidence, the counselor can explore client strengths and provide career information and resources that might increase the client's self-efficacy to pursue their preferred career.

Middle Adulthood

The stereotype about middle adulthood is the midlife crisis. From an Eriksonian perspective, the "self-focus" (Arnett, 2004) transforms into an "other" focus (Karcher & Benne, 2008). People 35–64 years old could be considered in middle adulthood (Juntunen & Schwartz, 2016). The middle adult often channels their giving back (generativity) toward people in earlier ages and stages of life, whereas the midlife adult in stagnation remains stuck in patterns of living that do not involve helping others (Karcher & Benne, 2008). In a study of 237 women near the end of middle adulthood, participants higher in generativity were more likely to report aging successfully (Versey & Newton, 2013).

For middle-aged individuals, the microsystems and mesosystems in their lives have likely changed since early and young adulthood. The individual might be married or in a long-term relationship. If this is not the case, the projections of the microsystem, mesosystem, exosystem, and macrosystem of marriage and children may decrease wellness whether or not this was part of the plan for a couple (Anderson, 2016; Williams, 2016). For example, for partners who are unable to conceive (or choose not to), they may feel a dissonance of being demeaned by the macrosystem while also imposed with the assumption that their lives should be more enjoyable (Moore, Allbright-Campos, & Strick, 2017). If a significant portion of the parent's self-concept is based on their ability as a parent, well-being can fluctuate depending on perceived daily and ongoing parenting outcomes (Whitbourne & Connolly, 1999).

The pressure to be successful in one's career by the time one arrives at middle adulthood can negatively affect a person who views that they have not achieved certain goals by this point in their life. A factor that can exacerbate the work–wellness relationship in midlife includes being a member of a marginalized group who may still encounter barriers to employment and promotion or incidents of microaggressions at work (Whitbourne & Connolly, 1999). Anderson (2016) claimed that divorce and transitions related to the parent–child relationship could affect wellness. As in all transitions, divorce can result in positive holistic change or foster recurrent problems for the members of the couple.

The quantity of roles for middle adults is staggering. Stop for a moment and reflect on the microsystem and mesosystem that make up the life of the adult in middle age. McAdams (2001) identified several responsibilities in the following statement: "In their roles as parents, teachers, coaches, mentors, leaders, helpers, and volunteers, generative adults serve as norm bearers and destiny shapers in families, schools, churches, neighborhoods, and the workplace" (p. 396). Again, the midlife adult is faced with a triple-bind of a societal assumption to involve oneself in multiple roles, yet the enormity of them can decimate the person's wellness. However, the midlife adult not involved in meaningful activity that nurtures others risks one's personal development being stunted. The confluence of age, identity, and culture also merits consideration. People who identify as lesbian, gay, bisexual, or transgender who did not come out until later in life may be new to exploring their sexual identity as they move into midlife (Kooeyman & Rogers, 2017). Middle-aged parents who immigrated to the United States might encounter strain in imparting their values with their children who have assimilated cultural aspects of the United States (Anderson, 2016).

Given the aforementioned factors, pursuing and maintaining wellness is imperative. There are substantial upsides of middle age, including the knowledge, skills, and experience that are acquired (Lachman, 2001). In fact, some research has shown that life satisfaction is higher in middle adulthood than both emerging and older adulthood (e.g., Maher, Pincus, Ram, & Conroy, 2015). Let's briefly look at how seeking wellness in one domain can translate to holistic well-being in midlife. Although the likelihood of incurring medical problems elevates in conjunction with age, attending to body wellness has key advantages (Merrill & Verbrugge, 1999). One lesson that has been repeated throughout the book holds true for many individuals in middle age: Wellness is interconnected. Therefore, body wellness has been shown to improve in relation to other wellness domains, such as emotion wellness, specifically positive affect (Dainese et al., 2011). The relationship between holistic well-being and body wellness is bidirectional. For instance, increases in physical activity had a favorable impact on life satisfaction for middle and older adults but not for emerging adults (Maher et al., 2015).

Wellness Interventions for Clients in Middle Adulthood

As is the case with emerging and young adults, one wants to understand the intersection of development, context, transition, and their effect on wellness and consequently the presenting concern. Middle adults are traversing a plethora of roles. Hence, psychoeducation and normalization about these phenomena can be therapeutic. Role overload can be effectively addressed by wellness interventions. Marlatt (1985) developed a useful wellness-related exercise in which clients list all the activities in their life that they "want" to do and all the life engagements that they "need" to do. The clients are then directed to notice the proportion of wants versus needs.

This exercise can be insight producing for clients who realize that their life consists predominantly of needs rather than wants. The client then explores how the imbalanced ratio of wants to needs has affected their well-being and presenting problem (*note:* have a wellness model nearby for the client to refer to). Now, the client can be empowered to decide whether to add a "want" to enhance well-being or potentially remove what they initially thought was a "need." A decisional balance activity from motivational interviewing can then be used to look at the pros and cons of making a change (Miller & Rollnick, 2013).

Another way of conducting this activity is to simply have the client list out all of their tasks and responsibilities on paper, using scaling questions to rank on a continuum whether the task is nurturing (wellness enhancing) or depleting (wellness decreasing). Keep a wellness model nearby to assist the client in identifying how their wellness is affected by different life roles and tasks. Similarly, the client can be exploring making adjustments that can support their well-being.

The following is a line of processing that is both assessment and intervention with a middle-aged client and integrates notions from the Transition Framework (Goodman et al., 2006) and solution-focused therapies. First, inquire about the client's hopes, dreams, and expectations for life during middle adulthood. Ask the client, "What does success during midlife look like for you?" This step enables the wellness counselor to avoid assuming what the stage of middle adulthood entails for the client, because this answer will be different for each and every client. You now have more of a template for what the client values.

Use the wellness model as a road map for this conversation, asking the client about midlife goals across wellness domains and overall (holistically). Ask the client, "What midlife experiences and milestones do you feel good about?" This question connects with the solution and strength-focused aspect of the wellness counselor. Wellness counselors want to know what has gone well. The insights from processing this question can be incorporated into self-talk when the client is feeling discouraged or lead to an additional prompt about "what thoughts, feelings, and behaviors can be mobilized from these experiences to aid in areas in which you are currently struggling?"

Finally, the counselor can examine the following questions with the client: "In what ways do you feel you have not met your midlife expectations?" "What have been the biggest barriers?" As the intervention continues, co-construct with the client steps that they can take that will represent positive steps on their life path, including ways to circumvent or move through barriers. Again, the wellness model can serve as your guide for brainstorming and talking about how positive steps can have a positive impact on one's well-being.

In Practitioner Spotlight 14.1, Allison M. Forti describes her use of wellness counseling with a client in middle adulthood who was experiencing a life-changing transition.

Older Adulthood

One of the ways that wellness counselors can potentially be ineffective when working with older adults is to adhere to one's own assumptions about older adults (Myers & Shannonhouse, 2013). Older adulthood is sometimes stereotyped to be a low point in life in all aspects of wellness. Counselors may unknowingly perceive that mental wellness—such as memory, intellectual ability, or interest in intellectual stimulation—becomes significantly dulled. Another misperception is that most older adults are severely limited in their capability to perform body wellness activities. Counselors may believe that most older adults are depressed (emotion wellness), grappling with existential and religious crises (spirit wellness), or lonely and isolated (connection wellness; Myers & Shannonhouse, 2013). Take a moment and reflect on the ideas you have about older adulthood. If you are an older adult, identify any biases that you may have about older adulthood based on your own experiences.

Older adults include individuals 65 years of age and older. The Eriksonian developmental task of integrity versus despair may compel the older adult to ponder the following: "What does my life mean, and how do I feel about that? What have I to grieve, to be proud of, to make up for, and what remains to be done about these things?" (Hearn et al., 2012, p. 2). One of the developmental markers that drives the older adult to wrestle with these questions is retirement (Hearn et al., 2012). Milne (2013, p. 6) asserted that the following factors contribute to a rewarding life in retirement:

Practitioner Spotlight 14.1

The Case of Anna

Allison M. Forti

Wellness counseling often takes a back seat as a type of counseling in oncology settings, where meaning-centered therapy and support counseling tend to be favored. However, I find wellness counseling useful with specific clients who present to counseling with a desire to improve their quality of life or holistic wellness following the completion of their cancer treatment. It should be noted that this includes clients on maintenance treatment. The following is a case example of how to apply wellness counseling in an oncology setting.

Anna—a 48-year-old White woman diagnosed with multiple myeloma, who had undergone an autologous hematopoietic stem cell transplant a few months prior and was currently taking Revlimid as a maintenance treatment—presented to counseling with a determined grit to make changes in her life. A self-described "Type A workaholic," she was struggling with how to adapt to her new normal that left her excessively fatigued and uncomfortable from joint and muscle pain. She also had a keen awareness that the median survival rate for her illness was 3 years, although her medical team was optimistic that she may live upward of 10 years. Anna was married without children and drew her primary identity through her job as an executive at a Fortune 500 company. Despite her husband's urging to step down from her position, she continued to maintain her work responsibilities with reduced hours (50 hours per week!). In a matter-of-fact manner, she proclaimed, "My job is quite literally killing me, and I have to change but don't know how." As her psychosocial oncology counselor, my first thought was that time was of the essence so Anna could begin seeing positive changes in her life. Anna was motivated to adapt to her realities but needed help.

Anna was a good fit for wellness counseling versus alternative approaches (e.g., support counseling, cognitive therapy, or narrative therapy) because her primary goal was to improve her wellness after she began maintenance treatment for her cancer. The first step was to assess her current level of wellness using the Wheel of Wellness model (Myers, Sweeney, & Witmer, 2000). I tend to rely on the Wheel of Wellness model because it presents a nice visual model for clients, but you may also choose to use the Indivisible Self model (Myers & Sweeney, 2004), which is evidence based, or the Five Factor Wellness Inventory (Myers & Sweeney, 2014). After thoroughly explaining the Wheel of Wellness and reviewing the tasks and subtasks of wellness, Anna reported that she was low in the category of coping self (which included subcategories of leisure, stress management, self-worth, and realistic beliefs) and physical self (which included the subcategories of exercise and nutrition). She scored high in the subcategories relating to work satisfaction, spirituality, and control. We mutually decided to begin focusing on her coping and physical self. Over the course of a

(continued)

The Case of Anna *(continued)*

6-month tiered approach (i.e., weekly appointments for 2 months, bimonthly appointments for 2 months, and monthly follow-up appointments for 2 months), Anna made the following changes to improve her energy level, reduce stress, increase her quality of life, and improve her overall wellness:

- To affirm her commitment to make lifestyle changes, Anna discussed with her oncologist the pros and cons of continuing to take Revlimid because of the harsh side effects. Ultimately, she decided it was better to take the medication and make lifestyle adjustments to account for her fatigue and physical discomfort.
- Initially, Anna reduced her work hours to 9–5 and learned to delegate her responsibilities. Over time, as she grew more comfortable with the changes, she truncated her work hours further.
- After challenging the idea that she needed to be the perfect wife, Anna allowed her husband to assume more household responsibilities so that Anna could schedule energy-improving naps.
- Anna set boundaries with her friends and only participated in social gatherings that energized her instead of depleted her. She learned to say "no"!
- Given her husband's proclivity toward sweets and fast food, Anna overcame her fear of his disapproval and adopted a healthier diet.
- After reducing her work hours, Anna had more time to take daily walks. She also learned to be mindful of her body. On days when she felt extra fatigued, she realized it was okay to walk less or skip her walk entirely. She minimized her black-and-white thinking.
- Anna began enjoying movies and television shows, something she had not allowed herself to indulge in throughout her adult life.
- Anna began spending more time with her husband in shared activities, deepening their relationship.

Over the course of 6 months, I noticed the visible improvements in Anna. She appeared happier and more energetic. At each session, we reviewed a copy of the Wheel of Wellness and used it as a guide to target our focus. By our last session, Anna was confident that she had reached her optimal wellness, given her diagnosis, and could maintain her lifestyle changes. After our time together ended, I would occasionally see her in the hospital for routine medical follow-up appointments. Anna relished in sharing her updates and she continued to monitor her wellness with the Wheel of Wellness and make necessary tweaks. As one of my mentors was fond of saying, "Counselors ultimately want to work themselves out of a job," as clients learn to independently maintain and promote their own growth. Wellness counseling was the easiest way to work myself out of a job with Anna.

• • •

Resources (e.g., sufficient money)
Exercise
Coping strategies
Intellectual activity
Purpose
Engagement (social support)

The components of the RECIPE acronym are an indicator of the importance of holism during retirement, because the five domains of wellness can certainly be located within it. One can also deduce that, similar to the interconnectedness of wellness, deficits in one or more of these areas could create a negative snowball effect, resulting in decreased wellness in retirement. Conversely, wellness assets can help someone maintain their well-being (Milne, 2013). Individuals who are forced into unemployment may be at risk for increased symptoms of depression (Mandal & Roe, 2008). The good news is that if the person can subsequently find work, these depression symptoms alleviate.

What fosters and detracts from wellness in older adulthood? This is an important question for at least two reasons:

1. Wellness seems to increase in older adulthood (Blanchflower & Oswald, 2008), whereas the prevalence of mental health problems is lower than any other time in life (Substance Abuse and Mental Health Services Administration, 2017). Yet, older adulthood can consist of unique issues such as declines in physical health (Milne, 2013). What is the secret to wellness that older adults possess?
2. Wellness may be a protective factor against negative changes in physical health. Individuals with self-reported positive emotions, meaning, and rewarding social life show fewer biological markers of deficient health such as inflammation (Friedman & Ryff, 2012).

Practitioner Spotlight 14.2 includes reflections by Dr. Matthew Fullen on wellness and older adults.

From a mind wellness and spirit wellness perspective, Kampfe (2015) noted that older adults who have a favorable outlook on life and who are adept at cognitively restructuring negative life experiences and deriving meaning from them are more likely to thrive. Despite losses in mind wellness that can occur with dementia for some older adults, spirit wellness can be sustained.

Practitioner Spotlight 14.2

Interview (Part 1)

Matthew Fullen

Question 1: What do you think counselors need to know about wellness in older adulthood?

Answer: Wellness in older adulthood is incredibly important. Unfortunately, research and clinical application related to wellness in later life is in its infancy. With that in mind, there are three things that counselors should know about wellness in older adulthood. First, it is important to be aware of biases about aging, to which many of us ascribe. Whether these take the form of implicit stereotypes about aging or explicit ageism, the attitudes that we have shape our willingness to approach older adulthood from a wellness perspective. Second, wellness must be holistic in scope. Aging well consists of a variety of important domains, including traditional domains such as physical, emotional, relational, and spiritual wellness. However, there are additional domains that are quite important to the study of aging well. These include cognitive wellness, contextual wellness, developmental wellness (i.e., How does your older adult client perceive growing older?), and vocational wellness (i.e., How do older adults maintain a sense of "calling" throughout their lives?). Last, but not least, it is important to remember that wellness is a strengths-based approach. When we approach older clients with an eye toward identifying and cultivating strengths, we replace negative cultural stereotypes with an expectation that most older people are resilient, capable, and worthy of our best efforts.

● ● ●

Connection to loved ones was a significant theme that arose in a qualitative study on people with dementia (Trevitt & MacKinlay, 2004). To that end, older adults whose spirit wellness is bolstered through their family (connection wellness) are part of a family who holds relational skills that enable them to adjust and support each other, given the fluctuations that occur as they matriculate through life, address issues that arise, and make meaning through narrative and tradition (King & Wynne, 2004). There are distinct implications for the counselor here that are discussed later in this chapter.

Older adults can reap benefits to their well-being from low-intensity physical activity (body wellness; Bae, Ik Suh, Ryu, & Heo, 2017). Taken further, physical activity is positively correlated with meaning for older adults and may be a reason why older adults who are more active feel more energetic (Ju, 2017). Older adults with body well-ness concerns are frequently able to navigate them through alternative means. For instance, when a research participant was asked about how she was able to bathe, given that she had a medical problem that affected the ease of this process, she remarked, "I bend at the knees and gently roll into a sitting position and put my bum on the edge of the tub and then I put one leg in at a time. Then I reverse this process to get out of the tub" (Yuen & Vogtle, 2016, p. 597). Instances such as this example are helpful in understanding the finding that one can be well while living with medical problems in middle and older adulthood (Friedman & Ryff, 2012).

Emotion wellness plays a substantial role in older adult well-being, as one might expect with people at any stage in life, and interacts with the remaining domains of well-being. Researchers found that participants who lived alone and those experiencing more feelings of loneliness were at an increased risk of death during this longitudinal study (Teguo et al., 2016). The authors concluded that these two variables work collectively so that persons who both live alone and feel lonely are affected. Older adults diagnosed with depression are at risk for several wellness issues (Fiske, Wetherell, & Gatz, 2009). Figure 14.1 shows the variables that are predictive of depression in contrast with those that reduce the likelihood of depression in older adults.

One can see the role of context in this model as well as the holistic nature of it because the variables portrayed involve the domains of wellness (Fiske et al., 2009). Stressful life events are another important element of the model. Of note are the findings that traumatic experiences from one's youth correlate with mental health problems in older adulthood (Raposo, Mackenzie, Henriksen, & Afifi, 2014). The impact of these traumas continues throughout the person's life. Moreover, risk of mental health problems increased for older adults exposed to multiple categories of abuse or neglect (Raposo et al., 2014).

Counselors working with older adults must use a contextual lens that is inherent in wellness counseling (Myers & Sweeney, 2004). This requirement is because the lives of older adults have been affected by the time in which they grew up and matriculated through life. Living through the Civil Rights Movement or World War II, for example, carries with it different experiences and perspectives (Blando, 2010). These historical experiences intersect with other factors, including race and ethnicity, sexual orientation, socioeconomic status, and so forth (Blando, 2010). The counselor must remember to be client centered to maximize empathy with the client. The environmental aspects of a wellness approach offer the advantage of guiding

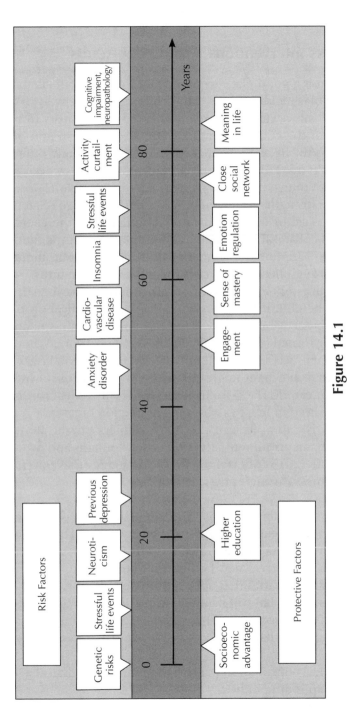

Figure 14.1

Variables Predictive of Depression in Older Adults

Note. From "Depression in Older Adults," by A. Fiske, J. L. Wetherell, and M. Gatz, 2009, *Annual Review of Clinical Psychology*, Vol. 5, p. C-1. Copyright 2009 by Annual Reviews. Reprinted with permission.

one toward a holistic understanding of the client that informs effective intervention.

Wellness Interventions With Older Adults

A place of strength is a good place to start when working with clients of any age, particularly older adults. My (Phil) most effective work with older adult clients occurred when I conducted an inventory (formal or informal) of the client's strengths. The assessment in and of itself resulted in as much or more therapeutic value than any other intervention I might do. This result was largely because I was working with clients with cognitive impairment. It is easy for people to lose awareness of their strengths if they happen to be having age-related problems with physical or cognitive health. The family of the client can provide useful collateral information about the client's inner and external resources. The family members can develop insight about their loved one through hearing the client identify their strengths.

Simply using the wellness assessment procedures described in Chapter 9 can be helpful. If the older adult client has medical problems that affect their activities of daily living, you might administer an assessment of their formal or informal activities of daily living. When doing so, place an emphasis on (a) identifying any instrumental (task-based) supports that the client might need and (b) problem solving ways that the client can do the tasks by him- or herself (only if this is safe) or still be involved in helping with the completion of tasks.

Physical activity is a key piece of the body wellness puzzle. Body wellness, in turn, has a prominent effect on other domains and overall wellness. Kampfe (2015) offered the following suggestions for enhancing body wellness through physical activity:

- Use a decisional balance to aid the client in processing the pros and cons of engaging in physical activity. (*Note:* The counselor's understanding of the Transtheoretical Model/stages of change from Chapter 11 may be helpful here.)
- Discuss feasible activities that appeal to the client.
- Pinpoint resources that will facilitate implementation of physical activity (programs or places).
- Acquire assurance that the client will strive to adhere to the plan.
- Obtain medical consultation prior to initiating the physical activity (this step is imperative).
- Ensure that physical activity or exercise is light when the client first embarks on their plan.

A similar format can be followed for enhancing the client's level of mind wellness and connection wellness through hobbies and social activities. Family counseling, when appropriate, can be a valuable way to build connection wellness (Myers & Harper, 2004). The family wellness counseling principles described in the next chapter may be helpful.

Fullen and Gorby (2016) co-created the Resilient Aging program, which was implemented with older adults at an adult day center. Each of the nine group sessions composing the program centered on a different facet of resilience and wellness, ranging from social through spiritual domains. The group leaders prompted attendees to disclose anecdotes representative of persevering through challenging times and how this related to holistic and component-specific well-being. This model holds great potential for the wellness counselor.

Any thoughtfully selected wellness model can serve as a structure for stimulating the communication of favorable or meaningful narratives. To begin this process, the counselor could pose questions such as, "Can you share about a recent or past wellness success?" (Randolph, Hermann-Turner, & Fullen, 2017). It is then the counselor's job to draw out key details of the narrative, including moments of insight for the client or ideas that might be fruitful in maintaining and enhancing wellness currently. Be sure not to allow the client to "speed" through parts of the story that connect to meaning. The counselor should deconstruct the anecdote by asking questions such as the following: "What did you learn about yourself from this experience?" "What did you learn about wellness from this experience?" "What was the most meaningful part of this experience?" "What specific thoughts, feelings, or behaviors that you exhibited in your story can be applied currently to enhance your well-being?"

For more reflections on wellness interventions with older adults, read Practitioner Spotlight 14.3 by Dr. Matthew Fullen.

Conclusion

Much of the adult life span has been addressed in this chapter. Because of this expansiveness, a multitude of highly significant topics were not discussed within each age and stage of life. However, we attempted to provide an overview of some relevant developmental, environmental, and life transition facets of adult living. Furthermore, we sought to demonstrate that wellness is a central component to all of these factors.

Practitioner Spotlight 14.3

Interview (Part 2)

Matthew Fullen

Question 2: What are some key considerations for counselors when incorporating a wellness counseling approach with older adult clients?

Answer: When working with older adult clients, it is important to operationalize key terms such as holistic wellness, resilience, and strengths-based counseling. You may want to include these core concepts in your informed consent paperwork or incorporate them as they come up during your initial sessions. Next, it is important to do your homework on key theories of adult development and aging and how these relate to aging well. For instance, many counselors learn about Erikson's (1963) Eight Stages of Psychosocial Development, but have you considered Baltes and Baltes's (1990) work on the life-span perspective and how older adults maintain their well-being using the framework of selective optimization with compensation? Developmental theories that focus specifically on older adulthood provide a rich foundation for the application of wellness counseling with older adults. My last suggestion is to balance a focus on wellness with the human realities of suffering, loss, and death. We must communicate to our clients that we wish to discuss wellness, resilience, and strengths in a manner that honors our human capacity for grief, pain, and the challenges associated with aging. As the early 20th century poet Kahlil Gibran has described it, we are "suspended like scales" between sorrow and joy, and in older age these two qualities are particularly "inseparable."

● ● ●

Reflection Prompts

1. What notable transitions do you recall from your life in early/ young, middle, or older adulthood? How did these experiences affect your well-being? What insights can you apply from this reflection to your understanding of wellness and transitions?
2. What biases or assumptions do you hold about early/young, middle, or older adults? How might these assumptions affect your work with clients? Create a specific plan to ensure that any biases do not negatively affect your work with clients.
3. Refer to Bronfenbrenner's (1979) ecological model, which is discussed in Chapter 13. Stop and reflect on the role of context in the life of one of your current or past clients.

Note: If you discuss this with peers as part of a class, be sure to not share any identifying information.

How do or did these systems affect the client's wellness?

4. What are your reactions to Dr. Forti's case study of counseling an adult during an extremely difficult transition? What are your takeaways from this example on how to implement wellness counseling with adult clients?

5. A developmental lens is critical, hence its coverage in this book. However, what (if any) cautions exist when applying a developmental lens as part of wellness counseling with clients? How can you address any potential risks of integrating wellness and development?

Learning Activities

Adult Development Interview

Interview someone in a different stage of life from yours. Your goal should be to find out about:

1. Rituals or markers that let the client know that they had transitioned to a new phase in life
2. Life transitions that have occurred during their current stage in life
3. Most challenging aspects of life at this stage
4. Positive and growth-producing experiences at this stage—ask for specific examples with each prompt

Wellness Interventions for Older Adults

Review the risk and protective factors for depression in older adults shown in Figure 14.1. There are multiple possibilities for intervention points, including prevention (Fiske et al., 2009).

- Pick one risk factor and one protective factor to target with a wellness intervention.
- Conduct a review of the literature and try to identify at least one evidence-based practice that addresses this risk factor in older adults.
- What additional ideas do you have for wellness approaches across modalities (community level, family, couples, individual) for effectively addressing these depression risk factors in older adults?
- What steps do you need to take to incorporate the results of your literature review into practice with your older adult clients (e.g., seek training on the approach, prepare materials during session preparation time, read a book on the topic)?

Resources

Association for Adult Development and Aging (AADA)
http://www.aadaweb.org/

A division of the American Counseling Association, the AADA is an organization for counseling students and professionals interested in adulthood and its corresponding developmental processes. Conference, membership, and resource information can be found on this website.

Midlife in the United States:
A National Longitudinal Study of Health and Well-Being
http://midus.wisc.edu/index.php

A clearinghouse of research studies on middle adulthood that were borne out of a large-scale study occurring over multiple years.

Society for the Study of Emerging Adulthood
http://www.ssea.org/

Organizational website for professionals and students interested in consuming and fostering knowledge on the period of emerging adulthood. Conference, membership, and references to readings and online information on emerging adulthood can be found on this website.

Substance Abuse and Mental Health Services Administration—
Selecting Evidence-Based Practices for Treatment of
Depression in Older Adults
https://store.samhsa.gov/shin/content/SMA11-4631CD-DVD/SMA11-4631CD-DVD-Selecting.pdf

This resource is a literature review of interventions that have benefit for older adults as evidenced by research studies. Each section of the document includes references to treatment manuals and readings.

Substance Abuse and Mental Health Services Administration—
Tools and Resources (Older Adults)
https://knowledge.samhsa.gov/resources?field_taxo_populations_served_tid=97

This webpage has a search function allowing perusal of numerous types of useful information, including literature on domains of well-being, mental health assessments, and interventions for older adults.

References

Anderson, M. L. (2016). Supporting adaptation to new family roles in middle age. In C. L. Juntunen & J. P. Schwartz (Eds.), *Counseling across the lifespan: Prevention and treatment* (2nd ed., pp. 337–354). Thousand Oaks, CA: Sage.

Arnett, J. J. (2000). Emerging adulthood: A theory of development from the late teens through the twenties. *American Psychologist, 55,* 469–480.

Arnett, J. J. (2004). *Emerging adulthood: The winding road from the late teens through the twenties.* New York, NY: Oxford University Press.

Bae, W., Ik Suh, Y., Ryu, J., & Heo, J. (2017). Physical activity levels and well-being in older adults. *Psychological Reports, 120,* 192–205.

Baltes, P. B., & Baltes, M. M. (1990). Psychological perspectives on successful aging: The model of selective optimization with compensation. In P. B. Baltes & M. M. Baltes (Eds.), *Successful aging: Perspectives from the behavioral sciences* (pp. 1–34). Cambridge, England: Cambridge University Press.

Blanchflower, D. G., & Oswald, A. J. (2008). Is well-being U-shaped over the life cycle? *Social Science & Medicine, 66,* 1733–1749.

Blando, J. (2010). *Counseling older adults.* New York, NY: Routledge.

Bronfenbrenner, U. (1979). *The ecology of human development: Experiments by nature and design.* Cambridge, MA: Harvard University Press.

Dainese, S. M., Allemand, M., Ribeiro, N., Bayram, S., Martin, M., & Ehlert, U. (2011). Protective factors in midlife: How do people stay healthy? *GeroPsych: The Journal of Gerontopsychology and Geriatric Psychiatry, 24,* 19–29.

Erikson, E. H. (1963). *Childhood and society.* New York, NY: Norton.

Fiske, A., Wetherell, J. L., & Gatz, M. (2009). Depression in older adults. *Annual Review of Clinical Psychology, 5,* 363–389.

Friedman, E. M., & Ryff, C. D. (2012). Living well with medical comorbidities: A biopsychosocial perspective. *Journals of Gerontology Series B: Psychological Sciences and Social Sciences, 67,* 535–544.

Fullen, M. C., & Gorby, S. R. (2016). Reframing resilience: Pilot evaluation of a program to promote resilience in marginalized older adults. *Educational Gerontology, 42,* 660–671.

Goodman, J., Schlossberg, N. K., & Anderson, M. L. (2006). *Counseling adults in transitions: Linking practice with theory* (3rd ed.). New York, NY: Springer.

Greeson, J. K. P., & Thompson, A. E. (2015). Aging out of foster care in emerging adulthood. In J. J. Arnett (Ed.), *The Oxford handbook of emerging adulthood* (pp. 559–577). New York, NY: Oxford University Press.

Hearn, S., Saulnier, G., Strayer, J., Glenham, M., Koopman, R., & Marcia, J. E. (2012). Between integrity and despair: Toward construct validation of Erikson's eighth stage. *Journal of Adult Development, 19,* 1–20.

Holmes, T. H., & Rahe, R. H. (1967). The social readjustment rating scale. *Journal of Psychosomatic Research, 11,* 213–218.

Ju, H. (2017). The relationship between physical activity, meaning in life, and subjective vitality in community-dwelling older adults. *Archives of Gerontology and Geriatrics, 73,* 120–124.

Juntunen, C. L., & Schwartz, J. P. (2016). Prevention and treatment in a developmental context. In C. L. Juntunen & J. P. Schwartz (Eds.), *Counseling across the lifespan: Prevention and treatment* (2nd ed., pp. 1–18). Thousand Oaks, CA: Sage.

Kampfe, C. M. (2015). *Counseling older people: Opportunities and challenges.* Alexandria, VA: American Counseling Association.

Karcher, M. J., & Benne, K. (2008). Erik and Joan Eriksons' approach to human development in counseling. In K. L. Kraus (Ed.), *Lenses: Applying lifespan development theories in counseling* (pp. 199–228). Belmont, CA: Wadsworth Cengage Learning.

King, D. A., & Wynne, L. C. (2004). The emergence of "family integrity" in later life. *Family Process, 43,* 7–21.

Kooeyman, L., & Rogers, R. (2017, July). *Understanding the lives of midlife and older LGBT populations: Counseling implications and strategies.* Session presented at the Association for Adult Development and Aging Annual Conference, New York, NY.

Lachman, M. E. (Ed.). (2001). Introduction. In *Handbook of midlife development* (pp. xvii–xxvi). New York, NY: Wiley.

Maher, J. P., Pincus, A. L., Ram, N., & Conroy, D. E. (2015). Daily physical activity and life satisfaction across adulthood. *Developmental Psychology, 51,* 1407–1419.

Mandal, B., & Roe, B. (2008). Job loss, retirement and the mental health of older Americans. *Journal of Mental Health Policy and Economics, 11,* 167–176.

Marcia, J. E. (2010). Life transitions and stress in the context of psychosocial development. In T. W. Miller (Ed.), *Handbook of stressful transitions across the lifespan* (pp. 19–34). New York, NY: Springer.

Marlatt, G. A. (1985). Lifestyle modification. In G. A. Marlatt & J. R. Gordon (Eds.), *Relapse prevention: Maintenance strategies in the treatment of addictive behaviors* (pp. 280–350). New York, NY: Guilford Press.

McAdams, D. P. (2001). Generativity in midlife. In M. E. Lachman (Ed.), *Handbook of midlife development* (pp. 395–446). New York, NY: Wiley.

Merrill, S. S., & Verbrugge, L. M. (1999). Health and disease in midlife. In S. L. Willis & J. D. Reid (Eds.), *Life in the middle: Psychological and social development in middle age* (pp. 78–96). San Diego, CA: Academic Press.

Miller, W. R., & Rollnick, S. (2013). *Motivational interviewing: Helping people change* (3rd ed.). New York, NY: Guilford Press.

Milne, D. (2013). *The psychology of retirement: Coping with the transition from work.* New York, NY: Wiley.

Moore, R. M., Allbright-Campos, M., & Strick, K. (2017). Childlessness in midlife: Increasing generativity using a narrative approach. *The Family Journal, 25,* 40–47.

Myers, J. E., & Harper, M. C. (2004). Evidence-based effective practices with older adults. *Journal of Counseling & Development, 82,* 207–218.

Myers, J. E., & Shannonhouse, L. R. (2013). Combating ageism: Advocacy for older persons. In C. C. Lee (Ed.), *Multicultural issues in counseling: New approaches to diversity* (4th ed., pp. 151–170). Alexandria, VA: American Counseling Association.

Myers, J. E., & Sweeney, T. J. (2004). The indivisible self: An evidence-based model of wellness. *Journal of Individual Psychology, 60,* 234–244.

Myers, J. E., & Sweeney, T. J. (2014). *Five Factor Wellness Inventory (FF-WEL): Adult, teenage, and elementary school versions.* Menlo Park, CA: Mind Garden.

Myers, J. E., Sweeney, T. J., & Witmer, J. M. (2000). The Wheel of Wellness counseling for wellness: A holistic model for treatment planning. *Journal of Counseling & Development, 78,* 251–266.

Prochaska, J. O., & DiClemente, C. C. (1984). *The transtheoretical approach: Crossing the traditional boundaries of therapy.* Homewood, IL: Dow Jones-Irwin.

Prochaska, J. O., & Norcross, J. C. (Eds.). (2014). *Systems of psychotherapy: A transtheoretical analysis* (8th ed.). Stamford, CT: Cenage Learning.

Randolph, A., Hermann-Turner, K., & Fullen, M. (2017, July). *Wellness and resilience.* Session presented at the Association for Adult Development and Aging Annual Conference, New York, NY.

Raposo, S. M., Mackenzie, C. S., Henriksen, C. A., & Afifi, T. O. (2014). Time does not heal all wounds: Older adults who experienced childhood adversities have higher odds of mood, anxiety, and personality disorders. *The American Journal of Geriatric Psychiatry, 22,* 1241–1250.

Schwartz, S. J., Zamboanga, B. L., Luyckx, K., Meca, A., & Ritchie, R. A. (2013). Identity in emerging adulthood: Reviewing the field and looking forward. *Emerging Adulthood, 1,* 96–113.

Substance Abuse and Mental Health Services Administration. (2017). *Key substance use and mental health indicators in the United States: Results from the 2016 National Survey on Drug Use and Health* (HHS Publication No. SMA 17-5044, NSDUH Series H-52). Rockville, MD: Author.

Tanner, J. L. (2015). Mental health in emerging adulthood. In J. J. Arnett (Ed.), *The Oxford handbook of emerging adulthood* (pp. 499–520). New York, NY: Oxford University Press.

Teguo, M. T., Simo-Tabue, N., Stoykova, R., Meillon, C., Cogne, M., Amiéva, H., & Dartigues, J. F. (2016). Feelings of loneliness and living alone as predictors of mortality in the elderly: The PAQUID study. *Psychosomatic Medicine, 78,* 904–909.

Trevitt, C., & MacKinlay, E. (2004). 'Just because I can't remember . . .': Religiousness in older people with dementia. *Journal of Religious Gerontology, 16*(3–4), 109–121.

Versey, H. S., & Newton, N. J. (2013). Generativity and productive pursuits: Pathways to successful aging in late midlife African American and White women. *Journal of Adult Development, 20,* 185–196.

Whitbourne, S. K., & Connolly, L. A. (1999). The developing self in midlife. In S. L. Willis & J. D. Reid (Eds.), *Life in the middle: Psychological and social development in middle age* (pp. 25–45). San Diego, CA: Academic Press.

Williams, E. N. (2016). Navigating work and family connections across the lifespan: Preventing and managing role strain and conflicts. In C. L. Juntunen & J. P. Schwartz (Eds.), *Counseling across the lifespan: Prevention and treatment* (2nd ed., pp. 303–320). Thousand Oaks, CA: Sage.

Yuen, H. K., & Vogtle, L. K. (2016). Multi-morbidity, disability and adaptation strategies among community-dwelling adults aged 75 years and older. *Disability and Health Journal, 9,* 593–599.

Chapter 15

Wellness Counseling for Counselors

When the well's dry, we know the worth of water.
—Benjamin Franklin

• • •

In addition to promoting client wellness, attending to self-care and avoiding impairment are ethical requirements of professional counselors. One of the best avenues for accessing knowledge and experience on wellness counseling is to strive toward living a wellness lifestyle. In this chapter, we discuss how a holistic wellness approach to self-care assists counselors in maintaining a high level of personal and professional functioning to effectively work with clients. Additionally, we discuss how supervisors can help promote wellness with their supervisees. Finally, we describe strategies for mental health and educational organizations to promote wellness within the work environment.

Counselor Susceptibility to Burnout and Impairment

For counselors to effectively promote wellness and remain congruent in their professional relationships with clients, they must maintain a high level of personal wellness. The nature of counselors' work makes them exceptionally susceptible to experiencing threats to their wellness. In practice, clients often come to counseling at a low point in their lives. Counselors might experience empathy fatigue, characterized by exhaustion, despair, and hopelessness, as a result of constant exposure to their clients' suffering (Stebnicki, 2007). Counselors who frequently provide services related to trauma might experience vicarious traumatization, which can lead to impaired professional functioning, interpersonal relationship stress, and decreased emotional and physical wellness (Figley, 2002). Burnout is common among helping professionals and counselors in particular. Counselors who are burned out experience feeling emotionally drained from work, feeling detached from clients and "numb" to client issues, and feeling ineffective and unproductive as a helper (Maslach, 2003). When counselors reach the point that they experience burnout, it affects multiple aspects of their wellness. Counselors who are affected by burnout often experience physical fatigue and hopelessness and become cynical toward their clients (Lambie, 2006). When counselors experience burnout and impairment, it can also have a negative impact on their clients. Counselors who are impaired struggle to provide high-quality services to clients and are more likely to engage in unethical behaviors (Lawson & Venart, 2005).

Lawson and Venart (2005) recommended that counselors engage in continuous self-assessment of impairment and self-care activities. The authors suggested using the Professional Quality of Life (Stamm, 2002) instrument to measure compassion fatigue, compassion satisfaction, vicarious trauma, and burnout. To measure professional, spiritual, physical, and psychological wellness activities, counselors can use the Self-Care Assessment (Saakvitne, Pearlman, & Staff of the Traumatic Stress Institute, 1996). These assessments can help counselors identify when they are experiencing reduced wellness and guide them in planning self-care activities to improve wellness.

Self-Care

Leaders in the counseling field recognize the risks counselors experience and the importance of promoting self-care. The American Counseling Association (2014) has included self-care and wellness as part of the ethical code, which requires counselors to "engage in self-care activities to maintain and promote their own emotional, physical, mental, and spiritual well-being to best meet their professional responsibilities" (Section C). Research supports the importance of wellness in preventing counselor burnout. Puig et al. (2012) found that higher levels of coping self, physical self, and creative self on the Five Factor Wellness Inventory (Myers & Sweeney, 2014) were predictive of lower levels of emotional exhaustion. In a study by

Stevanovic and Rupert (2004), therapists rated the following activities as the top 10 most helpful career-sustaining behaviors:

- Spending time with partner/family
- Maintaining balance between professional and personal lives
- Maintaining a sense of humor
- Maintaining self-awareness
- Maintaining professional identity
- Engaging in quiet leisure activities
- Maintaining a sense of control over work responsibilities
- Engaging in physical activities
- Taking regular vacations
- Perceiving clients' problems as interesting

This list is a good starting point for counselors to start brainstorming ideas for self-care. What would you add to this list? Similar to that of your clients, your self-care should be customized to meet your individual needs, preferences, and goals. Counselors should be mindful of which self-care activities are important to them and which ones will truly be helpful. For example, have you ever taken a vacation that ended up being more stressful than relaxing? We recommend that counselors assess their wellness continuously and develop a proactive plan of self-care activities. Following is an example of a wellness plan template that counselors can use to guide their self-care activities. This plan can be modified for personal use or for supervisors or counselor educators to use with their supervisees or students. An important consideration is to design the plan in a way that it does not become more of a burden. If our example is too cumbersome for you, use the components that work best for your individual needs.

Wellness Intervention Plan

Develop an individual wellness plan for yourself. The plan should include the following components: (a) Use informal or formal wellness assessments (e.g., Self-Care Assessment) to identify your current state of wellness in each dimension (i.e., mind, connection, emotion, spirit, body) and the current challenges in each dimension, (b) develop one short-term and one long-term goal for each dimension, (c) create a proactive plan for each dimension to meet these goals and improve your overall self-care, and (d) discuss the strategies that you will implement to meet your goals and overcome the barriers to maintaining your wellness.

Cues of Low Counselor Wellness
Across the Five Domains

You need look no further than the five wellness domains when assessing for signs of declining wellness as a counselor. Here, we identify potential red flags that relate specifically to the role of the counselor and signal declining counselor wellness.

Signs of decreasing *mind wellness* at work include the counselor becoming increasingly distracted, less mindful of and present with the client, and losing track of what the client is talking about to the point of being a consistent issue. Some counselors may begin to lose a positive sense of being intellectually stimulated by their work with clients. Part of the counselor's distraction can be due to negative self-talk leading to declining self-efficacy of the counselor.

Body wellness cues can be particularly telling. For example, do you experience a visceral unpleasant reaction when approaching your workplace? Have you begun neglecting hygiene, proper nutrition, or exercise? Sleep problems can be caused by stress at work. Conversely, lack of sleep can exacerbate work stress. Are behaviors such as substance use increasing?

Spirit wellness warning signs can involve a lack of gratification in one's work as a counselor or a sense of loss of direction in one's life. The counselor may stop engaging in religious/spiritual beliefs or practices that were previously important.

Emotion wellness deficits may manifest as a lack of empathy or ability to connect emotionally with clients. This state can occur because the counselor's emotional tank is empty. The counselor may experience consistent difficulty regulating their emotions at work. The counselor may avoid certain topics with clients to avoid eliciting strong emotions from the client, thereby making the counselor uncomfortable.

Significant dips in *connection wellness* can look like conflicted communication with coworkers, supervisors, or even clients. The counselor's social life can become unhealthy and bleed into the workplace—for example, overuse of substances with friends or family or inappropriate disclosure with a client. Conversely, the counselor may shrink away from people in their support network. Counselor may be less motivated to seek needed consultation from supervisor or peers.

Last, beware of your contextual well-being. What events are occurring in your life outside of work, and how are you knowingly or unknowingly carrying them to work with you? Are there events occurring in your family or community or worldwide that are being triggered at work? For instance, the #MeToo movement in which people are shining a light on the issue of sexual harassment, assault, and rape by sharing their traumatic experiences may be triggering for counselors who have experienced their own trauma.

To make the wellness model work for you regarding your counselor wellness, you must self-assess your own levels of well-being as mentioned in Chapter 11. Use some of the cues mentioned earlier and ones that are unique to you as warning signs to address these wellness deficits whether through personal counseling, supervision, or committing to a wellness plan. The catalyst to all of this, though, is taking time to self-assess your wellness on a daily basis; otherwise, you might not notice your own decreasing wellness and its impact on your work and home life.

Balancers and Boosters and Suggestions for Counselor Wellness

Counselors can apply many of the concepts in the Treatment Planning chapter (Chapter 10) and the Interventions chapter (Chapter 11) to their own lives. What wellness boosters do you use, and could use, at work during moments of lower wellness? Counselors can go for brief walks during pauses in the workday (body and spirit wellness). Healthy humor can be an effective way of changing one's perspective, eliciting pleasant feelings and staying well at work. Conversing with colleagues at your work site on light-hearted topics can be enjoyable and help you hit the reset button before your next client session (mind, emotion, and connection wellness). Deep breathing exercises can be enacted quickly to provide a positive effect before, during, or after counseling sessions (body and spirit wellness). Attempt to notice the sensation of your belly periodically during sessions. Are you flexing in your abdominal area and not breathing fully? This act may signify the holding of tension and may preclude you from being fully present. Therefore, simply open up a slow breath and release any existing tension. Last but not least, remember to eat and sleep (body wellness). Consume healthy snacks throughout the day as needed, and avoid skipping meals.

What about outside of work? You must have a wellness-enhancing life outside of work. One suggestion for accomplishing this is to find your "flow." Flow experiences are moments of becoming engrossed in a positive activity. This activity could entail playing with your child, practicing a musical instrument, reading a book, engaging in a game of chess, and so forth. Have connections with others who are not mental health professionals to avoid constantly thinking and talking about clients and mental health topics. Make sure your emotion wellness needs are met by others in your life and not your clients. Ensure that you have people to disclose your thoughts, feelings, joys, and failures to. Body wellness activities are extremely important for counselors because we often sit all day! Exercise and physical activity is key. Read and consume information on topics other than counseling (mental wellness). Search for people, places, and things in life that bring you satisfaction other than your work as a counselor (spirit wellness). In Practitioner Spotlight 15.1, Therese L. Newton discusses how she attends to her own personal self-care.

Wellness in Supervision

Ideally, counselors initially learn appropriate self-care strategies within their counselor education programs (Council for Accreditation of Counseling and Related Educational Programs, 2015; Witmer & Young, 1996). Some strategies counselor training programs can implement include incorporating wellness practices throughout the duration of the program, educating students about the risk for burnout and impairment, introducing students to the realities of the job that may cause stress, and requiring students to implement a personal wellness plan. Although initial training in self-care is an important part of burnout and impairment prevention, maintaining wellness is an ongoing personal and professional activity. Even though counselors are ethically responsible for attending to self-care and self-monitoring for burnout and impairment, supervisors also have a responsibility to monitor their supervisees and help promote their wellness (Association for Counselor Education and Supervision, 2011). There are multiple supervision models that address wellness within the supervisory relationship (Lenz & Smith, 2010) and several wellness-oriented interventions that can be implemented within group supervision sessions (Ohrt, Prosek, Ener, & Lindo, 2015).

Lenz and Smith (2010) developed a supervision model that integrates wellness concepts, referred to as the Wellness Model of Supervision (WELMS). The WELMS is an integration of the wellness development process of education, assessment, planning, and evaluation developed by Myers and Sweeney (2005) with the supervision process. The authors directly introduced their model to supervisees and dedicated up to 20 minutes of each supervision session to explicitly addressing wellness. The following list includes a brief summary of supervisor and supervisee activities during each phase of the WELMS:

Practitioner Spotlight 15.1

Self-Care and Clinical Practice

Therese L. Newton

In reflecting on how I integrate self-care into my clinical practice, I believe that it is important to first reflect on how I view my role as a counselor. I consider myself to be a person-centered clinician, believing empathically in the power of a strong and meaningful client–counselor relationship to influence treatment progression and outcome. Naturally, in viewing the counseling relationship as the foundation for my practice, I place great attention on cultivating strong, meaningful, and authentic relationships with my clients. In doing so, I strive to bring myself fully and genuinely to each encounter, because I believe it is the person-of-the-counselor—with our own individual dispositions and interpersonal style in addition to technical competence—who has the potential to transcend theory, technique, or intervention. However, as anyone in the helping professions can likely attest to, there are moments, cases, and even prolonged periods of time when being fully and genuinely present within the counseling relationship can be nothing short of a true challenge. It is no secret that life happens outside of the counseling session, for both clients AND counselors. Whether positive or negative, triumphant or trying, these moments that occur within and outside of our work with clients affect our state of mind, mood, interpersonal skill, and clinical effectiveness. This occurrence, as I see it, is inevitable. This circumstance is also something that we, as counselors, know yet easily overlook in times of struggle or challenge. In my experience, the ability to remain flexible in my approach to self-care, yet proactive and consistent in the attention I offer to my overall wellness, has proven to be most beneficial in mediating factors such as stress and burnout.

I take pride in having completed my clinical training within a counseling program that placed great emphasis on caring and cultivating the person-of-the-counselor—believing that clinical competence included cultivation of both technical skillfulness and personal awareness. In fact, it was early into my clinical training when I was taught to view wellness through a multifaceted and holistic lens. Conceptualizing overall wellness as the balance that emerges from the integration of mind, body, and spirit with self-care—including practical methods of caring for each of these facets—has been instrumental in allowing for flexibility in how I integrate self-care into my daily routine. Rather than viewing self-care as an activity to engage in when I was feeling the effects of burnout, self-care became small, practical, yet intentional acts that I am able to consistently integrate into daily or weekly routines. Although I would love to say that I have never slipped up, fallen short of

(continued)

Self-Care and Clinical Practice (continued)

my goal, or even avoided my care for one reason or another (and therefore have never felt the effects of stress or burnout), I can't. I have had, and still do have, periods of time when I prioritize nearly everything except myself and my wellness. However, as odd as it sounds, I am grateful for and find meaning in these periodic lapses, because they serve to remind me of how important and influential engaging in acts of care has been for my overall wellness and ability to offer the best version of myself to my clients and colleagues.

Exhaustion. Impatience. Cynicism. Anger. Interpersonal conflict. All of these traits, along with a plethora of other adjectives, reflect the effects of burnout. For me, they are the less-than-subtle indicators that I have been neglecting my own wellness. As a counselor, I do not operate in a bubble where burnout affects only me and my inner thoughts or feelings; it inevitably bleeds into my ability to work effectively with my clients, my coworkers, and those in my personal life. I can recall moments when I felt the root of my burnout was the client population I had on my caseload, or the climate of the agency I was working with, or even the state of my personal relationships. Although there was surely some merit in these thoughts, the greater truth was that the root of my burnout was my inattention to proactively replenish those areas of myself that had increasingly become depleted. Regardless of the specific nature of clientele, agency, or personal relationships, when we give of ourselves—as counselors do every day—feelings of depletion will happen unless we are also actively refilling ourselves in meaningful ways. When I become aware of the effects of my lapse in self-care, I often initially feel hypocritical and even shame as the counselor who does not practice what she preaches. Although these feelings and thoughts are unpleasant, this is an opportune time to offer myself grace and forgiveness. Moreover, it is with grace and forgiveness that I embark on my path back toward self-care and wellness. I also use these moments to reevaluate what areas of my wellness I have been neglecting, why I have been neglecting them, and if the methods of care I was offering myself before the lapse are still meaningful and relevant. Allowing myself the flexibility to change the way I care for myself ensures that I am engaging in meaningful activities that serve to replenish and refresh my mind, body, and soul; this method also allows for my continued journey toward greater self-awareness and increased intentionality. The process of assessing the facets of myself to determine what I need to find balance, rather than grasping at superficial or cliché activities, works for me. This practice has truly made all the difference in my ability to stay (fairly) consistent in maintaining meaningful self-care habits, thereby allowing me to bring myself fully and genuinely to each therapeutic encounter.

• • •

Brief Summary of the WELMS

Phase and Activities

Education
- The supervisor and supervisee work to define what wellness means for the supervisee.
- The supervisor educates the supervisee on formal wellness models.

Assessment
- The supervisee participates in informal or formal personal wellness assessment.
- The supervisor reviews the results of the assessments with the supervisee and collaboratively processes how the factors influence the supervisee's personal and professional life.

Planning
- The supervisee identifies a desired area of change.
- The supervisor helps the supervisee develop a written developmental wellness plan.

Evaluation
- The supervisor checks in with the supervisee about progress toward wellness goals.
- Formal and informal assessments are used to assess progress.
- The supervisee is encouraged to discuss wellness progress, and the supervisor provides positive encouragement about wellness progress.

The specific plans and approaches within the model can be tailored to meet the unique needs of the supervisee to best meet their personal wellness while also fostering clinical skills development.

In a related approach, Ohrt et al. (2015) developed an intervention to help promote wellness and prevent burnout with supervisees in group supervision. The intervention was intentionally designed to be brief so as to not distract from clinical skill development and client case consultations. The intervention included a 1.5-hour psychoeducational presentation during the first session on wellness models, burnout, and impairment risks; group discussion and brainstorming activities; and wellness goal setting, followed by weekly check-ins with supervisors about progress toward wellness goals. The components of the intervention are outlined in Table 15.1.

Table 15.1

Burnout Prevention and Wellness Promotion
Intervention Outline

Intervention Component	Content or Activity

1.5-Hour Psychoeducational Presentation	Burnout
	   Definitions
	   Occupational and environmental risks
	   Warning signs
	   Consequences
	   Prevention strategies
	Common Wellness Model Components
	   Intellectual
	   Emotional
	   Social
	   Occupational
	   Spiritual

Wellness Worksheet	Physical • Supervisees identify physical and emotional signs of stress. • Supervisees identify anticipated challenges and potential wellness barriers during the upcoming semester. • Supervisees discuss these aspects together as a group.
Wellness Brainstorming	• Supervisees brainstorm wellness strategies within each wellness domain. • Supervisor creates a list of the activities.
Wellness Goal Setting	• Supervisees develop two wellness goals for the semester. • Supervisor works with supervisees to ensure the goals meet the S.M.A.R.T. (specific, measurable, attainable, realistic, and time-related; Doran, 1981) goal criteria. • Supervisees share their goals with other supervisees in the group.
Wellness Check-In	• Throughout the semester, supervisees work on their goals. • Each week, supervisees spend about 10 minutes sharing their goal progress with the group.

An advantage of applying wellness concepts in supervision is that supervisees can typically use the strategies they are learning with their clients. It is helpful for supervisors to process with supervisees what they are learning about themselves and how they can use the skills with their own clients. Brooke Wymer discusses how she addresses self-care with her supervisees in the Practitioner Spotlight 15.2.

Organizational Wellness

Considering the strong emphasis in the counseling field on promoting client wellness, it is equally important for work environments to

Practitioner Spotlight 15.2

Supervision and Self-Care

Brooke Wymer

I started my career, like most who enter the helping professions, because I care about people and want to assist them in improving their lives after adverse experiences. I do not recall hearing buzzwords such as "self-care" and "burnout" when I was completing my education and supervision. I started my career in a child advocacy center providing forensic interviews for child abuse investigations and counseling children and their families who had endured trauma, primarily sexual abuse. After years of working in the field and stewarding a multitude of children's trauma narratives, I did not know how to name my experience. I knew I was physically, mentally, and emotionally exhausted. I no longer felt effective with my clients. I had become cynical about making a difference, and I viewed the world and people differently. At that time, I had to take a job elsewhere because I was one of the burnout statistics we now talk about in our field. I am one of many who left the field for a period of time because I did not have the tools I needed.

Given my own experiences, I knew that we had to do something different in supervision before new counselors enter the field to prepare them for the experiences they will have and help them implement prevention methods before they experience burnout. I had learned that supervisors should continually monitor beginning counselors for signs of burnout and to ensure supervisees are implementing self-care practices for overall wellness. I have had the opportunity to supervise students in field placements, those seeking licensure, and individuals who are newly entering the field within organizations. One of the main emphases in my approach to supervision is to develop and maintain a strong supervisory working alliance because this aspect is an essential aspect of an effective supervisory experience. Another reason I emphasize the supervisory working alliance is because a strong alliance has been noted in the literature as a prevention factor for vicarious trauma, secondary traumatic stress, and burnout symptoms in counselors (Saakvitne et al., 1996). The establishment of a supervisory working alliance is essential for supervisees to feel they can candidly express their thoughts and feelings related to working with their clients within an empathic, collaborative supervision environment. Another reason I focus on the strength of this relationship is because it is essential to my ability to confront the supervisee about countertransference responses and changes in the supervisee's overall wellness and functioning that could inhibit their work with clients and lead to burnout.

I have found it important to begin supervision by educating novice counselors about burnout, secondary traumatic stress, and

(continued)

Supervision and Self-Care *(continued)*

vicarious trauma responses so that we can create a dialogue about these topics that will continue throughout the supervision experience. Supervisees will often begin self-monitoring practices when they have been made aware of these responses. I have found it helpful to educate supervisees about how their ability to engage in overall wellness translates into their work with clients because many novice counselors have difficulty making connections regarding how their functioning affects their ability to work effectively with clients. I also work with supervisees to create wellness plans that meet their individual needs (i.e., physical, psychological, emotional, spiritual) to continually work toward improving their overall wellness. I often encourage beginning counselors to engage in their own counseling and to continue this practice throughout their career as needed. I also teach relaxation, mindfulness, and reflective practices to supervisees and have them engage in these activities for homework between supervision sessions to increase self-care practices. In every supervision session, I make it a habit to address how the supervisees are currently functioning, how they are feeling about their clients and their work, and what they are doing to maintain wellness in their life.

Finally, I have also found it essential to be a supervisory advocate for novice counselors. Burnout prevention and encouraging self-care practices start at the organizational level, and I believe that, as supervisors, it is our job to notice when structures are not working to support supervisee wellness. I know that if the organization is not supporting my supervisees, they are not likely to be able to provide effective services to clients. There are some key topics I have continually had to advocate for on behalf of supervisees. One key issue is organizational structures that allow for adequate time for clinical supervision that goes beyond administrative supervision experiences. I have also found that beginning counselors need opportunities to engage in peer support through clinical teams, case staffing, and peer support groups to share ideas and feel a part of a team that supports their work with clients. It is often essential to advocate for organizational structures that allow novice counselors to engage in healthy limit-setting and self-care practices (i.e., allowing for balanced caseloads, time for administrative paperwork, not being required to access e-mail outside of work, taking all of their vacation days). I believe that the impact supervisors can make in improving the wellness of supervisees translates directly to better, more effective services to the clients they will counsel and increase the likelihood that the novice counselor will develop into a seasoned professional who stays in the field. It requires supervisors to take the time and effort to build strong supervisory alliances and to provide education, monitoring, and advocacy.

• • •

be conducive to counselor wellness. Unfortunately, organizations often face challenges in creating well environments for counselors (Ohrt & Cunningham, 2012). Organizational factors that may affect counselor wellness include large caseloads, lack of supervision, unsupportive peers, long workdays, or low salaries (Lawson, 2007; Lloyd, King, & Chenoweth, 2002). Additional factors include agency culture (i.e., supervisor support, agency morale), agency resource, and time management. Counselors in schools often experience high counselor-to-student ratios and conflicting job expectations. Counselors who work in community agencies tend to experience higher levels of burnout, vicarious traumatization, and compassion fatigue than counselors in private practice (Lawson, 2007). Some factors may be challenging for clinical directors and supervisors to control, whereas other factors are easier to address. Each organization faces unique challenges and opportunities. However, the following recommendations provide guidance to directors of organizations to help counselors sustain their personal wellness:

- Reduce paperwork and cut "red tape"
- Adopt a collaborative management style
- Improve teamwork
- Provide professional development (Young & Lambie, 2007)
- Advocate for reasonable caseloads
- Have wellness days for staff
- Develop wellness committees (Ohrt & Cunningham, 2012)
- Have on-site exercise facilities
- Provide healthy food options on site
- Include break stations
- Develop support groups
- Allow social activities
- Provide health-risk assessments
- Have employee counseling
- Provide self-care information (Stokes, Henley, & Herget, 2006)

This list is not exhaustive, but it does help to get the brainstorming process started related to organizational wellness. We acknowledge that organizations often face ever-changing external challenges related to funding, laws, policies, or documentation that can make it difficult to prioritize counselor wellness. We encourage clinical directors to make time to address counselors' wellness needs. It is important to consider the counselors' own perspectives on helpful practices. Directors might consider forming a wellness committee among the staff or conducting a needs assessment to prioritize wellness initiatives.

Conclusion

Counselors have the difficult challenge of keeping their "emotional wells" full at all times. There is no hiding from clients' psychological and emotional distress. Prevention of burnout and impairment are vital in maintaining effectiveness as a counselor. We encourage counselors to be proactive in developing self-care strategies, engaging in supervision that attends to personal development, and contributing to organizations that have a culture of wellness. When we realize that our wells are dry, we must take a step back and fill it up to be able to help our clients grow.

Reflection Prompts

1. What are your biggest challenges to maintaining your wellness? How might you overcome some of these barriers?
2. How do you believe your supervisor could best help you maintain your wellness and avoid burnout with your clients?
3. Think about yourself as a supervisor (either now or in the future). What strategies do you believe you could implement to support counselors in maintaining wellness?
4. Think about your current work environment. How is the environment conducive or detrimental to wellness of the employees? What initiatives are implemented to help support wellness? What services are available to staff members?

Learning Activities

Take the Professional Quality of Life and Self-Care Assessment

Process the results with a partner. How well are you doing with self-care? Do you have any specific areas of concern? What are some areas of strength for you?

Develop a Wellness Plan

Develop an individual wellness plan for yourself. The plan will consist of the following:

  a. Identify your current state of wellness in each dimension (i.e., physical, social, intellectual, emotional, spiritual, occupational) and the current challenges in each dimension.
  b. Develop one short-term and one long-term goal for each dimension.
  c. Create a proactive plan for each dimension to meet these goals and improve your overall self-care.
  d. Discuss in detail the strategies that you will implement to meet your goals and appropriately navigate the challenges to maintain your wellness.
  e. Pick one short-term goal you will focus on during this class.

Resources

American Counseling Association Self-Care Resources for Counselors
https://www.counseling.org/knowledge-center/
self-care-resources-for-counselors

Professional Quality of Life Website
http://www.proqol.org/Home_Page.php

References

American Counseling Association. (2014). *ACA code of ethics*. Alexandria, VA: Author.

Association for Counselor Education and Supervision. (2011). *Best practices in clinical supervision*. Retrieved from https://www.acesonline.net/sites/default/files/ACES-Best-Practices-in-clinical-supervision-document-FINAL.pdf

Council for Accreditation of Counseling and Related Educational Programs. (2015). *Council for Accreditation of Counseling and Related Educational Programs: 2016 standards*. Retrieved http://www.cacrep.org/wp-content/uploads/2017/08/2016-Standards-with-citations.pdf

Doran, G. T. (1981, November). There's a S.M.A.R.T. way to write management's goals and objectives. *Management Review, 70*(11), 35–36.

Figley, C. R. (2002). *Treating compassion fatigue*. New York, NY: Routledge.

Lambie, G. W. (2006). Burnout prevention: A humanistic perspective and structured group supervision activity. *Journal of Humanistic Counseling, 45*, 32–44. https://doi.org/10.1002/j.2161-1939.2006.tb00003.x

Lawson, G. (2007). Counselor wellness and impairment: A national survey. *Journal of Humanistic Counseling, 46*, 20–34. https://doi.org/10.1002/j.2161-1939.2007.tb00023.x

Lawson, G., & Venart, B. (2005). Preventing counselor impairment: Vulnerability, wellness, and resilience. In G. R. Walz & R. K. Yep (Eds.), *VISTAS: Compelling perspectives on counseling 2005* (pp. 243–246). Alexandria, VA: American Counseling Association.

Lenz, A. S., & Smith, R. L. (2010). Integrating wellness concepts within a clinical supervision model. *The Clinical Supervisor, 29*, 228–245. https://doi.org/10.1080/07325223.2010.518511

Lloyd, C., King, R., & Chenoweth, L. (2002). Social work, stress and burnout: A review. *Journal of Mental Health, 11*, 255–265. https://doi.org/10.1080/09638230020023642

Maslach, C. (2003). *Burnout: The cost of caring*. Cambridge, MA: Malor Books.

Myers, J. E., & Sweeney, T. J. (2005). The indivisible self: An evidence-based model of wellness. *Journal of Individual Psychology, 61*, 269–279.

Myers, J. E., & Sweeney, T. J. (2014). *Five Factor Wellness Inventory (FF-WEL): Adult, teenage, and elementary school versions.* Menlo Park, CA: Mind Garden.

Ohrt, J. H., & Cunningham, L. K. (2012). Wellness in mental health agencies. *The Professional Counselor: Research and Practice, 2,* 90–101.

Ohrt, J. H., Prosek, E. A., Ener, E., & Lindo, N. (2015). The effects of a group supervision intervention to promote wellness and prevent burnout. *Journal of Humanistic Counseling, 54,* 41–58. https://doi.org/10.1002/j.2161-1939.2015.00063.x

Puig, A., Baggs, A., Mixon, K., Park, Y. M., Kim, B. Y., & Lee, S. M. (2012). Relationship between job burnout and personal wellness in mental health professionals. *Journal of Employment Counseling, 49,* 98–109. https://doi.org/10.1002/j.2161-1920.2012.00010.x

Saakvitne, K. W., Pearlman, L. A., & Staff of the Traumatic Stress Institute. (1996). *Transforming the pain: A workbook on vicarious traumatization for helping professionals who work with traumatized clients.* New York, NY: Norton.

Stamm, B. H. (2002). Measuring compassion satisfaction as well as fatigue: Developmental history of the Compassion Satisfaction and Fatigue Test. In C. R. Figley (Ed.), *Treating compassion fatigue* (pp. 107–119). New York, NY: Routledge.

Stebnicki, M. A. (2007). Empathy fatigue: Healing the mind, body, and spirit of professional counselors. *American Journal of Psychiatric Rehabilitation, 10,* 317–338. https://doi.org/10.1080/15487760701680570

Stevanovic, P., & Rupert, P. A. (2004). Career-sustaining behaviors, satisfaction, and stresses of professional psychologists. *Psychotherapy: Theory, Research, Practice, Training, 41,* 301–309.

Stokes, G., Henley, N., & Herget, C. (2006). Creating a culture of wellness in the workplace. *North Carolina Medical Journal, 67,* 445–448.

Witmer, J. M., & Young, M. E. (1996). Preventing counselor impairment: A wellness approach. *Journal of Humanistic Education & Development, 34,* 141–155.

Young, M. E., & Lambie, G. W. (2007). Wellness in school and mental health systems: Organizational influences. *Journal of Humanistic Counseling, Education and Development, 46,* 98–113.

Index

Figures and tables are indicated by "f" and "t" following page numbers.

(continued)

(continued)

(continued)